WOODEN MONKEY WITH CORAL EYES (*no. 114 in the Bieber Collection*)

SUBSTANCE AND SYMBOL
IN CHINESE TOGGLES

Chinese Belt Toggles from the
C. F. Bieber Collection

Text by
SCHUYLER CAMMANN

Illustrated with Photographs by

Hedda Hammer Morrison and Laura Gilpin

Philadelphia
University of Pennsylvania Press

Library of Congress Catalog Card Number: 62-7202

Printed in the United States of America

To the memory of
Langdon Warner

CONTENTS

Color plates face pages 30 and 31

PREFACE

THIS BOOK PRESENTS to the reader a collection of Chinese belt toggles, as miniature works of art. They were assembled by Miss C. F. Bieber, of London, Peking, and Santa Fe, New Mexico, most of them being acquired during her residence in North China in the late 1920's and early '30's. She was one of the first to appreciate these Chinese toggles and collect them in a systematic way, although there has long been a vogue for the somewhat related Japaneses toggles known as *netsuke*. Her collection of Chinese toggles is not only the largest known, numbering over two hundred, but it is also the most comprehensive, including representative examples of nearly every basic type, in a great variety of materials.

Miss Bieber was also the first person to enjoy the Chinese toggles in their wholeness: considering their original, practical use, studying the materials and techniques used to make them, and tracking down the ideas expressed by their makers in the subjects and symbols which they employed to decorate them. She never kept her findings to herself, but has generously shared them, guiding others to appreciate these small carvings as she did herself. Displaying them privately or in occasional museum exhibitions, she has helped others to understand and share her own deep feeling for them, and for the larger field of Chinese arts and crafts in general, of which they are a part.

During her years in China, Miss Bieber also helped the Brooklyn Museum to acquire a small but very representative collection of belt toggles, with a number of unusual specimens. Another small collection, formed in Peking by Dr. George N. Kates, is now in the Chinese Collection at Columbia University, while a third is owned by Mrs. William Gleysteen of Jenkintown, Pennsylvania, who also collected them in Peking. All three of these other collections, as well as random examples in various museums in Europe and America, have been carefully studied during preparation of this book, and references to some of these other toggles will occasionally appear for comparison.

The first photographs of the Bieber Collection were made by Mrs. Hedda Hammer Morrison in Peking. She is well known for her exceptional photographs of life in North China and in Borneo, where she now lives. The later photographs and the color plates were taken by Laura Gilpin, a distinguished American photographer who has won fame for her work in the Southwestern United States, particularly in the Valley of the Rio Grande, about which she has published an outstanding book. Only fine artists such as these could do full justice to the Chinese toggles, as they are so small that it is very difficult to bring out the full variety of their textures and the intricacy of their details.

Speaking personally, as the author of the text, I had collected some netsuke on my first visit to Japan in 1935, and a few of the Chinese toggles during some four years of residence and travel all over China (1935-38, and 1945), but I did not fully appreciate the toggles until Miss Bieber taught me to do so, through her own enthusiasm for them. Her subsequent generosity in helping me to make a detailed study of her remarkable collection finally led to the writing of this book.

In preparation for it, I undertook to study these toggles in all their aspects, to be able to present the subject as comprehensively as possible. For these were objects of utility with a long historical background, as well as miniature works of art: they are living examples of the old Chinese feeling for variety and diversity of materials, as well as former skill in craftsmanship, now lost; and most of them contain symbolic expressions of profound religious ideas or of deep-felt human needs and desires. It seemed obvious from the start that, in order to understand them at all fully and transmit this understanding to others, they must be approached on all these levels, and considered in their totality.

After a long period of study and preparation, this book finally emerged. Its first and second chapters discuss the purpose of these toggles and their specific uses, along with some historical background, and a listing of the chief types found in China and her dependencies. The next five chapters describe the materials of which they were made, explaining why the Chinese considered these particular ones especially suitable, along with brief descriptions of the tools and techniques used in making them. The remaining chapters take up the philosophic and religious ideas that informed the minds of the toggle makers, leading them to produce certain designs and use certain symbols in preference to others. We hope that the total study: text, catalogue, and illustrations, will demonstrate that the Chinese belt toggles, though they may be called "products of a minor art," are not only representative of the finest aspects of traditional Oriental Art, but can also give any Westerner who approaches them with understanding, new and richer insights into the Old Chinese art and civilization, and philosophy in general.

Many others have helped on this book, by encouragement, advice, and expert information; without them this book would not have become so complete a study. The list begins with the late Langdon Warner of Harvard University (to whom the book is dedicated), and Laurence Sickman, Director of the Nelson Gallery in Kansas City, both of whom urged Miss Bieber to carry out this book project, and encouraged her in its initial stages. In addition to the many librarians and museum curators, botanists and geologists, who have patiently helped us with our researches, answering specific questions as they arose, we owe special gratitude to Dr. B. Francis Kukachka of the U.S. Department of Agriculture, Acting Director of the Forest Products Laboratory in Madison, Wisconsin, who analyzed the wooden toggles to identify the materials from which they were made. We also would like to extend our special thanks to George Kalmbacher of the Brooklyn Botanical Garden and Gordon Saltar of the Winterthur Museum in Delaware for their helpful suggestions.

All of us who have directly contributed to the making of this book, from Miss Bieber down, have done our respective parts in the hope that many others—not only students, collectors, and art lovers, but people of the most varied interests—would come to find in these toggles what we have been finding: subtle beauty, glimpses of inner wisdom, and sheer pleasure.

SCHUYLER CAMMANN

Philadelphia, 1959

Substance and Symbol

in Chinese Toggles

1

THE DEVELOPMENT OF
BELT TOGGLES

AT FIRST SIGHT, the appealing little objects that are described and pictured in this book might seem to be merely miniature art productions, designed to be admired as table ornaments. But their appearance is deceptive. Although most of them are beautifully constructed, and many of them depict traditional subjects from Chinese art or folklore, they were all made for strictly practical use. Their primary purpose was to serve as toggles, to fasten things to men's belts. As such, they belong to a venerable tradition, reaching far back in history.

Belt toggles have been worn over a wide area in the northern parts of the world. Wherever men wore long robes or tunics without pockets— and pockets are a relatively modern innovation—the only convenient way to carry things on one's person was to attach them to the belt or cloth girdle. Such things as knives and awls, in their respective sheaths, could hang free, while smaller objects could be stowed in belt-pouches or purses. All these were generally attached to separate cords, and the other end of the cord was then fastened to the belt. The securing could be done by tying the end of the cord directly to the belt, or to a ring or frog attached to the belt; or else the cord could be tied to a large lump, button, or bar, that could be slipped up behind the belt or girdle and be held in place by its breadth, or by its weight as a counterbalance to the thing it was helping to support. The last of these was what we call a toggle.

A closely related toggle type was an actual belt fastener, in the form of a knob or button of ivory, wood, or metal, attached to one end of the belt and arranged to slip through a loop at the other end. This type does not seem to have been used in China or Japan, Tibet or Mongolia, although it was common in other areas, as we shall see.

[15]

The use of toggles for securing things to the belt was a particularly convenient method, as the wearer could easily attach or disengage the object that it was helping to support, without having to undo his belt every time, or else being obliged to tie and untie small knots, which could be especially annoying in cold weather. The toggle itself had to be sufficiently large, or heavy enough, to prevent the weight of the object itself from pulling it down through the belt, but at the same time it could not be so big as to be awkward or uncomfortable for the wearer. Also, as it was often his only personal ornament, it had to be considered as an object of decoration, so it was generally made of some interesting or valued substance, and shaped or decorated in some attractive way. These considerations account for the convenient size and the ornamental appearance of most of the East Asian toggles, which in turn has inevitably led to their popularity among modern collectors.

Leather belts with permanent rings or frogs at their sides for securing personal possessions, belonged principally to the horse-riding aristocrats of the steppes, although they were also worn by the Mongols who ruled over China, Persia, and Russia in medieval times, and by the Manchu rulers of China, Mongolia, and Tibet, in more recent centuries.[1] But the less wealthy folk, even among the peoples just mentioned, generally would have worn simple cloth belts or girdles, and attached things to them with toggles; and even the nobles and gentry, on informal occasions, wore silken girdles and used toggles.

Sometimes both methods were employed at the same time. The nobles of Tibet and Mongolia customarily slung their personal possessions from silver-mounted leather frogs that hung from either side of the belt; but they often also tied a toggle near the lower end of the long cord that secured the flint-and-steel set, so that the latter could be hitched up tighter to the belt, to prevent its thumping against their legs while they walked or rode horseback.[2]

In trying to trace the origin and development of the toggles themselves, we immediately run into difficulties. Toggle-wearing was such a necessary, matter-of-fact trait that writers of the past usually took it for granted, and seldom bothered to mention it when they described the habits of their own group or discussed other neighboring peoples. The evidence provided by art is even more scanty, for a number of reasons. Unfortunately for our search, portraiture in the past was largely confined to pictures of the nobles and officials in formal attire, and the old

Chinese artists left very few detailed pictorial records to show how the masses of the people looked and dressed in their own times. Even when a comparatively ordinary person was included in a painting, such a trivial item as a toggle would have been omitted as a nonessential and hence distracting element. Lastly, the location of the toggles at the sides of the belt always made it difficult to see them, as the sides of the wearer were generally concealed by hanging arms or drooping sleeves.

Even archaeology has been of little help. Unless a toggle chanced to be found in place, on a body entombed in the colder regions of the far North, it would ordinarily be lost in the general accumulation of miscellaneous small objects and personal ornaments found in ancient graves; and it would be still more difficult to recognize one if it were found alone, in a city site or elsewhere, as they are easily mistaken for small amulets or other ornaments.

In view of this disappointing lack of old evidence—whether literary, artistic, or archaeological—it would seem to be easier to work back from the known examples of more recent periods.

Certainly the best known of the more modern belt toggles were the netsuke of Japan.[3] These were regularly worn as a customary item of costume for most Japanese until well past the middle of the nineteenth century. They persisted there even after 1868, when the formal abolition of feudalism brought about a radical change of styles, and lasted on until the introduction of cigarettes drove out the use of pipes and tobacco boxes which the netsuke had helped to secure to the *obi* girdles.

In spite of considerable variations in carving, subjects, and materials in the Japanese netsuke, we now know that these belt toggles came into Japanese culture rather late. They seem to have been introduced into Japan about the end of the sixteenth century of our era, during the latter part of the Ming Dynasty in China, probably following the Japanese attempts to conquer Korea in the 1590's.[4] The introduction of tobacco from the New World by the Portuguese, about the same time, apparently had considerable influence in helping to spread the custom. By the mid-1600's, the netsuke were widely used for supporting tobacco boxes or smoking sets. Their high popularity during the Tokugawa period (1603-1867), when overly strict sumptuary laws decreed that they were to be the only form of personal ornament permitted to those below the rank of samurai, and the rapid changes in popular taste during those two and a half centuries, could easily account for the multiplicity of types that we now find.

It seems probable that the custom of wearing toggles must have reached Japan from the mainland, either from China directly or else by way of Korea.[5] A Chinese form of seal, pierced for a carrying cord so that it could also serve as a toggle, seems to have been the earliest kind of netsuke. These and others of the early forms of netsuke were called *karamono*, literally, "Chinese things," while the early figure netsuke were called *tōbori*, meaning "Chinese carvings." Very few of the latter have survived, but from sketches of them in old Japanese books we can see that they included a variety of objects, some of which were in purely Chinese style.[6]

The origins of toggle-wearing in China itself are very obscure; but, considering the long span of Chinese history, they seem to have arrived rather late there also—although considerably before the netsuke appeared in Japan. They may have been used much earlier in Tibet and Mongolia, where we know from personal observation that they still lingered on into modern times, and it seems rather likely that they came into China along with other foreign influences during the Yüan or Mongol Dynasty (1280-1368), if not before. At any rate, by the time the Japanese borrowed the custom from the continent, at the end of the sixteenth century, the custom must already have been well developed in China, because we have seen examples that must date from the Ming Dynasty (1368-1644) which seem to indicate a broad, previous development.[7]

The Palace Museum Collection in Old Peking (now on the Island of Formosa) used to have a long horizontal scroll depicting a Ming emperor of the early fifteenth century, riding horseback with some of his courtiers, and in this painting one of the attendants seems to be handling or adjusting a toggle that secures his purse.[8] Other purses and pouches worn by his companions distinctly show a bead halfway down the double carrying cord, which must have been the prototype of the Japanese *ojime* bead that was regularly worn with the netsuke. This picture is rare, in that most of the surviving Ming paintings represent nobles and officials in more formal dress, with grotesque-looking hoop belts that projected outward from the body and hence did not permit the use of toggles; while, in the other hunting or riding scenes of that period, the very full Ming sleeves, or the loosely cut robes then in fashion, overlap or otherwise conceal the sides of the belts, making it impossible to see just how things were fastened to them.

From the succeeding dynasty of the Ch'ing (1644-1911), there is a painting in the same Palace Museum Collection which shows the Chia-ch'ing Emperor (reign: 1796-1820) sitting informally in a garden with several attendants.[9] His pages are depicted with objects hanging from various places on their belts, which must have required the use of toggles, although again the toggles themselves are not shown. (We would expect them here, with very casual dress; but the formal and semiformal belts of the Manchus had metal rings at the sides from which they could hang their knives and purses, etc.[10]) Such informal paintings are also relatively rare from the Ch'ing dynasty, and in these, too, the belts are usually hidden by hanging sleeves or overlapping upper robes.[11]

If the old Chinese paintings have been rather unsatisfactory for illustrating the early use of toggles, they do show something that seems to have bearing on our subject. Many of the Sung paintings of old men and sages depict them wearing, tied to their cloth belts, small gourds or bits of sacred fungus (ling chih).[12] Large bottle-gourds were commonly used by Buddhist pilgrims and other travelers in medieval Asia for canteens, to hold water or wine, but the ones worn at the belt in these pictures were too small to serve as anything but little medicine bottles, or as amulets to promote health or fertility. Similarly, the fungi could not have been used for anything except medicine for longevity, or for amulets with similar associations. In the primitive medical concepts of Old China, charm amulets were considered to be as effective in their way as were the actual medicinal potions.

These earlier ideas were also maintained in the toggles themselves, after their introduction to China. For, when we later review the materials used to make them and the kinds of symbols portrayed on them, we shall see that beliefs regarding supposed curative properties and auspicious wishes for health, longevity, and fertility were nearly always present. It would seem, then, that the idea of carrying medicinal substances or charm amulets at the girdle in older times had constituted a second line of ancestry for the Chinese belt toggles. Thus the latter seem to have developed from a fusion of two basic needs: first, the requirement of a handy fastener for securing things to the belt, and secondly, a portable bit of medicine or a charm for personal luck and protection against bad spirits, or against the diseases that they might bring.

These linked concepts apparently passed over to Japan in close relationship, but the Japanese seem to have misunderstood them; or at least they handled them somewhat differently. They generally used the netsuke as a toggle to support a small medicine box, called inrō, which carried one or more kinds of herbs or drugs in separate compartments.[13] Since the Japanese toggles were no longer drugs or charms in themselves, they could be made of any convenient substance, and their decoration ceased to be symbolic but became purely ornamental, in the Japanese artistic tradition. Eventually, the netsuke were used to secure many other things in addition to the inrō, but the close connection between netsuke and inrō was never entirely forgotten.

One reason for the scantiness of Chinese records regarding toggles, either pictorial or written, is that toggle-wearing was, during the Ch'ing dynasty at least, essentially a trait of the middle and lower classes or of the "barbarians" from beyond the frontiers—in which category most of the Chinese placed their Manchu overlords—while toggle-making was primarily a folk art in China. In fact, it would seem that men often carved toggles for themselves when house-bound in winter, or else they made them for gifts, such as wedding presents, to give their friends. Apparently, hunters, or farmers, herdsmen and shepherds whittled toggles of wood or bone, horn or antler, in their spare time; while the woodworkers and stonecutters of the towns and cities created them from leftover scraps of fine woods or from less expensive bits of semiprecious stones, discarded because of poor coloring or flaws in them.

Even in the case of Chinese toggles in jade or ivory, which must have been made for wealthier patrons by skilled artisans, there never seems to have been any established industry for producing them, even remotely comparable to the netsuke industry that flourished in Japan during the late eighteenth and early nineteenth centuries. If there were any outstanding toggle artists in China—and certain groups of toggles in semiprecious substances such as carnelian, made in the same general style, indicate that there may have been a few of these—their works were never signed as the finer Japanese netsuke were, so they remain anonymous.[14] Therefore, it is impossible to date the Chinese toggles with any certainty, and that also means that we are unable to trace any clear chronological development of types and styles, as one can with the netsuke.

A few clues for dating might be gained from the subjects depicted. For example, we know from other arts that certain animals or plants, like the flying bat symbolizing happiness or the artemisia leaf as a symbol of curative powers, would be popular at one period only to fall from favor at a later time. Also, special conventions for representing certain animals or birds might come into style for a time, later to be dropped again. For Chinese tradition was certainly not static, even though strong conservatism in the remoter provinces, further from the capital, might cause old traits to linger on there as survivals, long after they had been abandoned elsewhere.[15] Then, too, the age of a toggle is sometimes partially apparent from the degree of wear or the discoloration of its substance, but the latter can be misleading, especially when old ivory or ancient mammoth tusk has been reworked at a later time.

Most hazardous is the attempt to determine dating by "style" alone. Stark simplicity or even downright crudity in a Chinese toggle may be merely the result of an amateur or untrained carver. Certainly it cannot be taken as a sign of great antiquity. Similarly, an elaborately conceived or a very finished toggle is not necessarily the product of a "mature art" from a later period; it might well have been made at the same time as some of the cruder ones, but for a wealthier man, able to afford a trained craftsman to produce it for him. In short, all the sophisticated jargon of the date-minded art historian might as well be cast aside; for in most cases we simply cannot tell how old a given Chinese toggle is. Instead, we must try to appreciate each example for itself, as an expression of a now-forgotten folk art, reflecting in the choice of material and in its symbolic decoration the hopes and aspirations of the common people of China.

It would be equally rash to consider the Chinese toggles as "antiques." Even though a few of the surviving examples might be dated with some confidence as "Ming," which would make them several hundred years old,[16] this is still young by Chinese standards. Indeed, many of them might be quite recent, as toggles were still being used in the 1930's and early 40's. Miss Bieber and her friends used to see them being worn by occasional coolies and other men, in and around Peking; and I found them being worn by caravan men and muleteers in far western China, by Tibetans in the borderlands of Northern Yünnan and Western

Szechuan, and by the Mongols of Inner Mongolia. In fact, we have both purchased some of the examples now in the Bieber Collection directly from their wearers. But now, in China proper as in Japan, the custom is apparently completely dead.

Even the former distribution of toggle-wearing within Old China itself is something of a mystery. Although I have actually seen them being worn in Northern and Western China, as just mentioned, I have not noticed any toggles being worn in South or Central China, in spite of very extensive travels throughout those areas as well. Furthermore, the relative scarcity or total absence of such common or familiar South China substances as water buffalo horn or bamboo would suggest that toggles have not been commonly made there—at least, not in recent times. One might partially account for this by pointing out that the specimens in the collections that we have been studying were mostly acquired in North China; but, in the absence of any positive evidence to the contrary, it seems fairly certain that toggle-wearing was primarily, if not exclusively, a northern trait in China. This leads us to believe that it must have been introduced from the North or Northwest by another people.

Unfortunately, comparatively little information has trickled down to us about the details of costume of the so-called Scythians, or the ancient Bactrians (before and after Alexander and his Greeks came east and conquered them), or the Huns and the older Turkish tribes who came down from Northern Mongolia, to name just a few of the many peoples —nomads, seminomads, or more settled folk traveling as traders or raiders—who inadvertently dropped small bronzes in considerable numbers across the steppes of Central Asia, from the Black Sea eastward to the Ordos Desert of North China and Inner Mongolia. However, the Ordos finds, recovered in the two decades before the Sino-Japanese War, which began in Mongolia in 1936, included quantities of light-weight "ornaments," many of which were button-shaped, with loops, rings, or small perforated lugs on the reverse side, that would have fitted them for use as toggles.

Prominent among these Ordos finds were the so-called "Nestorian crosses," and birds that have been described as "doves" to make them fit into a Christian context, although many of the latter are eagles, some of them double-headed.[17] These crosses and bird-shaped bronzes look like a combination of toggle and stamp-seal—probably serving also as religious amulets—and it is extremely doubtful that their use was limited to the Nestorians. Cruciform symbolism was widespread in Asia long before Christianity, and there is nothing specifically Christian about a double-headed eagle.[18] Many other pieces among these "Ordos bronzes" could also have been used as toggles, and very probably a lot of them were; but it would be most difficult to prove it.

Moving further North and East, the evidence is somewhat clearer. When European anthropologists came to study the customs of the Chukchee and other native peoples of Northeastern Siberia, at the end of the nineteenth century, they found them wearing belt toggles, and formerly the trait was apparently widespread throughout Siberia, indicating a strong northern development that could have extended its influence as far as China.

The Chukchee belt toggles, as illustrated in the writings of the European explorers, seem to have been largely of the button type, usually made of walrus ivory, with a loop at the back for the cord.[19] However, certain of the old Chukchee amulets, preserved on rawhide strings as charms, in the form of little men, animals, and utensils,[20] look very much like old toggles of more varied inspiration, perhaps retained for their spiritual effect because they were still thought to possess some of the powers of the deceased ancestors who had worn them.

The custom of making toggles from walrus ivory was also found among the Alaskan Eskimo, who fashioned them in the shape of whales, polar bears, and seals, in addition to making larger, usually plainer, toggles for harpoon lines, dog-sled harness, and other gear. However, they seem to have worn them primarily as belt fasteners, rather than for securing things to the belt.[21] It is also noteworthy that a considerable number of togglelike objects, still unexplained, have been found in pre-Eskimo dwelling sites in the northern parts of Alaska and Canada, suggesting that the predecessors of the present aborigines probably had belt toggles of the securing type also.

From Siberia, the trait of toggle-wearing also seems to have extended westward into Europe. In Hungary, a type of belt toggle formed part of the national costume for men until the beginning of the twentieth century, and may have lasted even longer in remote areas. This was a decorated piece of steel with a dual function. It not only anchored to the man's belt a cord from which hung his flint-and-tinder bag and his pipe and tobacco pouch, but it also served as a striker for the flint when he wanted to make a fire or light his pipe.[22] These Hungarian metal toggles finally passed out of use, partly because of the disappearance of the national dress under the influence of drabber styles from Western Europe, and partly because the introduction of matches made the flint and steel unnecessary.

The Old Hungarian peasants also produced another kind of toggle that had an even greater resemblance to the Chinese belt toggles, although they were used in very different ways. These others were the "sheep toggles," small pieces of wood carved in matching pairs, and used much like the belt-fastening toggles to secure the two ends of a rope: the ropes being collars for the ewe and her lamb, respectively, so that the two could be easily recognized and reunited if the lamb strayed away.[23] Each set of these was distinctively made with an individual pattern, the pair being identical in subject; although the ewe's was slightly bigger because she had a larger collar. The shepherds, whittling these out of spare pieces of wood in their leisure time, carved simple reproductions of familiar objects in their daily life, as the Chinese did in their "replica toggles," which are discussed in Chapter 11. Among the Hungarian "sheep toggles" can be found miniature flutes, axes, spades and sickles, boots and bootjacks, chairs, beer kegs, milk-pails and yokes for carrying them, fiddles and ladders, keys and padlocks, and many other common domestic items. Particularly striking are the winnowing fans, because exactly the same subject often occurs among the Chinese belt toggles. Even when the subjects are similar, no two pairs of these Hungarian "sheep toggles" were ever exactly alike, because each pair was separately fashioned by an amateur carver. Like the Chinese belt toggles, they were true examples of a folk tradition, and not the products of any regular industry.

With such a well-developed tradition of toggle-making in Hungary, one might expect to find toggles also being made and worn in the broad intervening areas between Hungary and Siberia, in the steppes of Old Russia and in Central Asia; but here, again, we are hampered by lack of direct evidence. The Hungarian sheep toggles, however, need not have been the results of a widespread diffusion of toggle-making and toggle-wearing; they might just as well have arisen as an independently developed trait, to meet local needs. Forms of toggles are also found in two other areas of the Old World, which are neither anywhere near the areas previously discussed nor contiguous to each other, and the latter were most probably arrived at independently.

The first of these areas is West Africa, where belt toggles were being used until recently, in the form of large rounded buttons of some hard substance—probably wood—covered with neatly plaited leather in thin strips of two or more colors. For example, the University Museum in Philadelphia has a heavy whip from the Mandingo tribe, which has a stout thong at the end of its handle, ending in a huge button covered with interlaced leather thongs that could serve to secure it to a man's belt.[24] Other similar button-shaped toggles served to fasten the ends of their woven belts or sling straps to the sheaths of their knives and swords.

The second area is Northern Borneo and Sarawak. The costumes of the more southerly parts of Asia were usually not conducive to toggle-wearing. For example, we do not find belt toggles in the Near East or in the Indian subcontinent, because people there ordinarily wore free-hanging robes without belts or girdles, in order to permit easy circulation of air in an excessively hot climate. Similarly, in Southeast Asia the heat generally induced people to adopt a sarong-type costume that did not require a belt. Only in Borneo do we find a curious form of toggle used in connection with the headhunters' sword belt. This was made of wood, antler, or "hornbill ivory" (*Anggang gading*), a strange substance which comes from the head of a bird.[25] The Borneo toggles are usually described as belt fasteners (like the Eskimo toggles), but the University Museum in Philadelphia has an example that could only have been a toggle for securing a sword or pouch, rather than a fastener for a belt to support the latter. This is rather crude, being a simple disc cut from the base of an antler and pierced with two holes for the passage of a beaded cord;[26] but some of the more ornate toggles from Borneo are intricate examples of carving, true works of art.[27]

Our short sketch of the known distribution of toggles has necessarily been brief, because so little is yet known. This line of research should certainly be pursued further, not only to determine the entire range of the toggle-wearing trait in times past, but also to investigate more fully the nature and extent of little-known regional developments, such as the use of the steel toggles in Old Hungary. Only the Japanese side has hitherto been studied with any thoroughness. We can find numerous books and articles on the netsuke;[28] but, as mentioned above, the idea for these apparently came to Japan from the continent fairly recently, and, although their development in Japan was rather impressive, it seems to have been a very late and peripheral one compared to the development of the toggles in China.

Lastly, there is the question of evidence from choice of materials, which may also be able to furnish us with some more historical information. From the little that we now know of the past extent of toggle-wearing, it would seem that the use of toggles probably originated in the northern forest regions of Middle Asia, which is a midpoint in the area of their major distribution, and that it spread outward from there. If so, perhaps the earliest toggles were sections of twigs or gnarled rootlets.

The Japanese word *netsuke* means "root fastening," and possibly this preserves in altered form an earlier Chinese or Korean term reflecting some memory of the ultimate origin of toggles. Certainly root toggles were always very popular in Old China, as we shall see in Chapter 3.

Then, as the use of toggles was carried down into the steppe country where strong and durable hardwood was extremely rare, new materials had to be sought. Thus, they seem to have used thin bronze in the Eastern steppes (the Gobi and Ordos regions of Northwest China and Mongolia) and steel in the far west (Hungary). Meanwhile, in passing to the North, where there was a total absence of both wood and metals, toggle-wearing compelled the use of either bone or ivory, as found in the Eskimo examples.

In Ming and Ch'ing China, even more than in Tokugawa Japan, these and many other substances were used, in a great variety of ways, so we find almost as many variations in the materials used for the toggles as there were in their shapes or in the subjects depicted on them. This not only demonstrates that China had far greater resources than any other land of Eastern Asia and a more highly developed ingenuity, but it also seems to indicate that there must have been a long passage of time in which the evolution gradually took place.[29] The Chinese toggles must have been made and used for centuries, during which the urge of novelty and constant experimentation disclosed a vast number of possibilities. Thus the Chinese toggles progressively increased in sophistication and complexity by building on a borrowed trait which had begun far more simply among another people, many centuries before.

CHINESE TOGGLES: BASIC TYPES

WE HAVE SEEN that a belt toggle was a small object intended to be fastened to the end of a cord for attaching something to the belt. The Chinese variety, called *chui-tzŭ*,[1] was used in Old China to attach pouches and purses, knife-and-chopstick sets, flint-and-steel sets, tobacco pipes and cases, spectacle- and fan-cases, eating bowl containers (in West China and Tibet), and almost anything else that one might conceivably want to carry on the person. In the absence of pockets, toggle cords were indispensable for any man of action, except for the Manchu and Mongol nobles whose formal and semiformal belts were fitted with metal rings at each side for looping the suspension cords, following the earlier Mongol tradition. But even these dignitaries informally wore girdles of twisted cloth and secured things in them with toggles.

In many cases, the toggles of Greater China—that is, of the Chinese and their neighbors or dependents in Mongolia and Tibet—had other functions besides the primary one of fastening things to the belt. For example, when metal mirrors, seals, spoons, and other practical items were worn as toggles, they acted in a double capacity. In fact, we might call them double-utility toggles, since they form a distinct category by themselves. In contrast to these, most toggles were especially made just for the purpose of attaching things to the belt, with the secondary motive of providing a personal ornament.

As the Chinese toggles also had a decorative intent, it is necessary to make a firm distinction between these and other kinds of belt ornaments that had different functions. The word *chui-tzŭ* means pendulum or counterweight, describing the toggle's chief purpose; while simple charm pendants were called *p'ei ching*,[2] literally meaning "pendant scriptures,"

[27]

and the purely ornamental girdle pendants, usually made of fine stones, which hung from the sides of the belt in the traditional costume of nobles and officials of earlier dynasties, were called *p'ei yü* (or *yü p'ei*),[3] meaning "hanging jades." These last had no explicit function except perhaps as auxiliary marks of rank.

To serve as a proper toggle, an object had to satisfy several functional requirements, and the measure of its ability to fulfill them can distinguish a true toggle from similar-looking items such as belt charms, girdle pendants, and small religious figures. Every Occidental collection of Chinese toggles should be carefully examined with these points in mind, in order to sift out doubtful examples.

In the first place, a toggle had to be made in such a way that it could readily be fastened to a cord. This word "cord," by the way, must be taken in its fullest sense. We have seen everything from a crude leather or rawhide thong or a coarse hempen string to finely twisted silk, small-linked chains of steel, or braided metal cables of fine gold or silver wire. To attach the cord properly, a toggle must have what the Chinese call an "eye" (*yen*, or *so-tzŭ yen*[4]), that is, a hole or gap, or a projecting loop or an attached ring, through which to pass the end of the cord; or else it has to have a slender waist around which to loop the cord. An ordinary pendant might also have any one of these features, but the nature and use of a toggle required other qualities not necessary or even desirable in pendants as such, which therefore serve to distinguish the toggles as belonging to a separate class.

For example, in order to serve its primary purpose of securing things to a belt, a toggle must be either long enough crosswise or broad enough laterally to prevent its slipping back through the belt. Therefore, it must have some length in two directions, as in the bar toggles and the broad disc or button toggles; or else it must have bulk, as in the bun-shaped toggles or the three-dimensional figures. Ideally, a toggle should also be heavy enough to act as a counterweight to balance the thing it is helping to support, as its Chinese name implies. Often these qualities are combined, and we find bulk and weight together in a single piece, as in most examples of the ball-pendant type.

The words bulk and weight are purely relative in this connection, because a practical toggle could be neither too large nor too heavy. The Chinese belt toggles were rarely more than two and a half inches in maximum length or thickness. Anything much bigger would have gotten in the way, and might even have proved to be a distinct liability. If the wearer tripped and fell, for example, or were thrown from his horse, an excessively large toggle might break a rib or otherwise injure him. Also, to be an effective counterweight, a toggle could not be heavier than the object that it helped to secure; otherwise, it might drop and pull the suspended object right up to the belt. On the other hand, it could be considerably lighter, as most of the wooden ones were, provided that it was large enough to keep the cord from being pulled down through the belt. Thus, some small figures of stone or metal, because of their excessive weight, can immediately be recognized as having been made for some other purpose.

Since a toggle to be really effective must have length and breadth in at least two directions, it was usual to have the point of fastening at or near its center. By contrast, any small, ornamental carving with a loop or ring at its upper end was probably made for a mere pendant, unless it is long enough and heavy enough to hang vertically and to withstand the natural tendency of the suspended object to pull it down through the belt. Stone or metal toggles and some of very heavy wood or of ivory may sometimes be found with a terminal attachment, but the lighter ones were almost never fastened in this way.

Another very necessary aspect of the belt toggle's functional nature was compactness. Except in the case of the spike toggles, which were made from slender branches or antler tips, pointed at one end, for such specific secondary uses as loosening knots or for cleaning a horse's hoofs, etc., toggles were not pointed. Nor did they have sharp edges that could tear a cloth belt or girdle, catch in the clothing, or scratch a careless hand when thoughtlessly brushed against it. Generally, a toggle's edges and contours were gently rounded. If they were not originally smoothed, they eventually became so by constant handling. For the Chinese and the Mongols instinctively fingered their toggles or played with them while talking, just as the people of the Near East use "conversation beads," and thus the toggles received more than their share of rubbing, not to mention the natural friction from belt and clothing in ordinary use.

Furthermore, since the Chinese as a people seem to have specially developed the sense of touch, they delighted in substances that were pleasant to caress, such as oily-feeling jade or soapstone, or smooth satiny woods. Accordingly, the Chinese carvers in wood, ivory, or jade, including the toggle-makers, took special care to provide broad, flat or slightly rounded surfaces, avoiding sharp edges that would interfere with tactile appreciation. These concessions to the sense of touch were less necessary in Chinese pendants, which were commonly worn too high, or too low (if girdle pendants), for ease in handling. Consequently, some pendants have very acute angles or sharp edges that can immediately distinguish them from proper toggles.

To be fully functional under conditions of ordinary wear, toggles had to be made of very durable substances, or else special protective devices had to be added at the points of greatest friction. Such small objects, if made of a very soft or brittle wood, could not stand the wear and tear of daily use. Even hardwood or ivory toggles often show marks of erosion, such as obliterated features on the faces of men or animals, or indistinct patterns that must once have stood out clearly in relief. If a less durable object such as an ornamental nut or gourd was to be used as a toggle, it was usually transfixed by a metal bolt that could carry the principal strain, while metal caps or guard plates were attached to each end to protect them from wear. Such fittings were not attached to objects used for ordinary charms or pendants, so their presence usually indicates a true toggle.

The same requirements of durability made easily scratched substances such as amber highly impractical for toggles, except for ornamental ones worn by court nobles or members of the scholar-gentry on special occasions, for these, too, would not have survived ordinary use, even if a peasant had been able to afford such an expensive luxury. Indeed, as the toggles were objects of utility, generally, though not always, worn by the less wealthy classes of Chinese society, they were seldom made of any very precious substance. We have never seen a whole toggle of gold or of ruby or sapphire, or even of the precious apple green or *fei-tsui* jades. A small carving in any of these valuable materials would immediately fall into the "treasured ornament" or luxury amulet categories. The toggles in less valued kinds of jade were usually off-color pieces or reworkings of unwanted fragments, easily recognized as such by their odd shapes, and the crystal ones were also apt to be made of stones in the less desired colors, with obvious flaws. Even the ivory toggles often show by their form and quality that they were made from pieces of rejected scraps left over after creating some larger project. And yet, these little carvings in rejected substances often rise above the limitations of their

TOGGLES FROM NATURAL SUBSTANCES: DYED ANTLER, ARTIFICIALLY SHAPED GOURD, HORN (*nos. 17, 7, 20 in the Bieber Collection*)

TOGGLES OF STONE: WHITE JADE WITH SILVER, ROSE QUARTZ, TURQUOISE MATRIX (*nos. 29, 31, 28 in the Bieber Collection*)

TWO TOGGLES OF OLD IVORY (*nos. 214 and 215 in the Bieber Collection*)

FROG IN RED AMBER (*no. 136 in the Bieber Collection*)

material, showing once more how the Chinese could achieve miniature works of art with almost anything.

Now that we have considered some of the primary criteria for recognizing a Chinese toggle, the reader can perhaps begin to answer for himself that vexing question, When is a "toggle" not a toggle? This is a problem that especially plagues the beginning collector in the Western world, who has not had the opportunity to travel in Old China and see the toggles in actual use, or at least in their proper setting. But even experienced collectors are sometimes troubled by it. There is no short answer.

At this point, the reader is not likely to be taken in by a small carving that has no visible means for attaching a cord. He would immediately recognize that it must have been made for a sleeveweight, a paperweight, or some other light object of utility, or perhaps a mere ornament, but not a toggle. Similarly, he would know that a small carving which had a hole or ring only at its upper end, and was flat, thin, or very light, could only be a simple pendant, again not a toggle. However, there are many cases not nearly as clear-cut, and for these a few additional pointers might be helpful.

In the first place, any flat, button-shaped object of more than one inch in diameter is likely to have been a belt toggle. The buttons on Chinese clothing, purses, bags, and quivers, etc., were invariably very small, and they were usually spherical—until foreign influences inspired the flat metal or bone varieties familiar in the European tradition—and there were no other uses for large buttons in the old Chinese civilization. Here again, some discrimination must be used, though, because small bronze mirrors of olden times were sometimes recovered and used as button toggles; but on the other hand, every old Chinese mirror of small diameter was not used as a toggle. Indeed very few of them were, except in the Mongol and Tibetan border areas where there were no sophisticated scholar-collectors to revere them as antiques.

While it is obvious that not all perforated discs of ivory, wood, metal, or stone could have been used as toggles in China, many of them were. If such a disc is between two and three inches in diameter, and if the hole is large enough to admit a cord yet small enough to prevent a terminal knot from slipping out again, it could have been used as a toggle, regardless of whether or not it might originally have been made to serve some other purpose. Discs with larger apertures, or flat, narrow rings of jade or ivory, were also sometimes used as toggles by looping the string around one side; but these were not very typical, and most such cases were definitely instances of secondary utilization.

Secondly, a pendant or amulet would have been worn with the better side outward, to display it to best advantage; but with the toggles, the drabber side often seems to have been worn facing out, in order to receive the principal wear and tear, while the finer carving was protected at the back. Thus the rear of a toggle often shows the greatest marks of use, and in one particular style on which the subject is portrayed as resting on a giant leaf, the scratches and dents on the outside or lower surface of the leaf immediately show that that was worn outward to protect the principal carving.

Lastly, small figure toggles with attached bases are sometimes confused with little religious images made to serve as portable icons, and vice versa. Here the answer can be found by inspecting the bottom of the base. The undersides of the bases on images, whether large or small, were either left fairly rough or were smoothed off evenly, since they were intended to stand on a shelf or in a shrine box, so this part would ordinarily never be seen. On the other hand, the base of a toggle would not only be easily seen but it would also continually be felt. Therefore, even though the base would usually be left flat enough for it to stand upright if desired, it would ordinarily be finished off in some special way so as to appeal to the touch. Sometimes the underside of the base on the toggle figure would merely be smoothly rounded at the edges, but in other cases the whole surface was made slightly convex or concave, and often a symbol or a pattern was engraved or embossed at the center of the bottom to relieve the plain surface (as in No. 217). Any further question as to whether it had been a real toggle or merely an amulet could be settled by judging its general bulk and weight.

After these preliminary remarks by way of introduction, we can now go on to list the principal types of Chinese toggles, describing each, so that examples of it can be more easily recognized when encountered again.

1. *Ball Toggles* or *Ball Pendants*. These are usually rather heavy pendant-type toggles of the true counterweight variety. The actual sphere is usually made of ivory or some semiprecious stone. It is generally suspended by a metal bolt passing through it, with a suspension ring for

a cord at the top. Sometimes it is simply like a giant bead, pierced for a knotted cord.

2. *Bar Toggles*. These are notable for their greater length in proportion to the width. They include those made from a section of root, stick, or antler, fastened at the center. They may be pierced, transfixed by a short bolt with a ring, or, as in the case of the most primitive toggles, simply having the middle of the shank pared away to leave a thinner waist around which the cord could be looped without slipping.

3. *Box Toggles*. These are small containers, generally of a modified bun-shape, but sometimes in the form of a peach or another auspicious object, having a hinged lid or a small drawer swinging out on a pivot, and a metal loop, or bolt with ring, by which to attach it. Intended to carry small things, these were double-duty toggles, but they differed from others in that category because they were apparently originally made primarily to serve as toggles.

4. *Brick Toggles or Spreaders*. These are simple rectangular blocks of ivory, wood, or bone, etc., approximately twice as long as they are wide, and half as thick, pierced with two holes, one on each side of the center. Usually they are left severely plain, but sometimes one may be elaborately worked on the upper surface. These are known to have been worn with belt fittings, and they are found in most collections of Chinese toggles; but their construction would seem to indicate that they had probably originally been made for a different use. In view of the width between the holes, and the fact that the ornamented ones are carved in such a way that the ornamentation would be partly concealed by the string, it would seem more likely that they had probably served as "spreaders," placed farther down on a double-cord attachment for a bag or pouch, to prevent the two cords from becoming twisted together. Certainly, smaller pieces of the same shape were used in this way. Although an occasional example might have been made to serve as a proper belt toggle, it seems likely that they were primarily made for spreaders. As such, they would still belong in close association with the toggles, having the same relationship as that of the Japanese *ojime* bead to the netsuke. However, there was nothing to prevent their reuse as toggles, and many of the larger ones quite likely were so used.

5. *Bun-shaped Toggles*. These consist of thick, bun-shaped discs of various materials, attached by a ring or metal loop at the center of one flat side. They greatly resemble the Japanese *manjū* netsuke, which they

may have originally inspired. Like the latter, they are often pierced through the center by a ringbolt, which also serves to secure an ornamental metal plate to the front surface. (The Japanese call this particular combination *kagami-buta*.)

6. *Bun-pendant Toggles*. Although the basic form of the principal element is practically identical with the former type, the fact that it is intended to hang vertically, with either face exposed, gives this toggle an entirely different appearance, which adequately justifies placing it in a separate category. The two faces are sometimes lightly chased or engraved, but they were often left completely plain.

7. *Button Toggles*. These form another simple and basic toggle type, distinguished from the ordinary bun-shaped toggles by being much flatter and thinner. Sometimes, too, they are convex on the face and hollowed out behind, giving them a very distinctive appearance. When made of metal, they often have a ring or loop soldered to the back for a cord attachment; but when they were made of antler, bone, or wood, a small projection was generally left at the rear and pierced to make a way for the cord. Sometimes the face is richly worked, especially on the metal ones; more often it is merely smoothed and polished to afford tactile pleasure and to enhance the effect of the natural substance from which it was made.

8. *Cubo-octahedron* or *Bolthead Toggles*.[5] (The clumsy first name may be abbreviated as *cuboctahedron*.) Usually found as heavy toggles of the counterweight variety, these were given their distinctive geometric form by taking a cube and lopping off its eight corners, to produce a fourteen-sided figures, the faces of which comprise six equal squares and eight equilateral triangles. This shape is the one that was most frequently used for the heads of Chinese bolts and screws, hence the alternative name. An ordinary cube would be impractical for a toggle or a bolthead, because of its sharp angles and crisp edges which might tear things, but by cutting off the corners and rounding the edges slightly, a more practical as well as more decorative form was produced. Having shaped a cuboctahedron out of wood, jet, or some other suitable substance, the toggle-maker then either drilled it for the passage of a knotted cord or fitted it with a ringbolt. Actual toggles of this shape are not very common, but the form as such was frequently used for the heads of the ringbolts on toggles of all types, being pierced laterally to hold a small metal ring. It was eminently practical for this usage, as it pro-

vided a thickened section through which the ring could move freely, without danger of wearing through the bolthead, and at the same time it lacked any excessively sharp edges to catch in clothing.

9. *Cup Toggles.* These were small hemispherical metal cups, about an inch in diameter, ornamented on the outside and plain within, fastened by a ring at the top of the hemisphere. Like the Japanese "ash-pan netsuke" these were used for knocking out the ashes of a pipe when the smoker was seated in a house or tent. This type of toggle seems to have been more typical of Mongolia.

10. *Cylinder Toggles.* Cylindrical sections of solid or hollowed wood or of a naturally hollow bone were frequently used for toggles, as another of the basic types. The solid ones were generally transfixed by a ringbolt through the middle of the narrow side. If the hollow ones did not have openwork carving that could provide convenient gaps for the cord, they were sometimes drilled at the center of one side, then the cord was passed through and knotted, so that the knot remained concealed within the toggle. Essentially, these were like bar toggles, functioning on the same principle, but the arms tended to be shorter and their diameter was thicker in proportion to their length.

11. *Disc Toggles.* These formed another basic type. Although closely related to both the bun-shaped and the button toggles, which were also circular, they differed from each of those categories by being thinner than the former, and flat on both sides in contrast to the latter. The outside rim was often left flat, although the edges were sometimes slightly rounded to eliminate their sharpness. In the simplest varieties the disc was merely pierced to make a narrow hole through which a cord might be passed and knotted. However, on the more elaborate types a metal button was used in addition, with a long shank passing through the aperture and holding a loop or ring for the cord. Although the metallic face provided an interesting contrast of textures with the base material of stone, wood, or ivory, often the surface of the button was specially worked to provide additional ornament.

12. *Double-Utility Toggles.* We have already described how the Chinese and their neighbors used small bronze mirrors, seals, spoons, etc., as toggles, as well as for the other functions for which they were originally intended. All those fall into this category.

13. *Drum Toggles.* Frequently small cylinders of wood or ivory, or both in combination, were worked to resemble small drums. These could

be classed under replica toggles, but were numerous enough to form a category of their own.

14. *Figure Toggles.* A very large category of Chinese belt toggles consists of small figures in the round, representing popular divinities, or birds, animals, fish, or insects. Sometimes a human figure may be pierced through the head or back, or through the base, for the passage of the cord. More usually, no drilling was necessary, as arms held akimbo, or the loop made by a flying scarf, etc., offered natural gaps through which to pass the cord. The same is true of animals and plant forms; particularly the latter, where a looping stem or an arching leaf affords a convenient attachment point. Probably it is this category that offers the most traps for the collector, regardless of his degree of experience, because the fine lines of distinction between true toggles, pendants, small images, or miniature ornaments are very narrowly drawn here, and it is often difficult to decide for certain if a given example was really used as a toggle. In some cases a decision is almost impossible without careful consideration of the balance and a minute examination for points of wear.

15. *Flat Figure Toggles.* Sometimes the human or animal figures were worked in low relief on one side of a flat chip of wood or a thin, slightly arched section of bone or ivory rind. These are usually pierced with two holes like the brick toggles, unless some openwork carving provided gaps. Another form of flat toggle is the simple variety representing a thin slice or cross section of a lotus rhizome, with no decoration except for small holes representing the root canals, which also provided apertures for the cord. These rhizome toggles were almost numerous enough to be listed as a separate category, but they are too plain and undifferentiated to be very appealing.

16. *Natural-Object Toggles.* Often natural objects were simply picked up and used as toggles, without any more effort than the drilling of a cord hole when necessary. Under this heading we find such things as giant beans, small bottle gourds, light pebbles, or sea shells, selected both for convenience and for certain inherent decorative or auspicious qualities, as described more fully in the next chapter.

17. *Replica Toggles.* This broad category comprises a wide variety of toggles in the form of miniature copies of manufactured articles and utensils of daily use, often copied in a very ingenious way with movable parts. Sometimes, a portion of the original form would provide a convenient place for fastening the cord, such as the handle of a bucket or

the crossbar of a lock; but such things as saddles, hats, or bone dice were often pierced for a cord hole or fitted with a ringbolt. Typical examples from this category are described in Chapter 11.

18. *Reutilized Toggles.* This group comprises objects that were made for one purpose and then reused for toggles, sometimes after slight alteration to provide a place for the cord. These include old Mongol chessmen, antique mirrors no longer usable as such, and cast-off seals, etc.

19. *Root Toggles.* While these might be placed in the category of natural-object toggles or simply listed under materials, they deserve a place of their own as a very numerous group. Composed of oddly shaped sections of tree roots, they are usually totally amorphous, but sometimes Nature has been "helped," and the original root has been pared away here and there until it assumed the rough shape of a dog, a frog, or a miniature lion. These, too, will be more fully discussed in the next chapter.

20. *Scenic Toggles.* These generally present whole scenes, with rocks, trees, and temples, and usually people or animals in the foreground. They are among the most elaborate of the worked toggles.

21. *Spike Toggles.* As we have seen, these are a variation on the bar toggles, created by sharpening one end of the bar, or by taking a natural spike such as the prong of an antler, and were intended for various special jobs. Like the conventional bar toggles, they were generally secured by a hole through the center of the shank or by a ringbolt at that point. A popular variation was a section of bone or ivory carved into the shape of a green pepper, dyed the appropriate hue in a solution of verdigris.

22. *Storytelling Toggles.* Some of the scenic toggles represent episodes, or several episodes, from some familiar folk tale or popular drama, skillfully presented on a miniature scale. These are so complex and so distinctive that they deserve to be placed in a category by themselves. Particular examples of these will be discussed in Chapter 12.

The system of listing by the categories just given is admittedly a purely arbitrary way of classifying the principal types of Chinese toggles, being based primarily on their shapes and functions.[6] Other broad categories are provided by basic subject groupings, such as *Animal Toggles, Bird and Fish Toggles, Flower and Plant Toggles,* and *Human Figures.*

We could just as easily make other listings. One based entirely on subject matter, for example, would break down still further the headings last mentioned, on the basis of those most frequently repeated, and we would then have such groups as *Lion Toggles, Frog Toggles, Mushroom Toggles,* or *Lotus Toggles.* Or, again, one could classify them entirely on the basis of the substances and materials of which they were made, giving *Antler Toggles, Glass Toggles, Toggles of Jade,* etc., once more cutting across the lines of the categories already listed. The materials for the toggles make a fascinating study in themselves, and, as such, the principal ones will be discussed in detail in the chapters that immediately follow.

3

TOGGLES FROM NATURAL
OBJECTS

WHEN WE COME to investigate the various kinds of substances and materials that were used for making the Chinese toggles, either in their natural state or specially worked, the variety is astounding. At first glance it would seem that the possibilities were limited only by the materials available to the Chinese—including foreign importations as well as local products—with further variations provided by the different ways in which a given substance could be handled or worked. (This was apparently the case in Japan with the making of netsuke, for which they tried all possible substances.)

On examination, however, we find that in practice the Chinese exercised a considerable amount of selectivity in their choice of materials. They showed definite preference for some basic ones, while others they seem to have passed over entirely. In fact, it soon becomes apparent that the choices were by no means arbitrary, but were dictated by a definite philosophy and way of thought. Accordingly, a study of the toggle materials and the reasons why they were chosen is a basic requirement for any full understanding of the true significance of the toggles in Chinese civilization and their particular meaning to their wearers.

Often, natural objects were used as toggles with very little alteration, except for a little polishing, perhaps some light oiling or staining, and generally the drilling of a small hole for the cord. Ordinarily, these more utilitarian toggles were passed over by foreign collectors as being "too plain" or "not representative of Chinese Art." But, since they were so very common in Old China, and because their simplicity and essential practicality are so characteristic of the Old Chinese folk tradition, no collection of Chinese toggles could be considered complete without a few examples.

We have noted in Chapter 1 that toggle-wearing seems to have originated in the forested regions of Northern Asia, as the later distribution would imply, so the earliest toggles were probably made of twigs or roots. If so, we would expect to find this tradition continuing down into later times in any wood-growing area, including parts of North China and Manchuria. In any case, we do find that the North Chinese and the Manchurians seem to have had a special fondness for gnarled or oddly shaped roots of a conveniently compact size to use for toggles. In addition to the interest provided by their odd and varied shapes, in which a good imagination could sometimes make out human or animal forms, these would often have knotholes or perhaps even natural loops, to which one could attach a cord. Otherwise, they might have a narrower place around which a string could be tied without slipping; if not, it was a simple matter to drill a small hole.

In addition to their convenience and availability, roots had a special significance in Old China. The Taoists believed that roots represented the source or origin for the indwelling spirit in the trees or shrubs that sprang from them, and hence that the roots and lower trunk had in them the chief powers of the whole organism.[1] From such symbolic associations, it was only a step to ascribe actual magic powers to the roots, especially if they came from a tree that had any unusual qualities. Thus we find that the Chinese used roots of certain trees in their medicine and magical practices because of the powers of healing or the occult energies that these were supposed to possess.

Aside from the mandrake root, which had many of the same associations in Old China that it enjoyed in Medieval Europe, perhaps the best example is the folklore that has clustered around the root of a common North China shrub, *Lycium sinensis*, which the Chinese called *kou-ch'i*.[2] The first syllable of this Chinese name for it makes a pun on the word for dog, and the roots of this plant sometimes grow into a form that suggests the shape of a dog, in which case they were especially valued. The Old Chinese believed that these dog-shaped "dog roots" had extraordinary powers for curing and healing, and for helping people to prolong their lives or even to attain immortality. In these respects, they were thought to be fully as effective as the more familiar ginseng roots (the Chinese equivalent of the European mandrake) and other drugs favored by Taoist adepts who used them while seeking to become immortals.[3] On a more mundane level, these roots were supposed to exert special effects on the kidneys and reproductive organs, and were considered to be helpful in all forms of wasting diseases. But it was in magic that they figured most awesomely. Old Chinese wonder tales, which have found their way even into "respectable" Chinese literature, tell of occasions when one of these roots set all the dogs in the neighborhood howling, or even began to bark itself.[4]

Miss Bieber has no example of a "dog root" as such, but another dog-shaped root in her collection (No. 3) gives a remarkably lifelike impression of a Mongol or Tibetan mastiff, having been only slightly "helped" by a few deft cuts with a knife. In this case, it would have been considered to have the properties of the kind of wood of which it was made, and not the special ones that were attributed to true "dog root"; but it still would have had symbolic value and been credited with protective powers, because the dog in itself was a symbol of protection, especially against robbers and evil men.

In addition to these natural pieces of root used as toggles, we often find Chinese toggles carved from larger roots, but the subject of worked roots belongs rather to the larger topic of carved woods in general, and will be reserved for the next chapter.

Perhaps the next most obvious choice for toggles from the many materials available to the Chinese were small bottle gourds of the genus *Lagenaria*, called *hu-lu* in Chinese. These were formed of two spherical portions, a small one above and a larger one below, connected by a narrow neck. The different sizes of the spheres provided an interesting contrast, and their smooth surfaces were pleasant to the touch, satisfying the highly developed tactile sense of the Chinese; while the narrow neck between them was ideally formed for looping the cord around it. (See No. 5 for an example.)

Perhaps the surface of such a gourd might be lightly engraved, the scratches being filled with a darker pigment to produce the effect of an etched decoration; or sometimes a gourd might be lightly ornamented by pyrography, having patterns or symbols burned into it with a heated metal stylus. Others might even have embossed pictures, a symbolic form, or a grotesque shape, produced by having been grown inside special wooden molds. In general, however, the toggle gourds were left undecorated. Their natural coloration, perhaps enhanced by a light application of oil, and their distinctive texture provided sufficient ornament in themselves. This would be satisfying enough for the average Chinese peasant, partly because his simple life would have accustomed him to enjoy things for their own sakes and have made him suspicious of "lily-gilding," and partly because the very shape of the gourd gave it a deep significance in itself.

These small toggle gourds were miniature editions of the large bottle gourds that were traditionally used as symbols of medicine containers for the shop signs of Chinese druggists and apothecaries, and, as such, they were believed to be effective as health charms. Also, gourds, like melons, have numerous seeds; so, like the latter, they were natural symbols of fertility and numerous descendants. Furthermore, since gourd bottles had traditionally been worn by old men in the country districts for many centuries, as containers for water, wine, or medicine, they had gradually come to be symbols of old age and, by extension, of longevity.[5] Doubtless all these associations combined to contribute to the fact that, for at least five hundred years, a gourd of this form and shape has been called "Bottle Gourd of Great Good Fortune" (*ta-chi hu-lu*).[6] In short, such a toggle was a good luck amulet of the most comprehensive kind, believed capable of evoking almost any sort of good influence.

Occasionally, these small toggle gourds were opened at the upper end and, like the larger ones, provided with a small metal collar to prevent checking or cracking, then furnished with a stopper so that they could hold oils, medicine powders, or snuff, etc. This gave them a dual practical function, as containers as well as toggles. More rarely, another metal ring with a loop for the string was passed around the slender middle portion of either the plain or the container type, to ease the strain on the thin shell.

Not only bottle gourds but also the simple spherical gourds of small size were used for Chinese toggles. The latter never doubled as containers, but were always kept intact in their dried form with all the seeds still in them. The seeds were left there deliberately, to rattle about and make a pleasant sound, as audible symbols of the fertility which they were believed to represent. Sometimes they make so loud a sound when rattled that it would seem that scraps of metal or small shot had also been inserted in order to increase the noise.

Since the small round gourds lacked the convenient structural narrowing of their cousins, the bottle gourds, it was necessary to furnish them with some artificial means of attachment. This was generally done with a small ringbolt that pierced through the gourd vertically from the stem end through the base, and usually the top and bottom were capped with thin hemispherical plates of silver, to prevent their being chafed by the belt and to give them greater protection against hard knocks. Sometimes the silver caps had scalloped edges or light line engraving to suggest the petals in a floral form, but, in these cases, the gourds themselves were usually left plain.

Occasionally, to provide a contrast of textures, a very warty variety of gourd was used. The Brooklyn Museum has a fine example of this. Still more rarely, they might make a toggle from a molded gourd. A very interesting toggle in the Bieber Collection (No. 7) is made up of a small gourd that was apparently bound with wires while it was growing, so that its shell has a number of protruding lobes, creating an especially decorative effect. Furthermore, the usual ringbolt is here replaced by a slender pin of ivory, the upper end of which has been carved to represent a small clenched hand, which is pierced so that it clutches the cord. As both ends are also capped with metal having stamped designs, we have here three constrasting materials—vegetable, animal, and mineral—combined to make a very harmonious unity.

Large nuts or giant seeds were sometimes used as toggles in the same way. Seeds and nuts, from which new plants could grow, were natural symbols of renewal of life and fertility, and were recognized as such throughout Chinese folklore and magic. Hence any seed would have satisfied the unspoken but generally understood requirement for Chinese toggles, that in general the material of which they were made should carry special connotations. But, of course, practical considerations demanded that the seeds or nuts must be very large, of an appropriate shape, and heavy enough to serve as counterweights.

Perhaps the most characteristic examples of seeds used for toggles, and certainly the most striking, were the large, flat, shiny brown beans familiarly known as Gilla beans. The Chinese popularly call them k'o-tzŭ, "little wooden bowls," or hsiang tou, "elephant beans."[7] These come from a large woody climber of the legume family, called Entada scandens,[8] which grows widely in tropical Asia, in Africa, and in Central and South America, but in China is only found in the remote south, in the mountain forests of Southern Kwangtung. The plant produces its seeds in giant bean pods that grow up to six feet in length by about four inches broad, having a tough, woodlike, segmented shell. An early Chinese author described them as "pods like bow-cases, seeds like hen's eggs."[9]

The Gilla beans might suggest eggs in size, but not in shape, as they are characteristically heart or kidney shaped, flattened on the upper and lower surfaces, and rather flat around the rim. Although their rich mahogany color and lustrous sheen recall the chestnut, and a certain South China chestnut, the *Pan-li*, is not unlike it in size and flatness, the Gilla bean can easily be distinguished from any chestnut by the fact that it has an attachment scar at the lower end in the form of a small oval projection with a sunken center. This gives a marked contrast to the much larger "bald spot" found on all chestnuts. Also, the Gilla bean has an even more shiny surface, and handling would inevitably soon give it an even higher polish. In fact, the shiny seed case often presents the appearance of having been lacquered; very old, long-dried examples sometimes display a crackled surface like that of ancient, time-damaged lacquer.

In a few cases, perhaps the giant seeds may actually have been varnished with a clear lacquer before being mounted for toggles, but that was hardly necessary. The Gilla bean has an aesthetic charm of its own that needs no lacquer to enhance it. Its smooth surfaces with gently rounded contours were pleasant to the touch, while the soft brown color gave pleasure to the eye. But these obvious features were not the only reasons why it was so highly favored for making toggles.

Not only in China, but elsewhere in Asia as well, these seeds were credited with having medical powers, particularly useful in banishing fevers, but also effective for pains of the loins and for general debility. The drug made from the seed proper, inside the hard casing, was said to improve appetite, check fevers, and relieve pains, etc.[10] In addition, Li Shih-chên, the famous Ming writer on Chinese *materia medica*, noted that in his time people often extracted the inside of the seed— no doubt to make it into drugs—and used the outer casing as a medicine container to hang at the waist.[11]

This is one case where the old European beliefs regarding a substance seem to have been far more fanciful than the Oriental ones. At least the Chinese always knew they were dealing with a bean; but the Europeans down into modern times had very bizarre notions about it, largely because it came to them in a rather unusual way.

For hundreds of years the seeds of *Entada scandens* have been washed up on the North Atlantic beaches. People have found them from Kerry in Southwestern Ireland as far north as Spitsbergen. They also drifted up on the outer islands of the Faroe and Shetland groups and in the Hebrides, and for a long time the mystified peoples of these areas tried to account for their origin. According to old Norse beliefs, they were "stones floated on to the coast." People described them as "adder stones" or "eagle stones," and said that one of these "doth bring forth another stone when it is kept long." They carried them as amulets against witchcraft and the evil eye, until quite recently, and they powdered them for medicine.[12]

Later, more rational observers concluded that they must be seeds, but thought that they were the product of some marine plant or "sea tree." As early as 1570, the European author of a Latin herbal had guessed that some of these seeds found on the coast of Cornwall must be beans that had somehow drifted from the New World with favoring southerly or westerly winds. However, the old superstitions still persisted, even after Sir Hans Sloane, founder of the British Museum, published an account of them in 1696, suggesting that they must have drifted over from Jamaica, where he had found the original plant growing, while preparing his catalogue of Jamaica plants. In time, it gradually became more widely known that these were actually tropical seeds from the West Indies, carried across by the Gulf Stream. But such scientific notions percolated very slowly among the people who were actually finding them; and the "Molucca Beans," as they were called (no one now knows why), were still cherished as amulets along the northern coasts and in the outer islands, for a very long time. Especially in Scotland and in the Hebrides, they were prized for their usefulness in making snuff containers and tinder boxes, and ultimately for match cases, sometimes handsomely mounted in silver.[13]

Some Entada beans have been successfully planted (indoors) in Ireland, in recent times, to produce giant plants.[14] Perhaps an earlier attempt, long ago, gave rise to the tale of Jack and the Bean Stalk!

To return to the Chinese use of Gilla beans: in order to make them into toggles, they dried them thoroughly and furnished them with ringbolts for attaching the cord. They either transfixed the bean vertically to make a bun pendant, or else they pierced it transversely through the center, from one flat face to the other, to make an ordinary bun-shaped toggle of the more usual type. In either case, metal washers or small circular plates were added to prevent chafing, as in the case of the gourds. The Bieber Collection has fine examples of both types in Nos. 9 and 10.

While the rich chestnut brown Gilla bean, with its glossy texture set off by silver fittings, made an attractive ornament in itself, sometimes the sides were also engraved. The Bieber Collection has a bun-shaped toggle made from one (No. 10), with a picture of a man in a boat scratched into one side, while the reverse has a Ming poem inscribed in tiny characters. The poem is dated "Ming Dynasty: reign of Yung Lo," which lasted from 1403 to 1424 by our calendar. Although the date of a poem is by no means a guarantee of the date when it was actually inscribed, since we know from the writings of Li Shih-chên that these giant beans were known and used for other purposes during the Ming Dynasty, it is possible that this toggle was also made during the early Ming, in the period cited in its inscription.

Another giant bean seed, equally large or larger, but with a very different shape and texture, sometimes turns up among the toggles. Apparently from another member of the Entada family, this has the same small oval attachment scar, but it is situated at the end of the bean, rather than in the middle of one side (to speak technically: terminal rather than lateral). This second form of giant bean has a less regular shape, roughly rectangular, and longer than it is broad, with more bulging faces and sharper rims, somewhat suggesting the shape of a pillow. The outer surface is much rougher than that of *Entada scandens,* and it is a duller brown with a faint marking in purplish lines, like a network of coarse veins. With its rougher surface and even larger size, it seems even more worthy of the Chinese term "elephant bean." One of these has been published as a Japanese netsuke, but that is probably a mistake, as the method of attachment with a ringbolt is typically Chinese.[15]

Other forms of simple toggles were made of seashells or from pieces of shell. Seashells were considered as expensive rarities, increasing in value the farther they traveled from the source of supply, until, by the time they reached the West China borderlands and Tibet proper, they became objects of wealth in themselves.

A common form of toggle in the Tibetan area, sometimes seen among the Tibetans of Northern Yünnan and Western Szechuan, where I first came across them, is a circular section of conch shell, drilled through the center to make a hole for a knotted cord. They are generally worn with the concave side out. Some have been burnished to make them gleam brighter, but they are seldom decorated, although carved ones with simple designs in relief occasionally turn up. In addition to their treasure value as rarities in that inland region, they enjoyed special veneration from the Mongols and Tibetans as being important protective charms, because the conch is especially sacred in Lamaism, their special form of Buddhism. (The Danish National Museum in Copenhagen has several examples of such toggles from Outer Mongolia.[16])

The Bieber Collection also contains a handsome shell of the Purple Cowry (*Cypraea macula*, Adams), known in Chinese as *tzŭ pei*, which has been bored at one end to make a hole for attaching a cord, so it could be used as a toggle (No. 8). Not only is this shell very beautiful in itself, with richly variegated coloring and a smooth porcelainlike texture, but it would also have had many symbolic connotations.

Cowries were used for money in Ancient China and until recently among the tribes in the Southwest, and they have served as a form of jewelry, as wealth and status symbols, and as fertility charms among the outlying peoples of Yünnan and Burma until the present time. Even in China proper, the opening of the cowry shell, which strongly resembles the vulva, has led the Chinese to consider this shell as a sex symbol. Thus the concept of fertility is added to a well-recognized wealth charm. Lastly, the purple cowry is believed able to cure disease, more specifically to clarify the vision and remove inflammation of the eyes.[17]

Here, then, is a superb example of the thinking that led to the choice of a specific natural substance as a toggle. For this shell had a practical shape and just the right amount of weight, combined with inherent beauty and touch appeal, in addition to significance as an amulet for health, wealth, and fertility.

4

WOODEN TOGGLES

THE GREAT MAJORITY of Chinese toggles were made of wood, carved from the branches or roots of trees and shrubs. This might seem strange to those who know the Chinese toggles only from examples in Western collections, in which toggles of jade or other stones predominate. However, the relative scarcity of wooden toggles in the Occident probably results from the fact that many foreign collectors ignored them as being "too ordinary," passing them by in favor of the more eye-catching ones in more expensive substances. This tendency among collectors has led to an unfortunate and misleading imbalance in existing specimens, giving a totally false impression. The wooden toggles were not only the most common ones in China, but in their forms and in the subjects and symbols represented on them they also seem far more typical of the old Chinese folk art tradition that gave birth to toggle-carving and kept the craft alive into modern times. Luckily, a few collectors such as Miss Bieber felt an appreciation for the intrinsic qualities of the wooden ones as well.

Although in Mongolia and the uplands of Tibet wood was so rare that wooden toggles had a considerable value in themselves, most of China is (or was) rich in woods of many varieties, offering a wide range of choice to the toggle makers.[1] This very variety of available materials would seem to present a formidable problem when one begins to attempt an identification of the woods used for the toggles in any given collection. In the case of the Bieber Collection, we were saved from the perils of mere guesswork by the kindness of scientific experts who analyzed the wooden toggles and reported the substances from which they had been made.[2] It was then surprising to see how comparatively few types of wood had been used, out of the large number that were available, and it was also interesting to discover, through

[49]

further research, just why these particular ones seem to have been chosen in preference to others. Four considerations seem to have influenced the choice: the availability of a certain wood in North China where most of the toggles in this collection were made and worn; the auspicious connotations of the wood, which would give the carving power as a charm or amulet; the medicinal powers ascribed to the tree, which were thought to impart curative powers to the wood from it; and lastly, but not less important, the practical considerations of carvability and durability.

The great majority of the toggles from North China, and nearly half of those in this collection, were made from boxwood, which is known to the Chinese as *huang yang mu*. The ordinary box (*Buxus sempervirens*) is a small tree or shrub, common in European or American ornamental gardens for clipped figures or hedges, but growing as a timber tree in South and West China.[3] As it is very slow-growing, adding not more than an inch and a half or two inches to its diameter in twenty years, the wood is so fine-grained that it might be considered almost grainless. This makes it easy to carve and capable of taking the finest details of miniature work, while its compactness and freedom from splitting render the resulting carvings very durable.

These qualities in boxwood have made it very popular in the Far East for making printing blocks, ever since the Chinese invention of printing, several hundred years before Gutenberg,[4] and it is also much used in the making of combs and seals. Large quantities of the wood were therefore brought into Peking and other North China towns for such purposes, and one way in which the toggle carvers probably obtained their raw materials was by utilizing the scraps that were discarded by the block-cutters and the comb-makers.

But the boxwood was not used just for its availability, durability, and ease in carving. The plant from which it comes is an evergreen, and evergreens in general were considered to be highly auspicious, so their wood was highly valued for charms, amulets, coffins, and other objects of ritual. These beliefs apparently arose because, in retaining their leaves through the winter and during periods of drought, they visibly resisted the change of the seasons and periods of hardship, and thus they showed themselves to be infused with vital energy. The Chinese felt that they were imbued with the essence of the *Yang* or active element in Nature, and as such, they considered them as symbols of longevity, and capable of granting long life.

Although the more spectacular evergreen trees such as the pine and the cypress have been more prominently featured in Chinese literature, art, and folklore as symbols of longevity, most evergreens were considered to be auspicious long-life plants. Also, the soft wood of the pine or the cypress was not very practical for anything that would have to undergo as much hard wear and handling as a toggle. (There are no pine toggles at all in this collection, and only one of cypress [No. 123], which is badly worn.) Therefore, the harder, more serviceable boxwood was used in preference to these others.

In Chinese medicine the leaves of the box are used, as they are supposed to contain the *Yang* element that keeps them green for some time after plucking, but the wood was also believed to be useful if reduced to ashes. The powdered leaves or ashes were recommended as being cooling in fevers, and soothing for prickly heat or summer boils, and they were thought to be useful for women in difficult labor.[5] Thus, in wearing a boxwood toggle a householder had with him a medical substance that could be quickly utilized for various kinds of emergencies.

Another wood very frequently used for toggles in North China was birch. In fact, birchwood toggles form the second largest group in the Bieber collection. Several species of birch trees flourish in North China, Manchuria, and on the borders of Inner Mongolia, and the wood of several types is known by the general Chinese name *hua mu*. However, the one most often used by the toggle-makers was probably from the White Birch (*Betula alba*[6]). The Chinese considered the white bark of this tree an important medicine, using it especially in decoctions for jaundice and bilious fevers,[7] and it is probable that the ghostly color of the bark led the country people to consider this kind of birch a "spirit tree," possessing supernatural powers. Quite apart from these more superstitious considerations, birchwood was very practical for toggle carvings because of its availability and ease in carving. It, too, is eminently carvable, having a very close grain—although it is not quite as "grainless" as box—and being resistant to splitting.

Quantities of birchwood were continually being brought into Peking, Kalgan, and other manufacturing centers, to be made into wooden bowls, boxes, cheap furniture, saddle frames, handles for tools, for fuel, and for house construction; while the roots were prized for making all sorts of carvings, because of their wavy grain and fine texture.[8] These many uses resulted in plenty of chips or discarded pieces for the toggle makers, some of whom were probably the carpenters and wood-workers themselves, idly whittling in their spare time.

The third largest group of wooden toggles in this collection contains those of fruitwood (*Prunus*), apparently from the peach tree (*Prunus persica Batsch.*), *t'ao mu* in Chinese.[9] Fruit- and nut-bearing trees were also highly auspicious in China, because their productivity implied the presence of special powers, and their wood was called *hsien mu* or "wood of the Immortals."[10] Among these, the peach led all the rest in the virtues ascribed to it. The wood itself was considered to have more vitality than any of the other *hsien* woods, and was credited with all manner of magical powers, especially for subduing evil influences or for suppresssing demons. Charms carved from peachwood, often in the form of rectangular blocks or plaques, were carried on the person, or fastened to the lintels of doors to keep out demons, and poles or posts of peachwood were often set up around a house for the same purpose.[11] The flowers, fruits, and kernels of the peach, the bark of trunk and roots, and the exuded gum, all had specific and important uses in Chinese medicine,[12] at least partly because they were supposed to quell the diseases caused by specters or other spirits. Both the exorcising and the healing powers ascribed to the peach therefore played their parts in influencing people to use its wood for toggles, so that they could also serve as protective amulets.

Another fruit tree also regarded as having extraordinary powers, both medicinally and auspiciously, was the plum; and as its wood is eminently carvable, this was also used in making toggles.[13] The heart-wood of the plum is especially handsome, being of a deep brownish red, resembling mahogany in color; but plumwood in general was prized, as it is heavy, close-grained, hard, and strong, making it very practical for objects like toggles that would ordinarily be subjected to much wear.

Other fruit trees besides the plum and the peach, which were also credited with having evil-averting and life-preserving *hsien* qualities, were the pear, the *hai-t'ang* (*Pyrus spectabilis*), the persimmon (*Diospyros kaki*),[14] the loquat (*Eriobotrya japonica*), which produces the luscious *p'i-pa* fruits,[15] and the jujube (*Zisyphus vulgaris*) that gives the so-called "Chinese dates."[16] The Old Chinese believed that the fruits of all these trees could confer health, strength, and long life, and they considered the woods as being correspondingly effective and auspicious, so they doubtless used them for toggle-making. Nineteen of the toggles in the Bieber Collection were definitely identified as *Prunus*, probably peach,[17] and another was declared to be certainly of loquat.

Of course, peach trees and other fruit trees were too valuable to chop down simply for their wood until they had passed bearing age, so only the wood of very old trees would have been available for toggles, unless some accident or deliberate pruning happened to detach a branch large enough to produce pieces for carving. But one could always saw off burls or other excrescences without doing too much harm to the tree. In fact, in both evergreens and fruit trees, a great part of the magic spirit or inner essence of the tree was believed to be concentrated in the burls on the lower trunk or upper roots,[18] so they were especially prized for toggle amulets. We shall return to the burls in a moment.

Not only perpetual greenness or fruit-bearing made a tree or its wood medicinal in Chinese eyes. Another quality that was thought to produce the same beneficial effects was a wood of strong yet pleasing scent, which might be capable of discouraging demons and averting evil.[19] Perhaps the most highly scented woods in this category were camphorwood, sandalwood, and eaglewood or lignaloes.

The camphor tree (*Cinnamonum camphora*) grows in South China, on the islands of Hainan and Formosa, and elsewhere in tropical Asia. It is one of the most beautiful and effective shade trees. It used to be a common sight in South Hunan or neighboring Kiangsi to see a single huge camphor tree arching its branches protectively over a cluster of small houses. There, giant trunks over twenty feet in circumference were not uncommon.[20] The rich-smelling hardwood of the camphor tree is superior to almost any other kind of timber for keeping away insects and resisting fungus growths, so the Chinese rank it with the pine and cypress as a possessor of vital power. Like them it is an evergreen, as it belongs to the laurel family, and as such it was also considered as a "long-life" tree.[21] Unfortunately, its superior natural qualities and the auspicious powers ascribed to it, together with its valuable by-products (solid camphor and camphor oil), have led to a large-scale cutting of these trees, with the careless disregard for the future that has been a characteristic of Chinese wood-cutting for centuries.

Camphorwood comes in a variety of handsome colors, ranging from a grayish white to a dark reddish brown, and it is also easy to work. These characteristics, along with its auspicious and medical qualities,[22] made it popular with carvers of amulets. A camphorwood toggle can usually be easily recognized by its distinctive odor, but not always. Age may dry out the oil cells, causing it to lose its scent completely. Furthermore camphorwood was a valuable product of South China, rare in the North, and whenever something was rare or valuable, there were always clever Chinese who would seek to counterfeit it. Thus we find some imitations.

An example of this is a toggle shaped like a peach, in the Brooklyn Museum.[23] Purchased in Peking some twenty years ago, this still has a rather strong scent of camphor, and yet the material does not seem to have the proper consistency of camphorwood. The clue is provided by a small ring-shaped mark on one edge, which clearly indicates the presence of an inserted plug. It would seem that the maker had drilled a small hole in which to introduce a piece of raw camphor or a few drops of camphor oil, securing it by the plug, so it would only gradually seep out, pervading the whole piece with its characteristic odor. The plug was smoothed off so skilfully that it is barely visible, except with a strong hand lens.

This was an ingenious application of a very old trick. Much of the Cantonese "sandalwood wares," in the form of such things as the delicate fans cut to resemble lacework, which were so greatly admired by foreign visitors in the Clipper-ship era, were actually made from soft absorbent wood of cheaper varieties impregnated with sweet-scented sandalwood oil imported from India.

Real sandalwood (*Santalum album*) was very expensive, being not only highly valued but an expensive importation from the lands to the South, so it was a rare luxury in North China. It is also a rather soft wood, unable to stand much rough wear. For these reasons it does not appear to have been used for toggles. At least, we have never seen one of sandalwood.

The third fragrant wood with a distinctive scent that earned it a reputation for special efficacy was eaglewood, also called aloes wood, lignaloes, etc. This comes from an evergreen tree (*Aquillaria agallocha*) that grows on Hainan Island and in the lands south of China; and the Chinese have been importing it for over a thousand years.[24]

It is a very special thing, since it does not come from the healthy living tree, but from one sick or dead. After the tree is injured or decays, its heartwood becomes filled with a dark resinous substance which provides the highly distinctive scent. This resin-impregnated wood keeps off lice and fleas, and has long been used in medicine, in India and Europe as well as in China. The Chinese ascribe to it tonic, stimulant, carminative, aphrodisiac, and diuretic properties,[25] and also feel that it possesses certain occult virtues as a demon chaser. Thus it is highly prized as an auspicious substance for amulets and toggles. Miss Bieber has several toggles made from it.

One of these (No. 75), in the shape of a cluster of gourds, retains the typical scent very strongly. However, it is made from the sapwood, so the resin, instead of predominating, as it usually does, is here present only in thin, purplish veins that stand out sharply against the grayish brown wood of a rather wooly texture. Two others (Nos. 223 and 226) are made from the heartwood itself, and are so thoroughly saturated with the thick resin that they cannot float in water. This explains why the Chinese speak of the best quality of eaglewood as "sinking incense wood" (*ch'ên hsiang mu*). Two other eaglewood toggles in this collection, like the first one described above, do not have sufficient concentration of the resin to affect their specific gravity to that extent, and they will still float; but their strong fragrance as well as the characteristic structure of the wood itself identifies them beyond question.

Even though eaglewood was an expensive importation, it was brought to Peking in considerable quantities for making incense, Buddhist rosaries, and precious images, so there would have been spare chips available for the carvers.

Another expensive imported wood also used for toggles was rosewood. The Chinese used several varieties, ranging from a lighter, reddish type, known as *huang hua-li*, to a deep purple one, which they called *t'an mu* or *tzŭ t'an*. All these seem to have come from various kinds of *Dalbergia* trees, of the legume family, from Hainan, Indo-China, the Philippines, and the East Indies.[26] Some of these woods are rather light pink when first carved, but they rapidly become dark. One variety has fine gold fibers within it, causing the Chinese to call it "gold thread *tzŭ t'an*."[27] Two toggles in this collection (Nos. 21 and 161) show the fibers clearly. All five of the rosewood toggles in the collection, ranging from *hua-li* to *tzŭ-t'an* by Chinese standards, have been identified as

Dalbergia, and all five sink like stones in water. Rosewood was imported in quantity for fine furniture, carved ornaments, boxes, or stands for porcelains; so, again, there must have been scraps available for the toggle-makers.

The rosewoods were considered auspicious because of their reddish *Yang* color, which also led to their use in medicine for cleansing the blood, checking hemorrhages, and healing bleeding wounds.[28] Once again, auspicious and medicinal virtues, as well as decorative qualities, carvability, and availability, seem to have dictated the choice of the toggle material.

One other wood represented in this collection deserves special mention, although it is only represented by a single example, (No. 76); this is palmwood. The Hemp Palm (*Camaerops fortunei*), from which this wood probably came, is the hardiest of all palm trees, and can grow rather far north in the temperate zone; in the last century they were common as far north as Shanghai.[29] This tree was known all over China for its coir fiber, which was used to make ropes, brushes, raincoats and many other things,[30] and for the medicinal properties ascribed to its buds, flowers, seeds, and bark;[31] but I have not previously heard of its wood being used for ornamental carvings. The beautifully carved melon into which this has been fashioned is a typical toggle subject, but it would be interesting to know how the carver happened to choose this material. Since palmwood is difficult to work because of its stout fibers —the ends of which are visible on the bottom of this toggle as large dots of darker color—it must have required special carving techniques, and very possibly some town on the South China coast made a specialty of this. In fact, this example may originally have been carved for some other ornamental purpose, then reused as a toggle.

Turning from the kinds of woods to a consideration of wood as a material, we find among the wooden toggles in general a comparatively large number that appear to be dotted with small dark-pupiled eyes, recalling the handsome effect of bird's-eye maple, or else with a wildly contorted graining, such as one sees in the "briar root" used for making expensive pipes. This material, which the Chinese call *hua mu*, or "patterned wood,"[32] comes from burls. Burls can develop on the trunk or root of almost any kind of tree; in fact, only two of the burl toggles in the Bieber Collection are actually of maple. They usually grow out from the base of the trunk, near where it joins the main roots, or else from the upper roots themselves, probably as the result of some early injury or infection. Within these growths a number of buds had once begun to form, but their development was thwarted, and their remains give the appearance of a number of small knots packed together in an involved formation. Around these swirl the lines of the grain, like water rushing around rocks in a raging river. One Chinese scholar, describing the burl of the *nan mu*, said, "When it is cut, within it there are the forms of mountains and streams, flowers and trees." Indeed, large pieces of burlwood were sometimes merely worked into large buttons, with the surface smoothed and polished to show off the fine figure, in which an imaginative person could fancy he saw all manner of interesting things. The effectiveness of this is especially apparent on the grotesquely large button toggle, No. 13.

Although the distortion is sometimes more extreme than usual, in any burl the fibers are very irregularly contorted throughout the growth, so the grain cannot be said to run in any particular direction. As a result, wood in this form is useless for planks or construction work, as it is both difficult to work and structurally unreliable. In the Occident, such wood is often sawn into thin veneers to make ornamental effects, and for inlays; but in the Orient, although fine pieces were sometimes sliced into sections for inlays, usually the burls were simply chopped off by the woodworkers and discarded. Probably this is one reason why they were used for making toggles, as such wood is comparatively cheap and easy to acquire in a region where fine wood was otherwise relatively rare and expensive.

But beauty and availability were not the only reasons why burls were used for toggles. Old Chinese tradition believed that an indwelling spirit in certain trees occasionally showed its presence in the form of just such preternatural swellings or excrescences; how else could one account for them? And, if the burl was from a *hsien* tree or a long-life evergreen, already known to be endowed with special powers and virtues, the growth was all the more significant.[33] It is thus no accident that the largest number of burl toggles in this collection are of peachwood, and the next largest group from box. Birch, which had no special magical powers ascribed to it, is not represented among the burl toggles at all.

Although this burl material must have been very difficult to work, because of the frequent obstructions caused by the tiny knots and the changes of direction in the graining, the final effect is very pleasing. It is seen at its best in some of the large button toggles, which seem to have been made from the cross section of a single burl, having no decoration except its own marvelous graining, with the color contrasts slightly emphasized by a light rubbing of oil.

It has been said that the Chinese often lacked the sensitive appreciation shown by the Japanese for the appearance of woods, their variations in graining, and their innate natural beauties, and that they were too often prone to paint and gild their wood workings. While these generalities might sometimes be true as far as Chinese architecture and the formal furnishings of temples and palaces were concerned, it certainly would not apply to the wooden toggles, especially the ones of burl.

The Chinese wooden toggles were rarely painted or lacquered, as so many of the Japanese ones were. Nor did the Chinese ever inlay them with ivory or other rare substances, as the Japanese often did. The only lacquered toggle in this collection (No. 174) is not of wood, but has a base of bark fiber and glue. With the wear and tear to which they were inevitably subjected, paint would soon have cracked or rubbed off, giving them a shabby appearance. However, aside from this practical consideration, there was undoubtedly some inner feeling in the folk tradition, as contrasted with the more sophisticated spirit expressed in the "palace arts," which led to a finer appreciation for the simpler things. Perhaps it was because the strict sumptuary laws, as well as their highly straitened circumstances, denied them the use of fine lacquer that the peasants came to enjoy wood graining for its own sake. Whatever the ultimate reasons might have been, Chinese wooden toggles afforded an excellent opportunity for enjoying the rich figures of choice woods, often skilfully brought out to enhance their best qualities.

How was this work accomplished? No account of the Chinese wooden toggles could be considered complete without at least a brief mention of the techniques that were used to produce them. Almost nothing has been written about the techniques of the woodcarvers in Old China.[34] This is most unfortunate, as they had a highly perfected art for centuries until modern industrialism and power tools (in the larger towns and cities) brought a loss of pride in craftsmanship, impatience on the part of the apprentices against the long training that was needed, and a consequent deterioration in abilities. Even before the Communists took over, fine Chinese woodworking was virtually a lost art except in the back-country towns of Interior China. It was in such places, during the late

1930's, that I had the good fortune to observe the old techniques still being practiced.

Professional woodcarvers in Old China used a wide range of knives, chisels, and gouges, with flaring blades set in handles of wood, horn, or bone. These blades were characteristically narrow, flaring near the end, to conserve weight and avoid a waste of precious steel. They also used numerous files, bowdrills of various sizes for perforated work, and wire saws set in an arching handle of elastic bamboo for fretwork. Most of the toggles were too small for the use of a saw after the first rough blocking out, but many show the marks of fine drills.[35] Except in the cases where professional woodworkers were turning out toggles in their spare time, however, most of the wooden toggles were probably simply whittled out with knives, without any elaborate chiselwork.

Many of the wooden toggles and a number of the ivory ones clearly show that they must have been turned on a lathe. Some, such as a small button toggle in the shape of a straw hat (No. 192) and another representing a mortar and pestle (No. 187), were obviously completely finished on the lathe. Others seem to have been begun on a lathe, to establish the basic shape, and then were completed by handwork. This technique seems to have definitely been used on some of the drums and other cylindrical toggles, as well as on some of the button-shaped ones.

The old Chinese reciprocating lathe—used not only by woodworkers but also by gem-cutters, pewterers, and other kinds of artisans—was a relatively simple instrument.[36] It consisted primarily of a horizontal cylindrical spindle, known as the lathe-pin, resting in slots at the tops of two short uprights; these in turn were secured to the top of a sturdy wooden frame. A leather strap or rope was coiled around the center of the lathe pin, and its ends were fastened to two foot treadles below, in such a way that every time the operator pressed down with his right foot the lathe-pin spun in one direction, and when he pressed with his left foot it spun in the other. If a small piece of wood was to be turned to make something like a toggle, it was secured in a cup-shaped socket at the projecting end of the lathe-pin, and worked with a metal tool as it spun in one of the two directions—usually in the direction determined by pressure on the right treadle.

This reciprocating lathe was also used for abrasion work, by fixing to the end of the lathe-pin a cast-iron disk, the face and edges of which were smeared with a soft mud, made of fine sand and water. Then, as this disk was spun, the object to be worked was pressed against it and ground into the desired shape. This process, which was used so effectively for working jade and other hard stones, was also employed for very hard woods, such as rosewood, that did not respond well to the knife or chisel. Other wooden toggles were probably finished off in this way, or at least buffed against the lathe-driven wheel to soften their contours, as were many of the ivory toggles.

Chinese woodworkers in general did not make much use of sand-paper, or of shark- or ray-skin, which were its common Oriental equivalents; but the toggles were intended to be smooth for handling, and it was necessary to tone down any imperfections that might chafe the clothing, so they used other methods to achieve this. For finishing woods that were especially hard, they used a wet piece of fine-grained sand-stone to smooth it, and for softer woods they used Scouring rush or Horsetail (*Equisetum hyemale*),[37] which contains a very high content of silica.

On woods like boxwood and birch, which naturally have a rather dull finish, a light vegetable oil may sometimes have been used to impart a gloss, but eventually even the untreated toggles of these woods took on a shine after much handling, or at least acquired a satiny smoothness. Other woods, such as the rosewoods (*Dalbergia*) and the even more aromatic eaglewood and camphor, had their own natural oils which added to their beauty, assisted in their preservation, and eventually enabled them to take on a very high gloss that was much prized.

Since toggles were considered "old-fashioned" by the late 1930's or early '40's, even though they were still being worn here and there, most of them must have been made before the degeneration of wood carving set in; and some were of course made many years before. Therefore, as we have already remarked, the obvious crudity or extreme simplicity seen in numerous examples of the Chinese wooden toggles are usually evidence of amateur experiments on the part of peasant carvers or the lack of sophistication of "primitive" craftsmen. They cannot be cited to show the decline of once-high professional standards, nor can they be used to illustrate any supposed inferiority of Chinese work as opposed to the Japanese. The unadorned simplicity of many of the Chinese toggles is seldom offensive; it usually enhances the impact of their symbolic message, and is often a source of beauty in itself.

5

TOGGLES IN IVORY AND OTHER ANIMAL PRODUCTS

WHEN WE COME to the toggles in ivory and other animal products, including such substances as antler, horn, and bone, we might suppose that, in contrast to the wooden ones, it was the subjects depicted on them which gave them their chief value as charms and amulets. But we shall see that these materials also had auspicious connotations of their own, as well as fancied medical powers, to an even greater extent than many of the woods.

Many of the plainer disc or button toggles were made from ivory, by simply taking a cross section of the tusk. The most elementary type was a flat oval or disc, with its center pierced to provide a hole for the cord. The cord itself was secured by making a large knot at the end, or by tying it to a small button or stud of silver, having a diameter larger than the hole, which would prevent its slipping out.

The ivory discs generally had rounded edges to prevent their abrading the belt or outer robe, but otherwise they were frequently left plain, either to serve as a foil or background for an ornamental button or just to be enjoyed for themselves. Their creamy coloring, varied by the natural markings characteristic of different types of ivory or with patterns of cracking due to age, made a pleasing enough effect in its own right. Occasional examples, such as No. 18, were engraved with Chinese characters making auspicous phrases, into which darker pigments were rubbed to render them more prominent. A considerable number were carved in the shape of twin fish or other auspicious figures that lent themselves to a compact circular composition, such as No. 148.

When we come to consider the actual figures carved in ivory, the expression "figures in the round" should not be taken too literally. If so, it would be rather misleading, since most of the three-dimensional ivory carvings tend to be rounded in front and flat behind, or *vice versa,* or else they are roughly triangular or wedge-shaped in cross section. This was caused by the nature of the original material.

We have seen that the toggle-makers generally had to work with less expensive materials, as neither they nor their patrons were apt to be wealthy people. That meant that they were forced to use the less-desirable smaller tusks, or more likely the tips of the larger ones that had been discarded by the image-makers, and they could not afford to waste very much of the pieces that were available to them.

Given a small section of ivory tusk, there were only a few possible approaches for the carver. In the first place, he could use the complete section to make a figure in the round; but, if it were too thick, this would mean that he would have to pare away, and hence waste, quite a bit of the valuable substance. Alternatively, he could split it in half, and make two toggles of the variety that have one side round and the other flat; or else he could divide it into four sections, by splitting each half again, which would provide him with four roughly triangular or wedge-shaped segments. In the case of other toggles based on less regular shapes, it would often seem that the toggle-makers had sought out and reworked odd scraps that the ivory-workers had discarded after cutting up a tusk to make other things. Perhaps they were ivory carvers themselves, doodling in their spare time.

Many toggles of the flat-figure type are made of slightly arched sections of ivory that obviously came from the hollow end of the tusk, rejected by the ivory carvers. Often these have the decoration worked on the concave inner surface, while the outside still has the coarse outer rind remaining on it. There were several reasons for this. In the first place, the inner part of the tusk was softer and easier to carve, and the carved work would be less exposed to abrasion. Secondly, although the rind was always removed by professional carvers in the process of preparing blocks of tusk for carving, the walls of the hollow portion were fairly thin, so any attempt to split off or chisel away the rind would be apt to leave a piece too thin for carving, if it did not smash it completely in the process. Thirdly, a portion of rind was desirable on a toggle, as it provided a surface that could be more readily filed away, without spoiling the finish, if some ivory dust were needed for medicine.

The dust or shavings from elephant ivory had an important place in Chinese medicinal lore. For example, to remove iron or other foreign bodies, such as splinters, which had entered the skin, they applied a poultice of ivory dust in water. Furthermore, when boiled in water, the ivory parings were supposed to act as a diuretic, but if they were first reduced to ashes they were said to be antidiuretic. They were also recommended in cases of epilepsy, for osteomyelitis, and for smallpox.[1] Thus, an elephant ivory toggle was like a portable medicine kit for use in several kinds of contingencies.

Elephant ivory as a material for carving was a substance of great antiquity in China. In the ruins of Anyang, China's early historic capital (c. 1350-1128 B.C.), archaeologists of the 1920's and early 30's found many remains of carved ivory, and they have assumed that at that time elephants may have roamed as far north as the Yellow River in North China.[2] Shortly before the beginning of our era they were no longer found in the wild state north of the Yangtze Valley, and by the end of the eighteenth century they were virtually gone from South China as well; although roving wild elephants have occasionally been seen in southern Yünnan in recent times, two stray herds having been reported in 1957.[3] Meanwhile, commerce in Indian ivory has been active for more than a thousand years, and African tusks were imported since the eleventh century, when the Sung Dynasty encouraged long-distance overseas trade.[4]

For hundreds of years the Chinese have imported from Siberia the huge tusks of the prehistoric mammoth (*Elephas primigenius*), using this ivory as a substitute for elephant ivory, but also appreciating it in its own right. In spite of the similar structure of the teeth—which they may not have noticed—they thought of the mammoth not as a member of the elephant family but as a giant rodent. This odd misconception apparently arose because of tales that filtered down from the North along with the trade in mammoth tusks.[5]

The natives of Northern Siberia occasionally came upon the frozen body of an extinct mammoth when a section of river bank or a marshy knoll crumbled in a Spring thaw and exposed it, where it had been preserved for millenia by the permafrost. Thousands of years ago, some of these heavy animals apparently sank into the soft ground on the margins of the northern rivers or swamps and were engulfed. Their soft trunks, held high, were apparently the last to sink, and were usually eaten away by wolves or other predatory animals. Discovering the great furry beasts, covered with coarse red hair, with their ratlike pointed snouts, the Northerners thought they must be giant moles, and as their flesh was in reasonably good condition—still fresh enough to feed their dogs—they assumed that the "moles" must have died shortly before they found them. It must have seemed to them that an underground, molelike existence was the only way to account for the fact that they never saw these huge creatures walking about, although the recent corpses would suggest that there must still be living relatives of the dead animals, hidden from the sight of men.

Such spectacular imports as the giant teeth from this half-fabulous "King of Rodents" out of the mysterious North naturally aroused a great deal of interest and curiosity, so it was inevitable that they, too, should have been credited with special powers. However, even these were not as highly valued as the much smaller walrus tusks and the long, slender, spiral teeth of the narwhal from the same dim region. Both of the latter were believed to be able to detect poison and staunch wounds, ever since they were introduced to China with these claims, during the Middle Ages.[6]

On toggles made from cross sections of the tooth or tusk, it is fairly easy to determine what kind of ivory has been used by examining the structure as revealed in the surface markings. For example, elephant ivory and ivory from extinct mammoths both have a distinctive form of pattern which differentiates them from any other type of ivory. In each there is a pattern of fine, arching lines that intersect with one another, giving the surface the general appearance of the machine-tooling inside the rear case of an old-fashioned watch.[7] This is usually rather distinct, unless the marking has faded from long exposure to strong light.

It is said that mammoth tusks, although very much larger than those of the modern Asiatic elephants, had more delicate markings. But this does not seem to be an adequate criterion, especially where prolonged exposure to sunlight has faded the ivory almost to a uniform tone. In such cases, the arching lines are still visible under side lighting, as they appear slightly raised, but their relative width or coarseness is difficult to determine. Actually, mammoth tusks were imported to China in great quantities during the last two centuries, and hence in recent times they were not valued nearly as much as the more readily workable modern tusks. Therefore they were more dispensable, and more likely to end up in toggles.

In contrast to the elephant and mammoth tusks, the walrus tusks had an outer layer of fairly uniform appearance, surrounding a core of mottled texture and somewhat darker color.[8] The latter, which is very prominent in cross sections, was formed by a secondary deposit of dentine, while the originally hollow tooth was growing outward from the animal's jaw. This core substance was considered so valuable in China, because of its fancied abilities as a poison detector, that it was often cut out to make individual objects. (These were frequently dyed green with verdigris, probably at first done to imitate jade, and later because they liked it that way.) We never happen to have seen any Chinese toggles of this highly valued substance, nor even ones of walrus ivory with some of the core intact, perhaps because the material was too expensive for the toggle-makers. However, it would seem that some of the flat, arched toggles of ivory, without natural markings to identify them, may have been made from the hollow upper portion of the larger walrus tusks, the part that would have been discarded by the workers in walrus ivory as being less obviously endowed with the magical and poison-detecting qualities, since it had no core.

Of course, walrus ivory was the most common material for the toggles of the Eskimo and the Chukchee, previously mentioned, and in the toggles of both these peoples the core material is usually quite evident. In fact, it often adds an ornamental quality because of the contrast of textures.[9]

Other ivory toggles, lacking the characteristic markings of the elephant or mammoth tusks or any traces of walrus ivory core, may have been made from the teeth of the other large sea mammals. Whale ivory can sometimes be recognized in cross section by very faint concentric lines demarking the layers of growth (these never cross or intersect as do those in elephant and mammoth ivory). Whale teeth often have a small hole at or near the center, marking the former passage of the nerve.[10] Obviously, this characteristic was usually cut away in drilling the comparatively larger hole for the cord in making a disc toggle, but it may sometimes be recognized in bulkier toggles of other types.

The narwhal tusks were hollow for most of their length, which sometimes extended to thirteen feet, and they were further distinguished by spiral ridges on the surface, which wound around them from the base to the tip. The ridges would usually have been pared away in making a carving such as a toggle, leaving only the concave shape and the intense whiteness characteristic of this form of ivory as possible aids in identi-

fication.[11] Narwhal ivory does not tend to become as yellow as ivory
from other tusks and, especially on the edges, it often acquires a very
high glossy polish in the course of ordinary use. One example that we
have seen in a private collection was fashioned to resemble a section
from a stick of bamboo.[12]

Hippopotamus ivory is difficult to identify in small pieces, although
the long curved canines and the straighter incisors can both be easily
recognized when the tusks have been carved intact—as they frequently
were in Canton—by the sharply beveled area near the tips.[13] However,
this should not trouble us now, since this kind of ivory was not commonly imported into North China, and does not seem to have been
used for toggles, as far as we know.

We have not yet found any Chinese toggles made of "hornbill ivory,"
although the Japanese occasionally used it for making netsuke, and
the Borneo sword-belt toggles were characteristically made of it.[14] This
substance was naturally less precious in Borneo, since that is one of
the few places where the helmeted hornbill (*Rhinoplax vigil*), the bird
which produces this material, makes its home. Indeed it was probably
the great value of this imported substance, esteemed in China more than
the best elephant ivory or even jade, which prevented its use for the
popular toggles. Another possible reason was its tendency to split and
flake off in layers with extreme changes in climate such as are found
in North China. However, the best reason may have been that this
substance had no particular medical virtues in China, although in
Malaya and the Near East it was believed capable of detecting poison.[15]
By now, we have seen that one of the popular requirements for a good
toggle was the virtue inherent in the substance of which it was made.

Bone was sometimes used in making the toggles, and it would be
easy to say that this was used as a substitute for ivory. But again it had
virtues of its own. Medicine made from the ashes of ox bones was supposed to stop vomiting and diarrheas, and to cure noxious fevers; while
the bones of horses—especially bones of the head and leg—were considered good for many ailments.[16] Bone can easily be separated from
ivory by the roughness of the interior, unless this is scraped away, or by
minute small checks or gashes on the surface, which generally show up
darker against the light background.[17]

If we still assume that the Northern forest region of Asia was the
place where toggle-wearing probably originated, one of the earliest

materials, aside from wood, would have been antler. Thus it is not surprising to find a good many East Asiatic toggles made from antler, especially those from Manchuria.

The Northern hunters and forest dwellers apparently found that sections of antler provided a convenient and accessible material for toggles. The simplest, most elemental type was made by taking a tine or a narrow portion of the main branch, drilling a hole for the cord, and perhaps rubbing or polishing it to obtain a smoother finish. The Bieber Collection has one of these (No. 4) which has been deeply stained by design or by use until it resembles a log of mahogany. We have already seen that another variation was the use of a pointed prong as a spike toggle for loosening knots, etc. The Columbia University collection has one plain one, and another very simply worked to represent a lotus root or rhizome. Still another type, which must have been very common, to judge by the large number of surviving examples, was the button form.

The latter was made by taking a fairly thick section of antler, generally a cross section, then rounding the front of it, and slightly hollowing the back, leaving a circular projection at rear center that could be pierced or undercut to provide a hole for the cord. The rather porous, almost spongy tissue at the core of the antler makes a surface covered with minute pitting,[18] but this was smoothed and polished as far as possible. Sometimes the buttons were dyed green with verdigris, perhaps to give the impression of turquoise or jade at a distance. Some of these buttons seem to have been turned on a lathe; others were simply rounded out by hand.

The antler material was not only fairly accessible for Manchus or Eastern Mongols, but it was also highly valued by them and by the Chinese. Even a small quantity of powdered antler was for them a wonder-working drug, believed capable of restoring lost youth and virility, especially if it came from the young antlers in velvet.[19] This was because they thought that the deer was the only animal able to discover and eat the sacred fungus of immortality (*ling chih*) and thus attain great age, which naturally made the deer a symbol of longevity.[20] Furthermore, since they believed that most of the virtue of the fungus was absorbed into the antlers, these must be especially effective in helping human seekers for long life to attain sexual rejuvenation and eventual immortality.

This concept seems to have been doubly reinforced in the button toggles made of antler, for their head suggests a mushroom cap, which they also resemble in both color and texture, and mushrooms, as we shall see in Chapter 9, where considered by North Chinese and Manchurians as symbols of fecundity. Since this form of mushroom is mostly found in the Manchurian forests, which were also the haunts of the deer that provided the antlers used to make these toggles, the double association may have been deliberate.

Not only deer horns in velvet, but the horns of elk and moose, even in their mature state, were important sources of *Yang* medicine. These animals themselves were considered as *Yin* animals, since they frequented river valleys, marshes, and deep, shady forests, but paradoxically, their antlers were among the most potent of *Yang* tonics.[21] One very large button toggle of antler in the Brooklyn Museum, more than two inches in diameter even after lathe-turning, must certainly have come from a moose or elk.[22]

We also find toggles made from other kinds of horn, for much the same reasons: accessibility of material and belief in their special efficacies. One of the handsomest kinds is the black horn of the water buffalo, especially if it is slightly oiled and highly polished. Although it was much used for carvings in South China, there are no examples in this collection. This was another cure-all substance. A few scrapings reduced to ashes were believed to be effective for headache, epidemic fevers, diphtheria, gonorrhea, and baldness, among other things.[23]

Last, and perhaps most fascinating of all the animal substances, was rhinoceros horn, which is formed from a concretion of hairs growing out of the skin atop the animal's nose. The Asian rhinoceros once roamed widely over China, but by the end of the eighteenth century it was rare even in Yünnan, and the great demand for its horn, together with the high value set upon it by the Chinese, has resulted in its virtual extermination elsewhere in Southeast Asia.

Among the other powers ascribed to this substance was the ability to sweat or disintegrate in the presence of poison,[24] so beautiful cups were made of it for court use.[25] It was also used for the belt facings of high officials during the Ming and earlier dynasties. The high prices paid for it would make it seem unlikely that one could ever find a toggle made from it. But the Brooklyn Museum has such a toggle, which was acquired for them in Peking by Miss Bieber.[26] Possibly it was made from a block of the material removed while making a cup. It represents a magnificent cicada, beautifully carved, down to the details of the segments of its abdomen and the veining on its wings. It is represented as standing on an inverted and empty sulphur tray of the type formerly used with the flint and steel in making fires. The burned-out fire tray may have been symbolic of an exhausted human life, but the cicada was also a symbol of triumph over death and resurrection in a new body.[27] Thus we have here a profound symbol in a rare and magnificent substance.

Both the depth of meaning and the value of the material would suggest that this must have been made for a nobleman. But doubtless even he believed that the substance would serve as an antidote to poisons, a cure for devil possessions, and a remover of hallucinations and bewitching nightmares, an expeller of fear and anxiety, and a sedative to the viscera, in addition to many other claims which were made for it.[28] Such beliefs were universal in Old China, and although they were so characteristic of the folk tradition, which produced most of these toggles, even the scholar-gentry and the aristocracy took them very seriously.

6

TOGGLES IN STONE AND
RELATED SUBSTANCES

THE WOODEN TOGGLES and those of antler and bone were, generally speaking, genuine expressions of Chinese folk art. The ivory ones were somewhat less so, although a well-to-do peasant or small merchant might still be able to afford a simple one made of discarded scrap ivory. However, when we come to toggles of jade and other semiprecious hard stones, we enter another realm. Not only the substances themselves, but also the difficult techniques required to work them, raised them far above the meager resources of the lowly. Indeed, strict sumptuary laws, issued by the Imperial Court, forbade people below the level of the officials and gentry from wearing ornaments of jade, and these laws remained in effect until the gradual breakdown of old traditions acquired increased momentum during the nineteenth century, to become complete with the fall of the Manchu dynasty in 1911. Even after that date, true folk toggles of jade would have been comparatively rare, and they would have tended to be in the cheaper off-color shades of that treasured material.

Jade was highly valued in China since the beginning of Chinese history, about 1500 B.C., although the general name for it, *yü*, was always extremely comprehensive. In addition to nephrite and jadeite, the two different minerals we describe under the name of "jade," the Chinese included a number of others, with or without other descriptive terms that might make clear which kind of stone they meant.[1] Medicinally, *yü* was credited with all kinds of miraculous powers,[2] even more than were ascribed to jade in post-renaissance Europe, after its rediscovery in the New World.[3] In particular, the hardness and relative permanence of jade led Chinese seekers after immortality to imbibe it

[71]

in powdered form, mixed in various magic elixirs. One Chinese medical writer candidly summed up the situation by saying that jade might be taken in either liquid or powdered form as a means to becoming immortal, although it frequently brought on fever.[4] Indeed several Chinese emperors died after taking "elixirs of immortality," some of which may have contained jade dust.

Regardless of its effects when taken internally, jade was still valued for curative and life-prolonging amulets, down to the twentieth century. Therefore, like some of the other substances we have been describing, it was well fitted to contribute to the toggles the second important quality of power as protective amulets.

In addition to its fancied properties for promoting longevity, the Chinese have treasured jade, down through the centuries, for its "purity," translucency, variations in color, its musical sound when tapped, and its highly polished, eminently tactile surface. In fact, some of these qualities are effective for distinguishing "jade" from other less-valued substitutes. Although nephrite and jadeite are quite different materials—nephrite being a silicate of calcium and magnesium, while jadeite is primarily a silicate of aluminum and sodium with small quantities of other minerals—the simple tests which the Chinese have always employed to distinguish "jade" from other stones are still equally effective for both; but more scientific methods are often required to distinguish between these two.[5]

In the first place, color is not particularly useful for determining authentic jade. In fact, Occidental viewers are often inclined to doubt that the jade toggles are really of that substance, since they are not often green. But both nephrite and jadeite come in many colors, owing to the presence of impurities: from dead white through cream, yellow, and orange to rather vivid reds, on through violet, soft blues, green, and various shades of gray and brown, to deep black. Often a single piece may show several colors.

Perhaps the most common shade found on the jade toggles was the off-white, familiarly known as "mutton fat," but one also sees the less-prized grays or browns, or even the grayish greens. Although color as such is not a reliable criterion, the experienced collector soon learns to tell from the quality of the color, considered along with the texture and other properties, whether a given object is of real jade; but he is never satisfied without trying further tests, long used in China.

First, there is the hardness test. While the various forms of "jade" are not quite as hard as the quartzes (which are hardness 7 by the Mohr scale), they can still resist steel, so a knife can never scratch them. The blade may leave a temporary mark, but the mark will be steel dust from the knife, and the surface of the stone will not be harmed. This very elementary test will immediately eliminate soapstone and other softer substitutes, which can easily be scratched; although these latter substances will also have the oily feel that provides the second popular test for jade and is particularly noticeable in nephrite. The absence of this slippery texture will quickly expose substitutes made from opaque glass. Thirdly, if one taps the piece lightly, preferably at a thinner place, it should give a pleasant musical note, which is another characteristic of real jade. Soapstone copies will give a dull clunk, while the sound of tapped glass is different again. Fourthly, one should closely observe the texture, as the texture of "jade" is dense, sometimes with irregular crystals, and totally lacks any of the minute bubbles or other interior blemishes usually found in the substitutes of glass.

To be completely certain whether an object is of jade, scientifically equipped modern museums run specific gravity tests, and these are also employed to distinguish between nephrite and jadeite in doubtful cases. However, the older Chinese methods outlined above are generally adequate for separating the real from the false.

In early times, the Chinese used nephrite exclusively. Modern scholars believe that they may have had some sources of this within China proper, but if they did, these were apparently soon exhausted. For at least two thousand years, the main supplies came from the western end of Chinese Turkestan, and the long journey from there, through lands that were frequently in hostile hands, added greatly to the cost of the raw material. The manufacturing costs were also high, since jade is extremely difficult to work, and this added to the total value. In short, jade was always valuable enough in China to make it worthwhile for unscrupulous people to try to counterfeit it.

Most of the jadeite came from mines in Burma, during and after the eighteenth century. When the Burma campaigns of the late 1760's made them more accessible, blocks of jadeite were imported into Southwest China in sufficient quantities to lower the price somewhat, and make it more widely available to others besides the very rich. But it was still very expensive by the time it got to Peking, and all the pieces of finest quality were automatically reserved for court use, being set aside for this purpose as soon as a jade caravan entered China.

Because the jadeite from Burma was imported through the province of Yünnan, it was generally known in China as "Yünnan jade"; although some was brought around to Canton by sea, and after being worked in the famous shops there, it acquired the name of "Canton jade." The most famous center of jade-working was Peking, where highly skilled artists turned out the finest pieces for the Imperial Court. They worked on raw nephrite from Turkestan or jadeite from Burma, and ultimately on imported jade stone from New Zealand and South Africa, brought to China in European ships.

The raw jade materials came to Tali or Yünnanfu (Kunming) in Yünnan, to Canton, or to Peking, in blocks or boulders, and it first had to be sawn into convenient sizes for working. Many of the jade toggles present odd or unusual shapes suggesting that they were made of rejected scraps left over from the preliminary trimming. This seems certain when they also show the rusty discoloration that is commonly found on the exposed surfaces of the natural boulders; for this was generally removed before undertaking the finer carvings, unless a brownish tint was desired for some element in the design.

The cutting of the raw blocks was accomplished with bow-shaped saws, usually operated by two persons, the wire blades being coated with wet jade dust or abrasive sand.[6] The actual working of the smaller pieces, such as toggles, was largely done by grinding with a metal wheel, also covered with wet jade dust or other abrasives, which was mounted on the lathe-pin of a lathe like those used by the woodworkers, previously described. Over the wheel proper they usually stretched an arching band of thin wood, like a segment of a broad hoop, which served as a shield to catch the flying slivers and jade dust that were removed in the process of cutting, and deflected them back into a shallow pan below, where they were retained for later use.[7] The most delicate work was achieved by drilling with special drills mounted on the lathe frames in place of the lathe-pin, or by smaller, diamond-pointed bow-drills, followed by cutting with a fine wire saw from one drilled hole to another.[8]

In addition to jade dust, the abrasives consisted of "yellow sand" from ground-up quartz crystals, "red sand" from pulverized garnets, "black sand" from emery or corundum, and "jewel dust" from powdered scraps of inferior rubies or sapphires, also brought from Burma.[9]

These tools and techniques were rather primitive by Western standards, but the results obtained with them were usually of the highest quality, because the jade-workers knew and understood their material so well, and had the time and patience to take infinite pains with each piece. Each worker had to serve a long apprenticeship, usually spent in working less valuable kinds of stone or inferior jade, and perhaps it was in this stage that they produced some of the toggles; although the finest jade toggles were evidently of superior workmanship, showing the skilled touch of master craftsmen.

In working a piece of jade to make a toggle, the carvers frequently showed great skill in utilizing changes of color within the stone to achieve special effects. They also were careful to leave broad, flat areas which the fingers could caress, to enjoy to the utmost the tactile possibilities of jade. Though the nephrite could be ground down fairly smooth, the jadeite could never be smoothed entirely by the Chinese methods, and the result was a slightly uneven surface, not directly observable unless the toggle—or other carving—is held so that the light falls across it at an angle to reveal tiny projecting planes, but offering more variety to the finger tips. Jade in general, and especially the more translucent forms of jadeite, is most effective when it is not carved too thin, so that the object still retains a certain amount of "body." With the breakdown of old traditions of fine craftsmanship in the twentieth century, the Yünnan jade-workers sometimes forgot this, and created objects of lacelike delicacy, remarkable for their technique, but doing violence to the intrinsic qualities of the jade itself.

Perhaps the simplest of the jade toggles were the round, rather flat buttons without decoration, like those made of antler, previously described. In fact, the antler ones dyed green may have been deliberately intended to imitate these, though the resemblance would not be very convincing at close quarters. Other types of jade button toggles could be rather fancy, with patterns in relief on their outer surface. The best-known jade toggles, however, were the carved figures, sometimes quite flat, but generally three-dimensional. Animals, fish, and flowers were commonly represented, but the most popular subjects were probably the human figures or divinities in human form. These will all be discussed in the chapters dealing with the subjects on the toggles.

Many of the simpler disc toggles had the disc part made of stone, generally jade. Allied to these were jade discs pierced with a square hole and inscribed with characters to resemble cash coins. Some of these may have originally been made simply as lucky pieces, symbols of wealth, but they made effective toggles when a stout cord was passed through the hole and knotted. Flat rings were also used, since jades of this shape were frequently produced in ancient times for ritual and other purposes, and some of these were dug up again and reused as toggles.

The jades that have been buried in tombs with human bodies suffer decomposition and acquire brownish stains. These were often recovered, and sometimes the larger pieces were recut. The Chinese refer to this discolored jade as "Han yü," although it need not date back to the Han period (206 B.C.—A.D. 220) as the name might suggest. It is also important to note that long burial with decaying organic matter may cause a change in the composition of the stone as well as in its color, so that its hardness is lessened to the point that some of the very old, long-buried ones can be fairly easily scratched with a knife. Another kind of change takes place when nephrite jade has been subjected to a severe fire. It then turns grayish white and more opaque, with numerous fine cracks running through it. The Chinese call this "chicken bone jade," and are quite fond of it.

Typical toggles often found in "Han jade" are the rather large figures of cicadas which, in the olden days, were buried with the dead as symbols of immortality (see No. 45). Dug up again in recent times, some of these have been made suitable for counterweights by boring a small hole through the head or upper thorax for inserting a cord. Of course these could not have been used without superstitious dread until the custom of placing them in graves had long gone out of fashion, but the symbolism of immortality apparently continued on. This is not very surprising, as observant Chinese of any period could have noticed the strange events in the life cycle of the cicada (as described in Chapter 10), which suggested an analogy with the passage of the human life into a higher one, after discarding the earthly husk.

Agate, carnelian, and onyx, collectively called ma-nao, were often included in the broad yü category, and all these were believed to possess medical powers in themselves,[10] so of course they were sometimes used for toggles. The stoneworkers showed great skill in making these into toggles, taking special care to utilize any changes of color within the stone to enhance the total effect. For example, the Peabody Museum in New Haven, Connecticut, has a toggle of carnelian in the shape of a stag with red body and white antlers, making a particularly striking combination. Frequently the particolored bandings of these particular stones were used to produce clever or amusing effects. Undoubtedly this kind of artistic manipulation added a great deal to the value of the toggles in their owners' eyes, as "conversation pieces," as well as giving pleasure to their carvers because they afforded them an opportunity to demonstrate their versatility.

Another handsome mineral with similar auspicious and medical associations which sometimes appears in the toggles is malachite.[11] This was generally imported from Russia, and was consequently very expensive by the time it reached China. Perhaps this is why we have never seen a whole toggle carved from a single piece of this material. Chips of it were often used, however, to decorate certain toggles of the disc type. The disc proper was made from chips of this handsome green-banded stone set into a dark matrix and retained in a frame of gilded bronze, with a small cylinder of the same metal at the center to line the cord hole.

Mongols and Tibetans commonly wore toggles made from turquoise matrix. The Tibetans particularly favored this mineral, regarding the less-flawed pieces as precious stones. For them turquoise was a sign of wealth, as well as a medical substance credited with specific curative powers.[12] From Tibet, possibly through the influence of the lama monks, this reverence for turquoise passed on to the Mongols, and eventually it reached the Manchu Court in Peking; but its wonder-working reputation never seems to have impressed the Chinese.[13] Turquoise does not seem to have been recognized in China until rather late, and although there are said to have been quarries in China proper, in the province of Hupeh,[14] it was not valued there. Turquoise never found a place in the Chinese *materia medica*, and in the old days it was usually reserved for trade with the Mongols and Tibetans. The latter commonly made simple toggles from flat or rounded lumps of turquoise matrix, drilled through the center to receive a knotted cord. These were often employed as secondary toggles for hitching to the belt the flint-and-steel sets.[15] Frequent handling tended to change the natural pale blue color of the stone to yellowish green, as it is a very absorbent material; so most such toggles are green.

Other materials esteemed by the Mongols and Tibetans, and by the Chinese and Manchus as well, were coral and amber. Both were expensive imports from distant lands, and both were credited with special

virtues and powers.[16] The coral came to China from the Persian Gulf—
by sea, through Arab traders, or overland by way of India and Tibet—or
else from the Caspian region of northern Iran, across Central Asia. The
long journey naturally increased its cost, and since it was also a wealth
symbol in Mahayana Buddhism, to which both the Lamaists and the
Chinese Buddhists belonged, it was doubly prized.[17]

The Drummond Collection in the American Museum of Natural History has an especially beautiful example of a toggle in red coral, a delicately fashioned replica of a reed mouth-organ, known in Chinese as a
shêng. This would have had triple significance, symbolically speaking,
because the instrument itself carried natural associations of music and
joy, while its name, *shêng*, also makes a pun on another word with the
same sound, meaning "rise in official rank," and finally the color red
was a traditional symbol of happiness. This highly symbolic toggle was
secured to a slender, flexible metal cord of braided gold wire. The form
of the *shêng* with its projecting pipes was scarcely the most practical
one for a toggle, but this one was obviously made for a man of wealth
whose life would not have been too active, so practical considerations
probably would have been less important.

Amber (*hu-p'o*) was imported for centuries from Burma, by way of
Yünnan, but in recent centuries it was also brought to China from
Europe.[18] The distance of Peking from the source therefore made this
expensive too. Even more than its cost and comparative rarity, its chief
value in Chinese eyes was the fact that it was an ancient pine product,
because of the reverence for pine trees and their products in general as
conducive to longevity.[19] Amber would seem to have been a rather soft
and easily scratchable substance for making toggles, but being so expensive, amber toggles were probably confined, as we have suggested, to the
less active wealthy classes of the great cities or the Court itself.

While the clear, golden "honey amber" was the most common in
Old China, as elsewhere, the Chinese were very fond of an even more
beautiful kind, "blood amber," deep crimson, of such pure quality as to
be transparent. The Chinese also like the cloudy amber, which was often
so dense as to be totally opaque. A special kind of opaque amber much
prized in China was a very dark variety, deep brown to black, which
the Chinese called "root amber," and described as coming from a resin
exuded from the life-giving roots, and hence full of *Yang* vitality. This
collection has a toggle of "root amber" in lustrous purplish black, which

has been fashioned to resemble a cluster of grapes. The American Museum of Natural History has a number of toggles in various forms of amber, including one notable one in the shape of an ornate lock, made from a cloudy red variety.

Since amber was so valued in China, it was much counterfeited there, especially in Canton;[20] and accounts as old as the sixth century A.D. warn that only the kind which when warmed by friction will pick up mustard seeds should be accepted as genuine.[21] (Lacking mustard seeds, any small scraps of paper will do for testing the magnetic qualities of true amber.) Another test is to touch the object with a red-hot needle. If it is of real amber, the singed portion will give off a soft piney fragrance, while a synthetic substitute will merely produce an unpleasantly acrid stench.

Allied to amber in the minds of the Old Chinese was jet. This is also a fossilized organic material from ancient trees, rather than a true mineral, but unlike amber it came from the actual wood, being closely related to coal. The Chinese scholars of the medieval period said that pine resin after a thousand years turned into amber, and amber after a thousand years turned into jet (*hsi*).[22] Therefore, if amber was a symbol of longevity, this was doubly so. In addition, it had to be imported all the way from the Turfan region of Turkestan, which made it quite expensive; and, lastly, it was also credited with medical virtues.[23] As a substance for carvings it was eminently suitable, as it had a hard, compact texture, a velvety black finish, which could usually take a high polish, and was always pleasant to the touch. The regular importation of jet from Turkestan stopped centuries ago, so it was comparatively rare in China in recent times, but Miss Bieber has a fine figure toggle and an octagonal bun toggle both made of it; while the Columbia University Collection has an unusually simple one, cut with facets to form a large cuboctahedron and then pierced down the center for a cord.

A common substitute for amber in North China was amber glass, of transparent yellow or pale brown. This could fool the eye, but was immediately apparent when touched. In fact, clear glass (*po-li*) was often used to imitate transparent stones, while opaque glass (*liu-li*) was used to copy the others, such as jade or onyx. However, glass itself was not cheap in China until about 1890. Before that, for some two thousand years, it was considered a relatively rare and valued material, on a par with semiprecious stones.[24] This was because the Chinese of old did not know how to blow glass, but had to manufacture it in lumps, and then work it by lapidary methods like any of the stones themselves. As a result, both *po-li* and *liu-li* were listed among the more valued stones, even in their books of drugs.[25]

Although the glass toggles were often passed over by Occidental collectors as being of a common and not very interesting substance, Miss Bieber realized and respected the somewhat different attitude of the Old Chinese regarding glass, and acquired several of them. Among these are a very simple pair of shoes in yellow amber glass (No. 175), and a remarkably lifelike copy of a sheep's knuckle-bone in transparent blue (No. 200). The fuller symbolism of both these subjects will be discussed in detail in Chapter 11.

The glazes used by the Chinese to ornament their porcelains were also made from melted quartz sand, and hence closely allied to glass. Glazed porcelain toggles were apparently extremely rare in China, but Miss Bieber has a simple one, also representing a pair of shoes (No. 177).

The natural rock crystal was always much favored for carvings in Old China, although the rarity of the substance and the difficulty in carving it put it far out of the reach of humble folk. It too had symbolic and medical associations, which made it suitable for charm amulets,[26] and it was sometimes made into toggles, presumably for richer folk. Such a transparent substance would have been marred by the view of a cord or ringbolt passing through it, therefore the crystal toggles were usually made from the less-valued, flawed pieces of the stone, in which the diffraction of the flaws hindered the transparency, and often contributed pleasing and unusual effects of their own. In addition to the clear quartz, smoky quartz, rutilated quartz, rose quartz, and amethyst were also used. A favorite type of toggle made from these was the ball pendant, in which a sphere of the stone was pierced by a ringbolt and fitted with metal caps at top and bottom.

Lastly, we have several less valued stones often used in China as substitutes for jade and, as such, sometimes referred to as "poor man's jade." Among these were various forms of steatite or "soapstone" (formerly called *agalmatolite*), and calcite.[27] These furnished pleasingly colored materials, soft and pleasant to the touch, capable of taking a high polish, and also valued for supposed medical properties. However, the steatites were so soft that when accidentally scratched or struck they retained disfiguring blemishes, and even the calcites were eventually eroded. This made them impractical for detailed carvings, but they were quite suitable for rendering simple forms that would not be spoiled by too much erosion.

The rather extensive use of stones in Old China makes one of the obvious distinctions between the Chinese belt toggles and the netsukes of Japan. The comparative absence of workable hard stones in the volcano-born Island Empire—except for the crystals of Gotemba, which have recently given rise to a modern lapidary industry—has prevented the Japanese from exploring the mineral kingdom until modern times. Thus they never exploited its many possibilities to the extent that the Chinese did. This would also explain why precious and semiprecious stones seldom entered into Japanese folklore,[28] as they formerly did in China, where jade became—quite literally—a substance to conjure with!

7

METALS IN THE TOGGLES

THE ANCIENT CHINESE grouped together gold, silver, and bronze, calling them the Three Noble Metals. Later they added to these lead (or tin) and iron, to make another group of five basic metals.[1] They did this to conform with a traditional demand of Chinese philosophy and "numerical science" which specified that all things should be grouped in auspicious sets of five to conform with the Five Elements. In the hands of the "Five Elements School" this tendency reached its height, but even when the school as such was discredited in a more sceptical age, its categories lived on. Thus, the Five Metals took their place in Chinese thought, religion, and magic, along with the Five Sacred Mountains, the Five Musical Sounds, Five Basic Colors, Five Tastes, and the Five Directions (North, South, East, West, and Center), to name just a few of the groups of five in Old Chinese tradition.

Each of the five basic metals was considered as a rather mysterious, potentially wonder-working, and even medicinal substance;[2] and the first three of these retained the reputation of being "lucky" down into modern times. It was probably partly for these auspicious associations that the Five Metals also figured among the substances that were specially favored for the making of toggles.

Gold was of course too soft and far too precious to use for whole toggles, even if its use had not been rigorously limited to the highest ranks of society, but it was used for gilding other metals, and it also appears in occasional inlays. Lead was not only too soft but also too heavy to be used alone, yet it figured among the alloys used with other metals of the basic group, and was a fundamental ingredient of the pewter that was sometimes used for toggles. The tin, too, figured prominently as an alloy, particularly with copper to make the bronzes that were so highly valued in Old China.

[83]

Toggles entirely of silver were naturally restricted to the rich and mighty, because of the rigid sumptuary laws as well as their expense, and even the ones of fine bronze were probably out of the reach of the peasants, and therefore worn only by relatively wealthy people; but both these metals frequently figured among the mountings that set off the toggles of other substances. Inlaid iron produced an effect much esteemed by the seventeenth-century Manchus, and by the Mongols and Tibetans down to modern times. They especially admired such pieces after a soft brown rust had developed, to form a patina, as this made a better contrasting background for the gold and silver inlays.

Regardless of the kind of metal used, the metal toggles were generally made in the form of relatively thin buttons or discs, or as hollow objects such as small containers, in order to keep them light enough for practical use. Figure toggles in metal were rare and were kept rather small and compact, with the emphasis placed on their weight—to serve as counter-weights—rather than on their bulk. The figure toggles are represented in the Bieber Collection by a grinning child in white brass (No. 209), a small brass horse (No. 103) and a white bronze lion (No. 131). Another solid metal toggle is No. 73, which has the form of a gourd, done in heavy bronze with traces of gilding. Its ornamentation is very ornate, done both in relief and in engraving, except at the end, which has been deliberately left plain. This end shows marks of heavy pounding, as though the toggle had some secondary function such as grinding medicine to powder. This would also account for its having been made heavier than usual. As a bottle gourd was the traditional symbol of medicine and healing, this may well have belonged to a druggist or doctor.

Some of the buttons or discs were simply cast with patterns in relief, but the silver ones were usually hand worked. To accomplish this, a circular plate of silver was first beaten out to the desired width and thickness, then it was placed face down on a wooden anvil covered with a thick layer of beeswax, after which the worker tapped with a hammer on a succession of small, rounded punches to produce the pattern. The hammered portions sank deeply into the soft beeswax, so that when this stage was completed, and the piece was turned over again, its principal design stood out prominently in high relief. As a final step, the decorated disc was then placed on the anvil face up, and the background was worked from the front by hammering with small cupped punches that left little rings or dots in relief. (Toggles Nos. 36, 37, and 38 were made in this way.)

This method of working silver was very commonly used in China for thin silver jewelry in general, and I used to enjoy watching the work in process, in places particularly famous for it such as Kunming, Sian, or Chengtu. It is a very old technique, having been popular back in T'ang dynasty China, more than a thousand years ago.[3] The T'ang Chinese probably got it from the Persians, and in turn they passed it on to the Koreans and the Japanese. It frequently appears on Japanese sword fittings.[4]

Handsome effects were often created by setting off the metal disc against a background of some other substance, which would also help to give it additional protection. Thus a disc of silver or thin bronze was often used as a facing for a larger disc or ring of stone, which would provide a contrast of color and texture. An instance of this is No. 29, in this collection, which consists of a flat ring of light-colored jade with circular silver insets at front and rear, the front one having been worked in high relief by the method just described.

More often, the Chinese took the flat discs of silver, copper, German silver, or bronze and merely soldered a ring to the back to make them into simple button toggles. Rarer examples might have a disc of one metal cut away to leave an openwork design, backed with another disc of a contrasting metal, with the attachment ring soldered to the back of the second one. One toggle of this type, which I found in Inner Mongolia at the close of the Japanese War, has an openwork base of red copper against a disc of yellow brass. When it was new, the brighter metal below must have flashed through the little apertures to make a dazzling background. The pattern itself represents the old classical fable of the fox and the grapes.[5] (See No. 35.)

The Brooklyn Museum has two notable examples of a more ornate type of button toggle that was very popular with the Mongols.[6] One is a silver disc nearly two inches in diameter, mounted with seven small semiprecious stones, set off by a six-part tendril design in silver wire, while more silver wire is soldered to the surface to form a double rim that frames the whole. The background is lightly painted with blue-green enamel, producing a warm contrast to the silver wire and the stones themselves. The second toggle is even more effective. Again having a silver disc as a base, it has a large carnelian bead in the center, around which eighteen petals are outlined in wire, creating a chrysanthemum effect; while the double border, also made of applied wire, is filled with a rinceau or meander of the same. Again enamel has been used to set off the silver wire, this time of a deeper green. No doubt the knives or flint-and-steel sets which these were made to support were similarly decorated, as the Mongols were very fond of matching sets, and a Mongol nobleman usually ordered all his belt fittings from a single artisan, to be made by the same technique. The mixed sets, commonly seen nowadays, resulted after parts of the original sets had gone into the hands of Chinese pawnbrokers, or after an old set had been divided through inheritance and the missing pieces replaced by substitutes.

Their fondness for silver and for disc toggles frequently led the Mongols and Tibetans to use silver coins for toggles. This was simply done by soldering a silver ring, or a loop to hold a larger ring, to the back of a large coin of the "silver dollar" variety. Such coins have been minted in the Far East only since the latter half of the nineteenth century, but "Mexican dollars," Maria Theresa thalers, and Russian coins would have been available before that. Russian silver pieces with the double eagle on them were especially popular in Outer Mongolia, before the period of strong Russian influence there. Several examples can be seen in the remarkable Mongolian collections of the Danish National Museum in Copenhagen, among them a silver ruble dated 1898 and a copper three-kopek piece of 1905. Each has been mounted with a metal loop holding a movable ring.[7]

Two other varieties of coins were especially popular for toggles. The first of these were the British trade dollars, circulated throughout the Far East, which had Britannia as Ruler of the Seas on the obverse, and a Chinese-style "cloud collar" motif[8] on the back. The Mongols and Tibetans were usually unimpressed by the figure of Britannia, although a Mongol toggle in the National Museum, Copenhagen, has her on the outside. However, the "cloud collar" was not only a meaningful symbol in itself, but it was here displayed framing a *shou* symbol, the traditional emblem of longevity in all the lands under Chinese cultural influence, making a combination that was especially significant in terms of Lama tradition. Therefore, the Mongols and Tibetans generally attached the cord-ring on Britannia's side, leaving the other exposed to view, as shown on No. 42b in this collection.

The third most favored type of silver coin for toggles consisted of any of the late Ch'ing dynasty issues, put out by provincial governments in China during the latter half of the reign of Kuang-hsü, around the turn of the century (c. 1890-1908). These always featured a coiled dragon, emblem of the dynasty, as their chief decoration. Particularly esteemed were some silver dollars issued by the province of Yünnan, as they had no writing whatever on the obverse, but simply a splendidly forceful dragon, fierce enough to delight the wildest Tibetan, with no external reminders of the vexing Manchu-Chinese rule. The Bieber Collection also has one of these (No. 42a, not illustrated).

The simplest form of coin toggle, available to anyone, was made by taking one or more of the pierced "cash" coins and threading them on a leather thong, after which the end was tied in a knot that could not pull through. As the single coins were rather small, the wearer often used several, so that their combined bulk would make a more effective counter-weight. Sometimes the Tibetans added a number of such coins to a light seal-toggle, both to increase its weight and to act as protective guards on either side of it. (See No. 41 in this collection.) The Mongols, who also used these simple "cash" toggles, called them *tagh*.

The coin-shaped amulets were worn in the same way, with a knotted cord or thong passed through the center hole. The Old Chinese had a wide variety of these. Some were exactly like coins in shape, even to the extent of having a square hole through the center; but most of them had circular holes to differentiate them.[9] They ranged in size from little ones about an inch in diameter to "cartwheels" four or five inches across. The very large ones were fairly heavy, probably too heavy to make practical toggles. The ones most frequently used for toggles were the middle-sized variety, about two inches in diameter. These commonly had on the back two concentric bands of decoration: the outer one contained the Twelve Animals of the Zodiac (described in Chapter 10), while the inner band had the characters for the Twelve Hours, commonly called the "Twelve Branches," which were interchangeable with the animals in Old Chinese tradition.[10] The patterns on the obverse varied greatly. Sometimes they just showed the stars of a magic-working constellation (generally the Big Dipper), but they usually portrayed a mythological personage or a symbolic deity. Most frequently shown was Shou Hsing, god of longevity, sitting under a pine tree with a crane and a tortoise, or else the Taoist exorciser Chang Tao-ling, with his spirit tiger, chasing specters. Some more specifically Buddhist ones showed six-armed guardian deities, with tamed spirits kneeling before them in adoration. Whatever the subjects, the intent of the amulets was to insure long life or to protect against evil, as their subjects indicated.

Some of the plainer amulets merely had auspicious characters or flowers or animals. Among these a common subject was a pair of dragons or a pair of fish, one shown ascending, the other descending, around the central aperture, to represent the endless sequence of the Yin and the Yang, just as the Zodiac procession did on a more ornate scale. These were often made in openwork with the same pattern on each side,[11] which made them much lighter and therefore more practical as toggles. The Bieber Collection has two of these (No. 46, *a* and *b*). The second has the more unusual motif of three fish, all circling around the center. (Its significance will be discussed in Chapter 10.)

Also made of metal were the cup toggles, which were briefly mentioned in Chapter 2 as one of the possible types of Chinese toggles. These were carried for knocking out into them the ashes of a pipe, to preserve the felt rugs in a Mongol tent or yurt, and to hold the still-living embers for a moment until they could be used to ignite the next small pipeful of tobacco. Hence they had to be made of a noninflammable substance, and metal was the most convenient one. The ash-cup toggles were commonly carried by the Mongols until recently, and I saw one in use in Inner Mongolia as late as 1945.[12] It was considered bad manners among the Mongols to touch the hearth, much less to knock out one's pipe on it, and the rest of the floor was covered with rugs or matting, which could easily catch fire, so the ash-cups were a practical necessity. Sometimes they simply figured among the numerous other gadgets that were suspended from the loops at the sides of a Mongol man's belt; but they also served as toggles in themselves, particularly as counterweights for securing such related things as the small clawlike hook used to detach the caked ashes from the pipe bowl.

The Brooklyn Museum has such a combination, the cup and the claw hook being linked together by a slender metal chain in place of a cord.[13] The cup is of worked iron, a little over an inch in diameter and about three-quarters of an inch deep, smooth on the inside with chiseled decoration on the outer surface. Four lobes of design surrounding the suspension loop at the top form a "cloud collar" pattern, while the principal ornamentation consists of a gourd vine with broad leaves and four small fruits, the latter embossed in gold, set off by a stippled background of tiny punched circles. This is more ornate than most of its kind, but the total effect is very pleasing.

Another common variety of utilitarian toggle was the flint-and-steel set. The larger ones were secured to the belt by toggles, but smaller ones often served as toggles themselves in Old China, and in the Mongol and Tibetan areas until very recently. Although not entirely of metal, they consisted of a heavy steel rim or "shoe" attached to a kind of leather pocket containing the chips of flint and cloth or fiber tinder, with an iron or steel suspension loop above, and usually some metal decoration on the outer flap.

Mongols or Tibetans often used for toggles the ancient Chinese-style mirrors of small diameter, which they sometimes found in old dwelling sites on the frontier or simply picked up on the desert where they may have been lost or mislaid centuries before. These mirrors made effective button toggles, because of the attachment loop formerly made for a braided cord handle at the center of the nonreflecting side. Strictly speaking, these were not "utilitarian toggles," because they usually had too heavy a patina to serve any longer as efficient reflectors. However, they did have another purpose aside from their use as toggles to secure things, and that was to serve as magical protective charms, because old mirrors were greatly prized as wonder-working amulets.[14] They were even listed as such among the Ming *materia medica*.[15] Probably because the Chinese themselves prized them even more, they did not risk using them as toggles, except along the northwest frontier, where Chinese and Mongol customs tended to shade into one another. Elsewhere, they were in high demand by the scholar-antiquarians, who wanted them for their private collections of antiquities.

The Brooklyn Museum has a very handsome and most unusual form of multiple-duty toggle in the form of a box-seal.[16] This consists of a cylindrical box of silver, on the base of which has been carved a seal, forming two phrases in the Manchu script, elegantly incised in reverse within a circular frame. The upper lid of the box, which screws on to prevent its becoming easily detached when it was worn as a toggle, is surmounted by a lion with an ingeniously contrived wagging tongue, and a wire ring for suspension is attached to the top of its head. When the upper lid is removed, there is a second, inner lid with a ring handle, which lifts off to disclose a container compartment. Around the out-side of the box is a continuous scene showing a woman and a boy, each carrying a magic Taoist fly whisk, together with a giant grasshopper or cricket. They are depicted among highly conventionalized plants and trees, the whole scene being set off by bands of swastika fret, above and below it. Probably the scene was taken from some folk tale or popular drama, but we have not been successful in tracking down the original story.

We have never seen another seal-toggle like the one just described; in fact it may have been unique. But metal seals were probably among the commonest form of toggle during the Ming dynasty and perhaps long before. We have seen that the first Japanese netsukes, contemporary with the late Ming period in China, seem to have been Chinese seals imported to Japan. While the Chinese made seals from a great variety of substances, including wood, stone, and ivory, as well as metal, among the small-sized personal seals, which had no bulk at all, only the metal ones would have had sufficient weight to double as effective toggles. It is quite usual to find Chinese metal seals with a square base, like the even commoner stone ones, incised with a name or other personal inscription on the under side, while the upper surface is surmounted by an animal with its body arched upward to leave room for stringing a cord beneath it. Doubtless many seals of this type were formerly used as toggles in China.

In the Tibetan districts, where old customs have continued on long after they had died out elsewhere, because of the power of ultra-conservative tradition, metal seals were still a very common form of toggle in the 1930's. Sometimes the Tibetan seals followed the Chinese type just mentioned, as illustrated by No. 40 in this collection; but more usually they were cylindrical below, with a flattened, somewhat oval handle, richly decorated with interlaced scrolls, pierced through the middle of the shank for a suspension cord.[17] A typical shape is illustrated by No. 41, which I personally bought from the belt of a Tibetan caravan leader in the Tibetan borderland of Northwest Szechuan in West China. Strung on the same cord with it is a lump of the sealing wax used with it. (Unlike the Old Chinese vermilion, which is applied wet, the Tibetan variety has to be melted by burning, like the European variety.) Generally the seal proper is simply a broad disc of iron, which would be more resistant to the hot wax, while the use of two metals would interrupt the conductivity of the heat so the sealer would be less apt to burn his fingers. The device for impression, deeply incised in the base, is usually either a single syllable from the Tibetan syllabary used as a monogram, or one of the well-recognized Buddhist symbols, such as the Wheel of the Law or a holy lotus.

The scroll decoration on the shank of the Tibetan seals of this type seems to reflect an extremely old tradition which penetrated as far west as Scandinavia and Celtic Ireland, and it must have been passed down in Tibet for many centuries. This conservative retention of ancient art traditions is most characteristic of Tibetan religion and culture; but that does not necessarily mean that the actual work of making the seals was always done by the Tibetans themselves. Down through the centuries, some of the finest examples of "Tibetan" metalcraft have actually been done by artisans from China or Nepal, working in the "Tibetan" tradition, which is itself a fusion of ancient Indian, Chinese, and Central Asian styles.

To return to the toggles of China proper, perhaps we could say that the Old Chinese skill at metalworking was best expressed in the small metal attachments or mountings on toggles of other substances, such as stone or ivory. Among these were the strong though slender ringbolts, with their delicately faceted cuboctahedral heads; the carefully fitted guard plates that also cap the ends of the gourds and giant beans; and the intricately contrived chains that sometimes replaced the cords for attaching the toggles. Not only were all these expertly fashioned, but they were almost always exactly suited, aesthetically as well as practically, for their intended functions, displaying that innate sense of "rightness" which characterized the workmanship of Old China, regardless of the medium employed.

8

GENERAL SYMBOLS
ON THE TOGGLES

WE HAVE SEEN that the Chinese belt toggles were usually made from some meaningful material, and when we go on to investigate the subjects depicted or the motives used to decorate them, we immediately find that they, too, almost always were deliberately chosen to convey symbolic meanings.

China's art in general and its folk arts in particular have always been rich in symbols. Very rarely was a definite shape or pattern used merely for ornament or incidental decoration. If it did not obviously picture an idea or suggest one to the mind, it would often turn out to be a more involved symbol by association, or even an elaborate pun-picture or rebus, calling to mind an auspicious phrase which was generally the object of a deep-felt wish or longing.[1] Moreover, they had a special reason for using symbolic subjects or motifs on the toggles, because these—like the symbolic substances used in creating them—helped to make of the toggles good luck charms or amulets to help or protect their wearers. This was one of the toggles' primary functions.

Although most of the Chinese symbols tended to be more or less pictorial, some of the most basic and fundamental ones could be quite simple abstractions. These were also among the most popular and commonly used symbols, and were often the most pregnant with meanings. Their very simplicity made it possible to give them broader interpretations, and frequently a single emblem could convey a number of ideas, on different levels of thought. They also could combine with other symbols to present more extended meanings, and in some cases they combined with others of the simpler symbols to form sets.

The most basic and elemental Chinese symbol was the traditional

[93]

Yin-Yang motif. This consists of a circle bisected by an S-shaped line in order to produce two interlocking, commalike figures, one of which is colored black and the other red or white. The two halves represented respectively the Yin and the Yang, the two elements that compose and pervade the substance of all Nature, according to traditional Chinese thought.

The red side is the Yang, representing the positive, dynamic, hard, or aggressive element in Nature. This is the masculine aspect, associated with light, heat, and life. By contrast, the black side, or Yin, represents the negative, passive, soft, or quiescent element in Nature, the feminine aspect, associated with darkness, cold, and inactivity. Although the two elements are fundamentally distinct and separate in the diagram, set apart by the dividing line, the Chinese recognize that they work together harmoniously, and that they are generally found mixed in varying proportions in the structure of living things, even in those which we would consider inanimate. As an example of this reasoning, they consider a man as being composed mostly of Yang, but say that he must have a little of the Yin element to temper it, otherwise he would be excessively violent and aggressive in his actions. Similarly, a woman, though mostly made up of the Yin, should have a little of the Yang in her composition, to give her spirit and initiative, and to prevent her from being too weak to cope with life. In symbolic recognition of this interaction, the Chinese usually place a dot or "eye" of black on the red Yang side, and a similar mark of red (or white) on the black Yin side.[2]

Such a basic Chinese concept naturally makes its appearance on the toggles, either directly or indirectly. It can be directly portrayed in the figure of the Yin-Yang, as on the horn toggle in this collection (No. 20), or as part of a larger cosmic pattern, to be discussed in a moment; or the idea of the two opposed yet complementary elements could be less directly suggested in other ways.

As an example of the indirect portrayal of the Yin-Yang, we find that the Old Chinese traditionally expressed the Yang by carvings in relief, calling this technique *yang wên*, while the Yin was indicated by incised or sunken work, known as *yin wên*. These contrasting techniques were often used on the opposite sides, or ends, of a single object, to convey the concept of the polarity of the two basic elements in Nature. Apparently as an expression of this philosophy, a number of toggles of stone, wood, or ivory, which have guard plates at each side or at each end, to protect them or to provide additional ornamentation, have the guard plates decorated in the two techniques. The plate on the upper or outer side—the face which would be most prominently displayed when the toggle was worn—has designs in relief, while the opposing plate is decorated by incisions or light engraving, in a Yin technique. This combination occurs so frequently on the toggles that it seems obvious that this was deliberately intended. On an otherwise plain toggle, this balanced decoration clearly provides an element of symbolic meaning that enabled the toggle to function as a charm or amulet. For the dual form of decoration transformed the whole toggle into a microcosm that symbolized the union of the two basic elements in the greater universe. Thus, the toggle itself became a symbolic token of the harmoniously balanced order of Nature, and also recalled the ideal of balanced harmony within the life of the individual.

Often the Yin-Yang symbol itself was included as part of a larger design. For example, it was frequently placed in the center of a circular or octagonal plaque, where it was framed by the Eight Trigrams (*Pa Kua*), as in No. 28. The set of Eight Trigrams traditionally consisted of eight rectangular figures, each of which is made up of three broad horizontal lines: either whole lines or lines broken in the middle. They range from three whole lines to three lines cut apart at the center (or six half lines, in three tiers), with the six other possible combinations of whole and broken lines, all set out one after another to form a circle. The Eight Trigrams were thought to represent the basic manifestations of Nature in which the Yin and Yang were believed to operate. Thus, the three whole lines ("pure Yang") stood for Heaven, while the three broken lines ("pure Yin") indicated Earth, and the other combinations typified Thunder and Lightning, Wind and Rain, Mountains and Swamps, in each of which the Yin and Yang were present in varying combinations.[3]

Chinese tradition, from the Sung Dynasty if not earlier, accounted for them as follows. First there was the Great Unity, symbolized by a single unbroken line. This then split into two complementary aspects, the Yang and the Yin, most simply represented by a single straight line and a broken one. Then, by a tripling of the lines, using both whole and broken ones, were created the Eight Trigrams, to symbolize the most significant or impressive manifestations of Nature. Thus, when they are shown grouped around the Yin-Yang symbol, the Trigrams should be considered as emanations from it, helping to complete its meaning.

In time, the Eight Trigrams acquired further associations. In some of the interpretations of them—said to have been written by Confucius himself, and found in the commentary to the *I Ching* or Book of Changes, traditionally but falsely ascribed to him—these eight symbols also stood for the various parts of the human body, or the principal forms of animal life, etc. In that book, and elsewhere, they were represented as symbolizing also the eight directions of space (North, South, East, West, and the four intermediate directions) in which the Yin and the Yang are thought to extend their functions.[4] Thus the Eight Trigrams carried still further the mystical idea of the Yin and Yang subtly pervading all things.

The composite diagram of the Yin-Yang framed by the Eight Trigrams was often painted in bright colors under the center of the ridgepole in West China farmhouses, to mark the metaphysical axis of the house as a universe in microcosm, and to provide spiritual harmony and magical protection for the household through its inner power and influence. For similar reasons, it was frequently pictured over the doorways of farmhouses, shops, and private dwellings, elsewhere in China, and it was often figured on personal charms and amulets, among which were included toggles, and lucky coins that were sometimes also used as toggles.

The Eight Trigrams alone were considered as symbolizing in themselves the harmony of Nature. As such, they often figured on bronze mirrors, amulets, etc., and they were sometimes used to decorate the rim of circular or octagonal toggles of the disc or bun types. More rarely, the two principal trigrams, the firm and the penetrated, representing Pure Yang and Pure Yin, Heaven and Earth, were used without the others, to symbolize universal harmony.

On many other forms of Chinese charms and amulets, as well as on bronze mirrors, the Eight Trigrams often appear surrounded by an outer row of animal figures, representing the traditional East Asian symbols of the zodiac. These zodiacal animals were used as calendrical symbols in China for at least two thousand years, to symbolize the twelve double hours of the day, the twelve months of the year, and the years in the sixty-year cycle. Therefore, in circular procession they contribute the concept of the passage of time, extending the meaning of the total pattern to make it a more comprehensive Space-Time symbol.

The Twelve Animals as a group do not seem to have been much used on Chinese toggles, except when lucky charm coins, on which they were so often shown, were reutilized as toggles, by passing a knotted cord through the central hole. However, the individual animals often appeared singly as subjects for toggles. This is because, as symbols of months and years, they were commonly used as we use birthstones in the West, for very personal lucky charms. Specific examples will be more fully discussed in the chapter on animal toggles (Chapter 10).

The Chinese and the Tibetans often depicted the Eight Trigrams, and other symbolic sets of eight emblems, on an eight-lobed figure intended to represent the cosmic lotus. On this, the eight lobes, or the petals which they represented, signified the four cardinal points of the universe and the four intermediate directions, just as the trigrams themselves did.[5] They also used this eight-lobed conventionalized lotus, or other highly stylized flower types with radiating petals arranged in multiples of four (four, eight, twelve, sixteen, and rarely thirty-two or thirty-six), to form the center of a diagram or a figure, as a symbol of the directions of space, like a compass rose in the Occident. Such flower shapes were often used for the washers or guard-plates on the sides or ends of toggles, setting off the bolthead or the rivet end of the bolt that transfixes the toggle. The presence of such a figure tends to transform any object it is used to decorate, especially if it is disc-shaped, into a kind of cosmic symbol or mandala representing the universe in microcosm, just as does the use of the Yin-Yang symbol or the circle of eight trigrams.

Sometimes, of course, such a floral shape or pattern might have been used as a mere decoration for relieving a simple guard-plate, because some ornamentation seemed needed. But the Chinese artists, and the Chinese folk artists in particular, seldom used decoration for decoration's sake. They almost always tried to include some inner meaning; so it is not too far-fetched to assume that they generally intended such patterns to express some cosmic symbolism.

Another, very definite way of indicating the primary directions of Space was by the use of a figure called the Cloud Collar. This was formerly actually used as a pattern for collars on robes (often detachable ones), hence the name; but it also served as a directional symbol in the center of cosmic diagrams, on bronze mirrors, etc., for nearly two thousand years.[6] To describe it as simply as possible, it consisted of a quatrefoil, or foliate Greek cross, on which each of the four equal

arms was shaped somewhat like the top of a fleur-de-lys, while the center
—which represented the fifth direction, or the universal axis—was either
left plain, as an open circle, or was filled with some other emblem. For
example, the one on the coin toggle, No. 42*b*, centers on a circular *shou*
character, symbol of longevity.

Among the more abstract symbols in old Chinese tradition were the
highly conventionalized *shou* emblems. There are no less than a
hundred of these symbols of long life or immortality, all more or less
recognizably developed from the written character for longevity, which
is pronounced *shou*; although some are so stylized that the relationship
would hardly be evident unless they were seen in the total group.[7] Since
the desire for long life amounted almost to an obsession in a land where
early mortality was a general rule, these *shou* symbols were used to
ornament almost anything, to convey a wish or hope for the most coveted
boon of extended years.

In the simplest, circular forms of the *shou* symbol, where the resemblance to the original character is sometimes very slight, it is
possible that they may once have been separate symbols, reused in this
context because of the resemblance to the *shou*. The most usual one
consists of a double pattern, filling two adjoining hemispheres. Sometimes they have details exactly the same; at other times, similar ones,
until one reaches the center of each, where there are slight differences.
The total pattern gives the general impression of a circle divided between
two complementary elements, like the Yin-Yang emblem, and this might
originally have been an alternative symbol for the latter. The rectangular
forms of the *shou* emblem are equally stylized, some of them are fully
as far removed from the original character, and they are often drawn
with exaggerated length to emphasize the concept of a long, long life
(*ch'ang shou*).

Sometimes highly complex circular *shou* emblems had incorporated
into their design a swastika (pronounced *wan*), to express by a pun the
concept *wan shou*, meaning "ten thousand years of long life." Again,
the stylized *shou* or a similar emblem of luck such as the *fu* character for happiness, may be surrounded by a meander pattern or some
other "endless" (*wu liang*) border pattern, to extend the meaning, as
illustrated on toggle No. 42*b*. Thus, they produced such pun phrases as
ch'ang shou wu liang, "a long, long life without end," or, if there was a
large happiness character within the enclosure, *ta fu wu liang*, "great

happiness without limits." Even the illiterate people in China were very well aware of these subtle ways for expressing auspicious wishes and felicitations, and most Chinese actually believed that such expressions in symbol form, on toggles and other things, could actually help to bring about the desired conditions that they represented.

Another simple wish symbol, evolved from the stylized form of a written character, was the *shuang hsi*, emblem of a happy marriage. The original character was composed of two linked joy characters, so the expression of intent was quite obvious. We have already noted that a toggle was considered as a suitable wedding gift for a man, and that is doubtless why we find this symbol occasionally used on toggles, instead of a more graphic paired-birds motif, for example. Generally, they merely inscribed the stylized *shuang hsi* character on one of the more conventionally shaped toggles; but they sometimes carved the form of the character itself out of jade or another valued stone, to serve as a flat toggle, with the cord looped around the central bar. The same was done with the *shou* character for longevity or the *fu* for happiness.[8]

Moving on to more complex symbols in the general category, we have several sets or related groups to consider. Unlike the Trigrams and the Twelve Animals, these were not cosmic symbols, nor did their use go back to such remote antiquity. The first of these is a Buddhist group that was introduced from India during the Middle Ages, undergoing slight changes in the process of transmission. Originally called the "Eight Precious Things" (*Pa Pao*), the set consisted of eight emblems associated with the Buddha: the lotus, a wheel, a vase, a conch shell, twin fish, a royal umbrella, a state canopy (resembling a broad umbrella without a staff), and an endless knot. Collectively, they were brought from India by Buddhist missionaries as emblems of the faith, with appropriate religious interpretations; but eventually, by late Ming times, they degenerated into mere luck signs, until people finally referred to them simply as the "Eight Lucky Things" (*Pa Chi Hsiang*). Although the Chinese very commonly used them as a group to decorate other things, they do not seem to have used them all at once on the toggles; but they did use some of them alone: notably, the twin fish and the endless knot.

The endless knot is generally formed by an interlacing tape, which makes a kind of double figure eight with additional loops at each end. As a pre-Buddhist symbol in India, it was explained as the mystic sign on Vishnu's breast; but the Buddhists, especially in China, interpreted it as symbolizing Buddha's intestines (*ch'ang*), or else they described it more spiritually, as a symbol of the futility of life unless one followed the way of Buddha—an endless, weary wandering—since it had no end, but always returned upon itself. However, to the later Chinese, at the time when these toggles were in frequent use, its endlessness caused this symbol to become associated with the much-desired longevity. Furthermore, since its name, *ch'ang*, made a pun on the word for long, the whole figure now symbolized a long long life, and came to be used alone as a wish-symbol with that meaning.

This reinterpretation of the endless knot is a very good example of the extent to which these Buddhist symbols had lost their original meanings; for the historical Buddha's basic teaching had emphasized that all desire was evil, most especially the desire for prolonged existence in this world of sin and pain. There was no place for long-life symbols in Orthodox Buddhism. Similarly, the twin fish as a symbol of marital happiness—its most frequent interpretation in later China—was very alien to the Buddhist monastic tradition, in which it was believed and openly preached that the celibate life was the preferred one for an earnest follower of Buddha, and marriage was merely a necessary concession to the difficulty some people found in conforming to the ideal.

As an individual symbol, the endless knot occurs among the incidental decoration on some toggles. We have also seen it carved out of flat pieces of jade or other stones in such a way that it could be used as a toggle by itself. The twin fish symbol was frequently rendered, in various substances, and will be further discussed in Chapter 10.

Another very popular set of Chinese symbols was also sometimes called the *pa pao*, and like the set just mentioned, it once had ritual connotations, too, but in another religion; for this was a Taoist set. Properly speaking, these symbols were actually the emblems or attributes of eight semidivine Taoist immortals.[9] Originally, each was held by one of the Eight Immortals as a means of personal identification, to insure recognition by the faithful. But, in time, the emblems came to be used alone, to recall their possessors, on the well-known symbolic principle that a part can stand for the whole. Then, with the further passing of time, they gradually lost that significance also, until they become symbols of longevity in their own right. Eventually, as a last stage, they lost even that meaning, until they were considered as mere luck-bringing emblems, like the eight Buddhist ones in their final period. Thus, they present an excellent example of the tendency toward deterioration of religious symbols, a process not confined to China.

This Taoist group also included a lotus flower, but it was a long-stemmed one, more usually presented in profile, so that it need not be confused with the Buddhist one. The other symbols were a magic fan, a pair of castanets, a flute, a magic sword, a basket of flowers, a musical instrument consisting of a bamboo tube and two sticks with which to beat it, and a crutch and pilgrim's gourd. The later two were the special attributes of Li T'ieh-kuai, who sometimes appears singly as a subject for a toggle: the only one of these eight to do so, in China. (See No. 224.) All eight of these Taoist symbols were sometimes used for decorating toggles, as shown on Nos. 74 and 185 in this collection. An occasional toggle in the form of a flower basket may have been made in allusion to the one included in this set; but, as we shall see, it was the symbolic contents of the basket, rather than the basket itself, which seems to have been significant in these instances.

Lastly, the Chinese had still another set of popular symbols which they also sometimes called the "Eight Precious Things" (pa pao), although they more generally spoke of them as the "Eight Jewels" (pa chu). Originally associated with Buddhism, these began as a group of "gems" or wealth symbols, usually seven in number, intended to represent offerings to the Buddha; but they went on to become symbols of the rich boons conferred on the faithful by Buddha's grace; until finally they too degenerated into mere wish symbols for desired wealth or luxurious living. Once again this was most un-Buddhist, for the Buddha had repeatedly preached against material desires as leading to sin and unfavorable rebirth. By this time they were shown in eights; since the Chinese characteristically prefer to present things in eights, just as we tend to use dozens. Unlike the previous groups, which contained a fixed number of objects, this one contained a rather indefinite amount. The Chinese artist had at least sixteen wealth symbols to draw upon, from which he would choose eight to depict at one time.

These included a branching stick of coral; one or two rhinoceros horns, one or two elephant tusks; various combinations of sacred pearls—generally one or three; gold and silver ingots, such as were formerly used for exchange, as a form of currency; and several types of gold or silver personal ornaments, as well as such specifically Buddhist "treasures" as holy books (sutras), sacred palm leaves (*pao yeh*), later misinterpreted as healing leaves of artemisia,[10] the *ju-i* jewels or scepters, and several additional ones.

An actual grouping of some of these wealth symbols appears on one of the toggles in this collection (No. 74), but the use of a complete set is rare on toggles, although so common in other branches of Chinese art. However, some of the gold ornaments, in particular, were sometimes depicted alone on the toggles, just as individual items from the other Buddhist set had been. Like the endless knot, for example, after their origins had been largely forgotten and most of their old significance had been lost as well, they were used by themselves and were given new meanings. Two of these were closely related symbols which had apparently been evolved in China, and were there added to the group of "gems" that had been brought from India or Central Asia. These were gold rings or gold rectangles, usually shown interlocked in pairs. In their original function they had been decorative hair ornaments, worn in pairs on the high chignon favored by court ladies of the T'ang and Sung dynasties, apparently secured by a metal bar which formed a link between them.[11] The proper term for these ornaments was *shêng*, but the same word was used in another sense to mean "success" or "victory," so in time they came to be used as pun symbols to signify successful accomplishment. By a still further extension of ideas, the fact that the symbol was formed of a linked or interlocked pair of precious things led to an association with success in marriage. Like the stylized *shou* characters and the endless knot, each of these *shêng* symbols—either the circular or the rectangular type—was sometimes rendered in openwork on a flat slab of ivory or jade, which could have been suitable for a toggle; but we do not know of any proved instance of their use as such. Their appearance on the toggles was usually as part of the decoration to contribute a pun meaning.

One of the most popular of the wealth series to be used individually was the "wish-granting jewel," or *ju-i chu*. This was commonly represented as a pearl mounted on a gold setting with three lobes, recalling the Chinese stylization of a cloud. Sometimes, this too was set off by smaller pearls at the extremities of the mounting. Frequently this "*ju-i* gem" was provided with a long, curved handle, to transform it into a "*ju-i* scepter," which was also included among the symbols of wealth in this final group.

Both the *ju-i* jewel and the *ju-i* scepter were considered as especially lucky symbols, not only because they were thought to be capable of granting wishes, but also because the qualifying name means "as (much as) you desire," which enabled either of them to join with other punning objects to form a variety of rebus combinations. For example, when either form of *ju-i* was shown with a large bat—whose name *fu* made a pun on the word for happiness—the whole composition formed a rebus, or pun picture, saying *ta fu ju i,* "(May you have) great happiness, as much as you desire."

The *ju-i* scepters were sometimes made in the form of the sacred fungus, *ling chih,* which was a traditional symbol of longevity in China, to convey the idea, "May you live as long as you desire." Conversely, the sacred fungus plant was often depicted on toggles and elsewhere in *ju-i* form, so that it would not only convey the idea of longevity but could also be used to serve as a pun element, conveying the *ju-i* phrase, in making rebus pictures. Some examples of this usage are shown on toggles in this collection, Nos. 117, 149, and 150.

These special uses of the sacred fungus, which has always been a traditional emblem of longevity and immortality in China, often associated with the Taoist immortals,[12] show very clearly how a plant symbol, already significant in its own right, could also be used to enhance the significance of other symbols, by helping them to convey extra, still more complex, ideas. Such instances are not uncommon in Chinese folklore and symbolism, as will be further demonstrated in the next chapter.

9

SYMBOLS FROM NATURE:
TREES, FLOWERS, AND PLANTS

THE SYMBOL-MINDEDNESS of the Chinese people in general has always been particularly apparent in their attitude toward gardens and their contents: the trees and flowers, and the ornamental rocks, often grotesquely shaped, which took the place of the garden statuary in other lands. Traditional Chinese gardens differed greatly from gardens in the West. One could not find in them the ornamental beds of flowers and clumps of shrubs, symmetrically arranged to produce balanced effects of color, which have always been considered the essential elements in Occidental gardens. The Chinese always put far more emphasis on landscape effects, in imitation of Nature, with a special eye to the symbolism of the individual elements and their combinations. The garden as a whole was laid out to suggest a miniature world in itself, a kind of universe in microcosm, in which they carefully arranged contrasts of artificial hills and pools, light and shadow, open areas and hidden nooks, to express the balance of the Yang and Yin. Like the Chinese landscape paintings (called *shan-shui*), the garden was considered incomplete unless it contained the two basic elements of mountains (*shan*) and water (*shui*), and these formed the basic setting into which trees, flowers, and shrubs were introduced in a seemingly careless, natural-looking way, to contribute to the whole their share of symbolic meanings.[1]

In fact, the trees, flowers, and plants were always regarded by the educated Chinese with an eye to their literary and symbolic associations; while the people in general mainly considered them in the light of their fancied powers to bring about the forms of good fortune which they symbolized—such as happiness or long life, wealth or fertility—or in terms of their supposed magical virtues and powers for averting evil.

[105]

Of course, the poorer folk could not afford to have large ornamental gardens; but they did enjoy potted flowers or small trees, even in the city, and sometimes they cultivated miniature ones, in a setting of small rocks, on a dish or tray, following an old tradition later taken over by the Japenese.

Among the subjects often reproduced in the arrangement of the formal landscape gardens or the humbler tray displays, since early times, was the Mountain of Longevity with the Sea of Happiness. These two symbolic features were originally referred to, separately, by passages in two different classics, saying "As long-lived as the Southern Mountain," and "As happy as the Eastern Sea." However, they balanced each other so neatly that they came to be used together as an auspicious couplet, considered as a single expression of much-desired felicity.

Various attempts to express, or at least to suggest, this idea resulted in some of the most elaborate of the toggles with subjects drawn from Nature. It was impossible to represent the sea effectively on a toggle, but it is mentioned on a mirror toggle in this collection (No. 182) which has on it the four characters *fu ju Tung Hai*, "as happy as the Eastern Sea." Even the depiction of the mountain sounds like an overambitious project, but the toggle-makers sometimes illustrated it simply as a rocky crag, taking advantage of the symbological principle that a part can stand for the whole, as in No. 226. Other times they would simply indicate it by a steep spur of rock rising behind a figure of the god of longevity, Shou Hsing, as illustrated in No. 223. Frequently, a few graven lines near the base of the "mountain" indicated a stream or water-fall, to represent the complementary element of water, and almost always pines and bamboos were depicted as growing out from crevices in the rock or sprouting from its ledges, to emphasize the idea of longevity.

We have already seen, in discussing the kinds of woods used to make the toggles, that the pine and the cypress, as hardy evergreens, were symbols of long life and vitality of spirit, credited with the power to promote or prolong great age. Chinese art in general often uses a pine tree with an accompanying crane to signify Winter among the Four Seasons, or the final years in a human lifetime; but the long and rather awkward form of the crane does not present a convenient shape for a toggle, and it is seldom represented on them. For that matter, the pine tree itself would seem to be very difficult to portray on anything as small as a toggle. One way of doing it was again to use a part to represent the whole. An interesting example of this solution is provided on a toggle in the Bieber Collection, where a convex rectangular section from an ivory tusk has been worked on the surface to give the impression of a pine trunk with its rough-textured bark, while against this a slender branch curves upward, giving forth fan-shaped clusters of long needles, to provide a final means of identification. (No. 51.)

A similar method of shorthand depiction was used in the case of the bamboo, where one or two jointed stalks and a few clusters of narrow leaves arranged in sets of three could suggest a whole grove of this ever-satisfying plant. (See No. 53 for a typical example.) The bamboo is also a symbol of long life, and of courage in adversity. This is because it stays green long after most other plants have succumbed to the cold weather, and it keeps its leaves in winter, even when weighed down by snow. The burden of the snow may even bow it to the ground, but after this melts, it again snaps erect, to resume its proud stance as a prince among plants.

A third symbolic element, the plum tree, was often combined with the pine and the bamboo to form a trio called "the Three Friends in Winter," symbolizing faithful companions, loyal even in times of stress. The plum was included here because it blooms in late winter, when the snow may still be on the ground, before any other trees have shown signs of renewed life, thus assisting the stalwart pine and the valiant bamboo to cheer and encourage a still-barren world.

Although the plum tree was considered as the herald of Springtime, before the end of Winter, it also figured as a symbol of the Spring itself, and its five-petaled blossoms were used in this way among the Flowers of the Four Seasons. Furthermore, because of their habit of early flowering and their cheerful hues, and because Spring is a happy time of renewed life, the plum blossoms quite naturally became a symbol of happiness and cheerfulness in general. As such, they were often displayed together with a magpie, the bird of joy. (They are shown together on toggle No. 152.) Also, by a still further extension of meaning, the plum blossoms referred to eternal springtime, or the spirit of youthfulness and rejuvenation in late maturity or old age, and thus they combined two longed-for wishes in a single symbol for happy longevity.

Another blossom that figured prominently in Chinese folk arts was the flower of the *hai-t'ang* tree (*Pyrus spectabilis*), a variety of crabapple. This was considered highly auspicious because its color, red, was the

Chinese happiness color; but it was also popular because the second syllable of its name made a pun on another word also pronounced *t'ang*, which made it suitable for inclusion among the rebus pictures.[2] However, we cannot recall seeing a *hai-t'ang* rebus represented on a toggle. Its characteristic color is, of course, no aid to identification when the flower is carved in wood, engraved on metal, or depicted on jade, but the *hai-t'ang* blossom is still readily identified by a conventional shape. It is regularly represented with four petals, of which the upper and lower ones are short and round, while those extending to the right and left are very much longer. By this shape, we can identify the *hai-t'ang* blossom as a fairly common subject for the metal guard-plates on the toggles.

Like the *hai-t'ang*, all the most prominent flowers in the Chinese artists' repertory were highly stylized, especially in the folk arts, since instant readability was one of the basic requirements for any popular symbol. Thus it happened that certain definite conventions for representing them were established centuries back, and consistently followed ever since. Apparently, long ago, keen-eyed observers carefully took each flower and singled out its chief characteristics, to find some particularly outstanding one that could be stressed or emphasized in reproducing it. Thus, its picture could not only be distinguished from those of rather similar-looking flowers, but it could also be easily recognized for what it was, even when rendered only in monochrome.[3] Perhaps this came about because the Chinese have tended to prefer paintings executed entirely in ink and, without the colors to aid in recognition, the shape had to bear the entire burden of communicating the spirit of the flower and passing on its meaning. Sometimes it is difficult, at first, for a Westerner to recognize a certain flower or fruit, because the high degree of conventionalization has taken it far from its prototype in nature; but it is characteristic of Oriental art in general that a symbol used in one medium is carried over into others in the same form, and often a given flower may be rediscovered, with the same shape but the addition of the appropriate colors, on such things as peasant embroideries or painted temple decorations.

The situation is quite different in regard to the leaves. Leaf forms were seldom as faithfully reproduced, and hence they cannot usually be relied upon as a guide for identification. In fact, they can be definitely misleading. For example, more ornamental leaves from a totally different type of plant were frequently introduced in the background to set off the flowers more effectively, and produce a more decorative impression; sometimes, other types of leaves and stems were deliberately included for a symbolic reason, such as the development of a pun meaning in a rebus. This is why one finds lotus, marigold, or peony flowers growing from continuous vines, instead of their own more rigid stems, with the smaller leaves appropriate for a vine, because the forms of good fortune implicit in the symbolic meanings of these flowers were thus given an aspect of unending continuity,[4] which was visually apparent even if that was not explicitly stated in a rebus. In all these cases, the flower itself is the essential symbol, and the way it is presented, in its commonly accepted stylized form, is thought to be sufficient identification, regardless of the rest.

After the blossoms from fruit trees, another group of highly conventionalized flowers was prominent in old Chinese symbolism. These were the chrysanthemums, of which it is said that the Chinese cultivators had produced at least one thousand varieties, and the related marigolds. The chrysanthemum was the emblem of Autumn among the Flowers of the Four Seasons, symbolizing a radiant middle age, while the marigold was called the "flower of eternal life" (*wan shou hua*), so both were frequent symbols of happy longevity. These popular flowers occur most frequently in Chinese Art, especially in paintings, on woven or embroidered textiles, or in ornamental carvings, and in highly stylized form they provided the inspiration for the form of the guard-plates on many of the toggles.

This collection has only one example in which the chrysanthemum has furnished the inspiration for the whole toggle (No. 50). The designer of this again used only a part to signify the whole plant, showing a mere segment of a single flower with its numerous petals, set off by a number of leaves; but he rendered the latter so realistically that from the leaf form alone the plant could be easily recognized. As we have previously said, such careful attention to the leaves is very unusual. Probably the chrysanthemum flower never became popular for entire toggles because the numerous sharp-edged petals would not only be less pleasant to the touch, but would also be apt to chafe or tear the belt and clothing.

The lotus plant provided the Chinese with some of their most frequently used symbols. The highly stylized eight-petaled lotus flower, which inspired the shape of many of the more formal toggles and provided incidental decoration on others, and the somewhat more natural but still stylized flowers that appear among the Buddhist or Taoist symbols in the popular groups of eight, were by no means the only lotus symbols used on the toggles. A great many toggles, especially the simpler ones of the folk variety, were modeled on the Chinese lotus plant (*Nelumbium speculosum*), and all parts of the plant were rendered, often with detailed realism, not merely the blossom.

The popularity of the lotus in Chinese art was of course due partly to the beauty of the flower, its great size, its elegant shape, and its clear pink color, in contrast to the blue-green of the giant leaves; but its use in the folk arts was more directly dependent on its function as a symbol. It served as such on many levels. We have seen that the mystical-minded Buddhists considered the eight-petaled lotus as a symbol of the Eight-fold Path of the Buddha's doctrine, or—when its eight petals were pressed out flat—as a symbol of the eight directions of space: in itself, or as the basis for a cosmic diagram. On a more popular level, the lotus was a Buddhist symbol of purity, because of the natural fact that it rises clean and fresh out of foul or muddy water. (Incidentally, this was why they used the lotus flower as a pattern for Buddha thrones or for the pedestals of images and holy ornaments.) Any of these symbolic meanings would be a sufficient reason for a devout Buddhist to wear a lotus toggle as a symbol of his faith.

The lotus in its connotation of purity also carried over into secular symbolism, and the honesty of an uncorrupt official was symbolized by lotus flowers with egrets. This bird was added for a similar association, because it manages to keep its plumage clean and white in the same filthy water from which the lotus rises unsullied. I have seen a few jade toggles with this motif, which might have been made as gifts for honest officials—or as a form of flattery for dishonest ones—but there are no examples in this collection. In the same circles, that is, among the scholar-literati, and even down to the folk level, the lotus flower was the emblem of Summer among the Flowers of the Four Seasons, conveying the idea of happiness in maturity. Probably some of the lotus toggles were made with this in view; however, by far the majority of the lotus toggles seem to have expressed personal wishes, based upon several possible pun meanings.

The lotus puns were chiefly based upon the plant's two variant names. One of the Chinese words for lotus, *ho*, is pronounced the same as the word for "unity" or "harmony," while the second, *lien*, forms a pun on the word for "successively," which makes it an appropriate element in rebus pictures referring to boons or desires which people hope will be repeated again and again, such as the coming of sudden wealth, increase in rank (for an official), or the arrival of children.

Wishes for fertility were quite frankly and obviously expressed in the many carvings of the lotus seed pod, which was apparently among the commonest and most popular of all the toggle motifs. While this subject was quite frequently rendered in jade, carnelian, and other stones, the most effective examples seem to have been those made of wood, often of figured wood from a root or burl. The wooden ones were usually cleverly contrived so that the seeds were carved separately but retained within the pod, so that when the latter was turned upside down they popped halfway out, without spilling out altogether, just as they would in the ripening pods of the actual plant.[5] This deliberate emphasis on the seeds may have been partly contrived as an amusing tour de force, or a display of the carver's dexterity; but the fundamental reason was certainly to call attention to the lotus seeds (*lien tzǔ*), which formed a pun on the phrase for "successive children." The frequent appearance of the lotus leaf (*ho yeh*) along with the seed pod increased the pun wish, so that it asked for "harmonious trade" or a "peaceful profession" as well. In short, such a toggle would have made an appropriate wedding present for a young shopkeeper or merchant.

Also suitable for a merchant or trader would be the toggles which express the most elaborate of the pun pictures, showing a goldfish (*chin yü*) wrapped up in a giant lotus leaf. The Chinese description of this combination, *ho pao chin yü*, meaning "lotus-enwrapped golden fish," after changing one character and taking alternative meanings for the rest, produces the hopeful phrase, "May you have an abundance of gold in the purse (*ho-pao*)." The Bieber Collection has two examples of this rather far-fetched rebus, Nos. 66 and 145.

The peach tree and its fruits provide the source for another extensive category of popular symbols. Since the peach tree has always been credited with especially auspicious associations in China, while its wood has been considered as one of the most powerful substances for helping the powers of good against the spirits of evil and misfortune, as we have seen, it seems natural to see it taking an important role among the symbols. While the peach tree itself figures rather prominently in

Chinese art, on anything as small as a toggle it would have to be condensed, so once again we generally find a part used to denote the whole. One exceptional toggle (No. 115) shows a whole orchard of peach trees, but we generally find only a branch with one or more fruits, and perhaps a few leaves and flowers in the background.

It is important to emphasize that the peach blossoms rarely appeared alone in Chinese art, because their tendency to fall from the tree prematurely caused them to be associated with early death, the exact opposite of that longevity to which most Chinese so avidly aspired. This early-falling propensity also led to an association with "fallen women," so prostitutes were often spoken of as peach blossoms (*t'ao hua'rh*), which was another reason for not representing them. Thus, when peach blossoms appear on the toggles at all, it is only on a branch with the fruits, wherein the peaches themselves, as symbols of longevity, would amply counteract and nullify the inauspicious implications of the flowers as such.

The peach fruits were always highly stylized, in accordance with the artistic convention by which certain inherent characteristics were highly emphasized to increase the ease in recognition. The Chinese distinguished the peach from other fruits by deepening and exaggerating the slight cleft on one side, and by prolonging the apex, until it often resembled a hooked beak, recalling extreme examples of the American Climax peach.

While Chinese folklore considered peach trees and their fruits as very potent in themselves, the truly wonder-working exploits in Far Eastern legends were ascribed to a very special kind of peach, the *p'an t'ao*, or peach of immortality, which grew only on the remarkable trees in the garden of Hsi Wang Mu, the Mother-Queen of the West, who ruled over the Immortals.

Some Occidental scholars think that this legend must reflect a distant memory of the Garden of the Hesperides, owned by Hera, the wife of Zeus.[6] Actually, the Greeks under Alexander the Great conquered Bactria in Afghan Turkestan in the fourth century B.C., and set up Greek cities there. From those centers, merchants and traders from the West may have come a great deal nearer China, in the Early Han Dynasty, which was the period just before this tale appeared in Chinese folklore, so it is not unreasonable to assume an ultimate Greek source supplying the garden motif for an already existing Chinese goddess.

It might seem a rather difficult task to portray a giant fruit on a tiny toggle, but the Chinese carvers were equal to the task, and they managed to convey the impression of vast size by making the fruit exceptionally large in contrast to the leaves and branches. Sometimes they also worked it in *Dalbergia* wood, to indicate by the deep purple color that these were no ordinary peaches. Some examples of this were cited in Chapter 4.

Due to its association with the Garden of the Queen of the Immortals, the *p'an t'ao* is naturally one of the chief symbols of longevity in China, along with the sacred fungus (*ling chih*), and some of its virtues pass down to peaches in general, which are also considered as emblems of immortality. As such, they take their place in the rebus combinations, where they stand for the word *shou*, meaning longevity, even though they are not true pun symbols. For example, a peach may appear with a happiness bat (*fu*) and a *ju-i* scepter, to make the auspicious phrase *fu shou ju i*, which means, "May you have happiness and long life, as much as you desire."

Also, the peach combines with two other fruits, the pomegranate and the "Buddha's hand," often displayed together in a basket, dish, or bowl, to form an auspicious group called the "Three Abundances." The Buddha's hand citron (*fu shou*) symbolized "much happiness," partly because of a pun on the first word of its name, while the peach signifies "much longevity," for reasons already given, and the pomegranate with its many seeds makes an obvious symbol for "much fertility." It would be one even if its chief attribute, the many seeds, did not make a pun on the phrase for "many children," which gives it a double emphasis. This composite symbol of the three fruits seems to have been a favorite one among the gentry, so one often finds it represented among the toggles of jade, while it is more common to find the individual fruit among the more plebeian toggles; although any one of these three fruits may occur singly in toggles for any rank of society, because each was a lucky symbol in its own right.

The Buddha's hand citron (*Citrus chirocarpus*) derives its Chinese name, and the alternative English one of "finger citron," from its odd shape. It is a bright yellow fruit with several fingerlike projections, suggesting the form of a human hand, partly clenched, with the fingers somewhat extended but held close together. Its rind is highly aromatic, with a rather pleasing scent, and, as scented things are believed to be demon-repelling, that is one reason why it is prized. Another reason is that its dried peel is thought to possess remarkable medical qualities.[7] Although much in demand in North China, the climate is too cold for it to grow there, so it is rather expensive, being considered as something of a treasure. It is therefore easy to see why it was considered symbolically important, and suitable as a toggle motif.

The pomegranate, originally imported from Persia,[8] was somewhat less rare, being grown in the gardens of the wealthy; but reproductions of it were even more highly valued, because it was such an obvious fertility charm, and the Chinese were obsessed with the idea of fertility, as we have already seen. The fruit, or a carved depiction of it, was for this reason an extremely popular kind of wedding present, so the toggles in this form may have been made as wedding gifts.

Just as the shape of the peach has been significantly altered, even distorted, by the Chinese artists to make it readily identified, they adopted a rather extreme conventionalization for the pomegranate, greatly exaggerating three sepals at the end of the fruit, and usually cutting a square hole through the rind on one side to disclose and emphasize the seeds. These do not seem to occur as frequently in the folk arts of the country districts as they do in the towns and cities, where closer contacts have resulted in upper-class luxury symbols filtering downward among the people, while parallel trends in the opposite direction often carried popular symbols upward.

Turning from fruits to vegetables, we find a great many toggles in all media made in the form of gourds and melons. We have already seen, in discussing the natural objects used for toggles, that small bottle gourds (*hu lu*) were often utilized for toggles, partly because of the convenience of their shape, since they had a pinched-in-waist around which the fastening cord could be easily tied, but also because of the connotations of fertility provided by their numerous seeds and, still further, because of their associations with medicine and healing, good fortune, etc. With all this wealth of significance to give them symbolic importance, the next step was to fashion all manner of other substances in the shape of gourds. Toggle No. 32 in this Collection gives some idea of how extensively this was carried out. Sometimes the replicas are perfectly plain, the simplest being two spheres with a connecting rod, turned on a lathe, but more often they show the fruit or fruits surrounded by a mass of vines and tendrils.

The vines and the stems added more to the significance of the gourd symbols; they were not merely used for their decorative effect, although they did contribute in that respect as well, but they served principally to help make up a series of pun symbols. This is because the Chinese word for the vine of a gourd or melon plant is *wan*, while the word for the stem or peduncle which holds the fruit itself to the vine is *tai*,[9] and together they make the phrase *wan tai*, meaning "(for) ten thousand generations," a phrase that often serves to express extreme duration in wishes for long life, success, many children, etc.

Most of the same associations apply also to the melons and the pumpkin—certainly those relating to fertility do—although these latter fruits lack the deeper associations with medicine that have clung so long to the gourd symbol. In addition, the pumpkin and the melons have the advantage of being valuable food producers (in contrast to the purely ornamental gourds), and this gives them an added connotation of abundance.

A pea pod or bean pod, swollen to show the growing seeds inside, is an obvious symbol of children in the womb, connoting fertility, and, as in the case of the gourds and melons, a succession of them on a continuous vine suggests the procession of countless generations of progeny.

Lastly, we have the eggplant (*chia*) represented in one toggle by a stone fruit with an elaborate iron cap to indicate the calyx and sepals. Since the word for cap is *kuan*, we apparently have here an expression of an official's hope to be promoted in rank (*chia kuan*). Both the character of the wish and the richer substance of which this toggle was made would indicate that this must have been intended for some person of higher standing, and is not just a folk toggle. (See No. 92.)

Turning from the garden vegetables, we find another extensive group of toggles devoted to representations of kinds of mushrooms. One of the problems that most puzzled us when we came to study the subjects depicted on the toggles was the exceedingly large number of mushrooms. Mushroom clusters obviously constituted one of the principal and most favored themes for the toggle carvers; yet they were not represented elsewhere in Chinese Art. They do not even appear in the rich symbol vocabulary of the folk embroideries, many of which were collected by Miss Bieber from the same districts in which she obtained her toggles.

At first it was tempting to assume that, since these particular toggles were all purchased in an area where there were many Manchus, they might have been Manchu toggles, and it was remotely possible that the Manchurians had borrowed from their more primitive neighbors in Siberia—such as the Chukchee or Koryak—a special reverence for the semipoisonous narcotic mushrooms which the forest-dwelling Siberians often ate with the deliberate purpose of inducing hallucinations.[10] However, although medieval Chinese literature contains a few rather vague references to a mushroom which, when eaten, caused the taker to laugh without stopping,[11] we have not found any direct evidence of either the Chinese or the Manchus deliberately eating poisonous mushrooms for the hallucinatory sensations they could produce. Furthermore, the mushrooms depicted on the toggles are never the dangerous *Amanita muscaria* taken by the Chukchee and the Koryak to induce the weird trances that have been so vividly described by European travelers to Eastern Siberia.

The care and accuracy with which these toggles were carved make it evident that their makers were simply reproducing common edible mushrooms of the *Agaricacea* family. This choice may have been partly in recognition of their food value, and an appreciation for the delicious contribution they would make to an otherwise drab diet; but obviously this was not enough to justify their use in toggles, among which the symbolic value was a paramount consideration. Also, it was probably not just a question of longevity, such as we find implicit in the sacred fungus, although some vestiges of the life-preserving qualities accredited to that might have carried over.[12] The most likely reason for the popularity of the mushroom motif, to judge from allusions in Chinese literature, was their fertility, their capacity to pop up in quantity one morning from seemingly barren soil, after the spores were activated by a summer shower. The Chinese literati, noting this, described the sudden flowering of a career, or a meteoric rise in fame, as being "like mushrooms in the morning" (*ju t'ung chao chun*).[13] However, this is a literary man's simile. Doubtless the peasants thought only of the idea of sudden fertility in an area previously barren, and in this, too, there must have seemed to them to be a quality of magic, which would inspire further respect in the minds of the credulous country folk.

A single example carved in antler (No. 90) apparently reproduces another variety, *Caprinus micaceus*. This mushroom cluster may have been represented for the same general reason as the others, but undoubtedly with a far greater emphasis on the idea of fertility. We have seen, in considering the material used to make the toggles, that antlers themselves were considered as furnishing important medicines for potency and fertility, and the crassly ithyphallic shape of these particular mushrooms undoubtedly led to similar beliefs concerning them, in terms of sympathetic magic; so, in combination, as found in this toggle, their effect must have been considered irresistible.

Quite apart from the problem of why they were used, how these mushrooms were treated, the ways in which the clusters were skilfully composed, reveals a versatility that can scarcely be found in any other single group of toggles. Several toggles in this collection have bilateral arrangements. Five of these have an even number of mushrooms on one side and an odd number on the other, apparently following a Yin-Yang system of number symbolism. Two more, although they have an equal number of mushrooms on both sides, have the heads all facing out on one side, and facing in on the other, thus producing a contrast between a smooth surface with projections in relief and a sunken surface marked by deep engraving, again following a Yin-Yang concept. These apparently deliberate symbolic arrangements indicate once more the deep underlying significance in what might seem to be merely trivial folk carvings.

One example (No. 83) shows all the mushrooms arranged in the shape of a ho-pao purse, apparently with a view to adding the idea of wealth to that of fertility. Another (No. 85) has them all spread out in a broad pattern, which when turned over reveals the shape of a butterfly, with the body and antenna added. Since the butterfly was itself a symbol of long life, this is an unquestionable instance of mushrooms being used in a longevity context, whether or not the mushrooms shared the reputation of their fungus cousins as bringers of long life. Two other examples of this complex theme have since come to light in other collections.[14] All three are so alike in size and appearance, although not quite identical, that they appear to have been produced by one man, working on a mass-production basis. This is a rare thing to find, as the Chinese wooden toggles were, in general, products of a folk tradition in which everything was individually made, often by the wearer himself.

In studying the mushroom toggles as a group, we have been struck by the fact that the more naturalistic mushroom clusters give a vivid impression of actively growing plants, in strong contrast to the rather static renderings of other products from the vegetable kingdom. It looks as though their makers actually intended them to express the miracle of growth in Nature. In any case, they certainly succeeded in achieving, in miniature, moving expressions of the principle that inspires all living things. As a result, these unpretentious mushroom toggles are just as effective as the more ambitious mountain toggles for conveying the idea of the universe in microcosm.

10

TOGGLES FROM THE
ANIMAL WORLD

THE ATTITUDE OF the Chinese toward animals often used to puzzle or even shock the Westerners who lived in China. Their harsh and cruel treatment of horses and dogs, or their sadistic savagery toward the captive animals in the few public zoos, where these could not defend themselves behind the bars, contrasted so strongly with their tenderness toward tame birds and caged insects. It was amazing to see the careful devotion they paid to their fighting crickets, or their strange sense of reverence for the ornamental goldfish. But the animals in Chinese Art were creatures apart, as far removed from the world of reality as the overbred goldfish. They were either purely mythical and auspicious creatures, like the various forms of the Chinese dragon or the Buddhist lions, or else they were actual animals, birds, or fish, credited with real or fancied qualities. Sometimes their use in art was based solely on far-fetched puns which gave them special symbolic or lucky connotations.

While we Westerners can enjoy the animal toggles purely for their skilful depictions and compact compositions, their humor, or even (God forbid!) their "quaintness," to a Chinese their primary importance lay in the messages they carried, and only secondarily in the ways in which the artists depicted them; although naturally a certain degree of skill was expected, and humor was always appreciated.

These attitudes should help, in part, to explain the feeling of the Old Chinese toward the fancy goldfish, which were actually semi-artificial works of art, having been bred very far from any natural fish, and which were virtually regarded as animated symbols of wealth and abundance, to bring increased fortune to their possessors.

The evolution of the ornamental goldfish came about from very practical considerations. The Old Chinese customarily left in their courtyards huge, open jars, called *shui kang*, filled with water for use in case of fire, an ever-present danger where the architecture was primarily of wood. They soon found that still water stagnated and offered breeding ground for mosquitoes; but experience taught them that this could be corrected by introducing fish to feed on the larvae, and thus destroy the noxious insects before they could develop. Practically the only fish suitable for this service was the humble carp, which did not mind having to live in motionless water; yet their sluggish habits and unattractively bulging contours did not offer very much to the viewer looking down into the jar from above. Then it occurred to some wise old Chinese that the answer was to breed them to obtain exaggerated fins and tails, which would project to give more character to the fishes' outlines when seen from above, and which would be almost constantly in motion, to make up for the natural stolidity of the fish themselves. Color was also a consideration, so they also bred them to encourage the red or golden hues.[1]

After generations of determined effort, the Chinese connoisseurs produced the ornamental goldfish now common in Occidental aquariums, although we usually view them from the side, through the transparent walls of glass tanks, in a way that the Chinese breeders never intended.

The Chinese term for goldfish is a literal description, *chin yü*, "fish of gold," but the word for fish (*yü*) makes a pun on the word for "overflowing abundance,"[2] so the whole expression, *chin yü*, makes a rebus signifying "an abundance of gold." This made the goldfish an obvious and very popular wealth symbol, either used alone or shown together with other punning objects to make larger rebus combinations. One of these we have already seen, in the case of a goldfish wrapped in a lotus leaf, as explained in the last chaper. An especially frequent rebus combination shows a goldfish carrying a lotus flower by its stem. This device was described in Chinese as *chin yü t'ung ho*, which makes a pun on "harmony together with an abundance of gold," two prime ingredients for a happy marriage. As such, the fish with lotus made a most appropriate subject for a toggle intended as a wedding present.

The twin fish that figure in the group of the Eight Buddhist Symbols were usually represented on the toggles as two carp or goldfish, and this pair tended to appear among the folk symbols with similar domestic connotations, rather than for any religious meaning. For example, the two goldfish were considered as representing a human couple living together in harmony, with an abundance of wealth as well as children, since the many eggs in fish roe made fish in general symbols of fertility. Even though such an ideal combination for marital happiness must often have seemed far from realization in a given family, the hope of attaining it was an object of intense desire; and in the folk tradition the representation or symbolization of a wish was believed capable of helping it come true. Thus, this was an appropriate theme for a husband's toggle.

The only other specific kind of fish to appear among the toggles is the catfish or mudfish (*Parasilurus asotus*), which was used because its Chinese name, *nien*, formed a pun on the word for "year," making it an appropriate word-picture in the vocabulary of the rebus language. These too were often shown in pairs. For example, a couple of them are depicted on toggle No. 150 in the Bieber Collection, along with a *ju-i* fungus and a leaf of the healing artemisia, to express the wish, "May you year by year enjoy long life with health."[3]

Some toggles may also show three fish. This collection has an open-work bronze lucky piece reused as a disc toggle (No. 46a), depicting three carp following each other around in the space between the rim of the central hole and the outer rim. This motif has been variously interpreted as intended to portray the succession of time: either as representing past, present, and future, or youth, maturity, and old age; or even as a symbolization of the "Three Regulators of Time" (*San Ch'ên* or *San Kuang*), that is to say, the Sun, the Moon, and the constellation of the Big Dipper.[4] But there were also many other triads in Old Chinese philosophy and folklore, so it is difficult to be sure exactly which one the three fish were intended to represent here.

A very interesting but rather crudely made folk toggle, formerly in the possession of Mr. Laurence Sickman of Kansas City, showed the three fish as three bodies of fan-tailed goldfish all meeting at the center in a single head. Dr. Carl Schuster has demonstrated that this motif goes far back in time, and has been found in many lands of Europe and Asia, always in the folk arts.[5] This indicates once again the common links at the folk level, in spite of the strong individual differences in the "higher arts" of each culture.

Another primitive folk toggle in the Bieber Collection (No. 23) shows four fish. They are depicted circling around a flat disc, on which is indicated a smaller disc labeled with the moon character (*yüeh*), and the latter is also dotted with seven small circles in the conventional Chinese way for representing stars, apparently to indicate the seven stars of the Big Dipper, with the moon, over the sun disc. The overt representation here of the "Three Regulators of Time" may help to identify the motif intended by the three fishes in the toggles previously described; but, since there are four fishes here, they must symbolize something else. Probably they just represent the continuity of Time, proceeding on and on in an endless succession; or else they may represent the four phases of the moon, or the four positions of the sun or the moon: rising, at the zenith, setting, and "under the Earth." On the bottom side of this enigmatic toggle are two snakes in high relief. Like the fish, they are *Yin* creatures, but they probably were included here with a more definite meaning.

The snake was not commonly used in the later Chinese tradition, except as one of the zodiac symbols, or as one of the five repellent creatures in a group known as the "Five Poisons." However, in Ancient China the snake was frequently figured on the funerary bronzes along with the cicada. Probably the snake was also a symbol of renewed life or immortality there, as the cicada was. As far back as the second millennium B.C., country people had probably observed how a dusty, bedraggled-looking snake could shed its old skin to emerge shiny and refreshed, as though it were taking on a new existence, which made it an excellent symbol of the conquest of age. Perhaps some lingering memory of this persisted on the folk level, although it was forgotten in the more sophisticated arts. In this case, the pair might symbolize a human couple who would share together a renewed life or rejuvenation in age. This is mere guesswork. It is also possible that two serpents could be used as another form of Yin-Yang symbol. In any case, these are the only snakes we have encountered on the toggles.

The birds most frequently depicted in Chinese art were highly auspicious ones, such as the *fêng-huang* (often miscalled "phoenix") and the crane. The *fêng-huang* was a symbol of the Empress, so it was forbidden to people of low degree, and consequently does not appear on toggles. The crane was more widely popular as a symbol of wisdom and longevity, but its overlong bill and legs made it inconvenient as a subject for figure toggles, so it is generally only seen on flat ones, such as the silver button toggle in this collection (No. 36). Note that on this particular example the concept of longevity has been further emphasized by having the crane carry a sprig of sacred fungus in his beak.

A more characteristic folk symbol, and hence far more common on the toggles, was the magpie. The first syllable of its name, *hsi ch'iao*, forms a pun on the word for joy, so it was widely used, in rebuses and elsewhere, as an expression of happiness. It appears most frequently with the plum tree, as shown on toggle No. 152 in this collection, to symbolize happy springtime, or a happy youth (including youth renewed). Two magpies together make up a motif, sometimes found on toggles, to signify *shuang hsi*, literally "paired joy," the term for marital happiness usually expressed in a single character placed on wedding gifts, as previously described.[6]

The most frequent marriage symbol in Chinese Art, aside from the *shuang hsi* character itself, was a pair of mandarin ducks (*Anas galericulta*), and these also appear on the toggles. When shown in paintings these beautiful birds are easily recognized by their distinctive coloration; but in unpainted carvings the identifying marks are a wedge-shaped crest, jutting out behind the head, and projecting scapulars. The latter are often abbreviated to a mere ridge above each wing cover. Two toggles in this collection (Nos. 155 and 156) depict them thus, but with their necks intertwined as an even more graphic symbol of conjugal affection.

The choice of these birds as a marriage symbol is based on a tradition that they mate for life, and that if one should die the other gradually pines away. However, the convention of the linked necks was a literary refinement, stemming from a story in a fourth-century Chinese anthology about an especially devoted couple who died and were buried separately. A tree grew from each grave, and their trunks gradually inclined toward each other until their respective branches met and intertwined, while their roots also grew together in the ground. Meanwhile a pair of mandarin ducks, a male and a female, perched together in the joined trees, with their necks intertwined, uttering plaintive cries, and people who saw them said that they must be the souls of Han P'ing and his wife who were buried there.[7]

Another rather literary bird symbol referring to marriage was the goose, as this traditionally did not mate a second time, and thus was a symbol of marital faithfulness. (We might remind the cynically inclined that the Chinese did *not* consider the goose a stupid bird.) In accordance with this symbolism, a live goose was usually given as an engagement present by the young man, and it is possible that a goose toggle may have been included among the return gifts presented to him. Nos. 153 and 154 in this collection are typical examples.

Among the other birds sometimes shown on the toggles was the eagle. This was a symbol of courage and bravery, but it also was an exorcising device to keep demons at bay, and as such it appeared on many printed charms, especially those directed against the dreaded fox spirits.[8] The Bieber Collection has one eagle toggle, No. 151.

Turning to animals, one of the commonest toggle subjects was the monkey. Few people in Old China ever had an opportunity to see live ones, except when a traveling circus came by with a few bedraggled specimens, unless they happened to live in Yünnan, in the far southwest, or else had made the pilgrimage to Omei Shan, the West Sacred Mountain, where wild macaques often come to be fed in the temple courtyards.[9] But monkeys and apes, as a kind of symbol for—or satire upon—the life of man and his works, have always appealed to the Chinese sense of humor. Furthermore, the general Chinese name for monkey or ape is *hou*, which makes a direct pun on the word for "marquis" (connoting noble rank in general) and also a less precise pun on "descendant(s)." The latter in particular has caused the monkey to be constantly used in a whole series of rebus pictures dealing with the subject of posterity, all of which were very dear to the family-conscious people of Old China, with their pride in the continuity of their lines.

Both these pun meanings could be combined in a single representation. For example, we find toggles that portray a wild-looking baby monkey riding on the back of its parent. In Chinese, this motif would be concisely described as *hou pei fêng hou*, literally: "crazy monkey behind monkey"; but, on replacing each character with a similar-sounding one, we get another phrase, meaning, "May the later generations (of the family) be ennobled as marquises." (When speaking of the substitution of characters, I am thinking of the process that went on in a scholar's mind when he saw the symbol and wished to work out its meaning. The illiterate majority, since they did not know any characters, would omit this step and merely think of another set of meanings for the same sounds, not knowing—or caring—whether they were different words or merely different meanings for the same word.)

Another popular toggle motif shows a monkey grasping a peach. First of all, this represented the folk hero Sun Hou-tzǔ, a mischievous semi-divine monkey who stole some of the peaches of immortality (*p'an t'ao*) while ostensibly guarding them.[10] The actual theft is depicted on toggle No. 115. In another case (No. 114), the monkey figure is definitely identified by having Sun's traditional hat. Such toggles also had a second meaning, however, because the descriptive words *fêng hou pao shou*, "crazy monkey grasping long life (peach)," makes a pun on another phrase, meaning "May you be ennobled and embrace longevity." It could also recall a simpler phrase, *hou pao shou*, in which one could replace the first word by its similar-sounding pun to say, "May your descendants embrace longevity."

In another popular and frequently encountered series of monkey toggles, a horse and a monkey are shown together: generally with the monkey riding on the horse's back. The most usual interpretation of this motif was *ma shang fêng hou*, "crazy monkey on horse's back," which by substitution becomes, "May you rapidly be ennobled." This message would be applicable only to an already-wealthy man or to a scholar official; it would be relatively meaningless to a peasant, who would well know that there was not much chance for this to happen to him. However, the latter, like anyone else, could still hope for the success of his children, or his children's children, so he would have read the pun differently, saying *Hou tsai ma shang*, "monkey is on horse's back", making a pun on the wish, "May your descendants be mounted on horse-back."

This last sentiment is a rather involved allusion to success in the Imperial Civil Service Examination, which was held every three years in the capital, because the winning candidate, the one who got the highest marks, was awarded the title of *Chuang-yüan* and was sent home on horseback. The height of ambition and the ultimate form of success, obtainable even for the sons of farmers and small merchants, if they were clever and could somehow gain the necessary advanced education, was to become an official; and practically the only way for an ordinary man to rise to a really high position was to take a first place in the Triennial Examination and become a *Chuang-yüan*. If he succeeded in this, his social and political success was assured and his family would rise with him.

The fact that this was considered a possibility for anyone accounts for the great popularity of the "Chuang-yüan returning on horseback"— the Chinese adaptation of the traditional Classical triumph scene—a recurrent motif on Chinese peasant carvings and folk embroideries.[11] The actual Chuang-yüan motif is depicted on one toggle in the Bieber Collection (No. 230), as described in Chapter 12.

The monkey and horse theme is most elaborately developed on another toggle (No. 123), which shows a monkey leaping up to mount a horse that stands with its front hoofs on a mounting block, while another monkey, on the off side, is crouching under the horse to help support it, to assist the first one. In this case, there seem to be two pun meanings. The first monkey, mounting the horse, is enacting the phrase *hou têng shang ma* ("monkey mounts on horse"), which makes a series of puns on the phrase "(May your) descendants mount the (Chuang-yüan's) horse," while the second monkey's act of assistance could be described as *pieh hou shêng pang*, "Other monkey rises to help," which is a rebus on "(May your) other descendants rise in rank."[12] Underneath the base is a carving of the three-legged money toad (to be described presently), which seems to convey a sly suggestion that all this promotion could be accomplished clandestinely by wealth: that is, by purchase of rank or through bribery.

The wishes that one's descendants might have long life, official advancement, and wealth were not enough; there was still the desire for fertility, as an ever-present element in Chinese symbolism, and there were monkey rebuses to express this idea also. One notable example of intricate wood carving (No. 122) portrays a monkey family with some eighteen small monkeys crowded around an elderly patriarch-monkey, who is seated in a formal arm-chair that is upheld by some of the smaller ones. From one point of view, this was doubtless intended as a humorous parody on a human family dominated by a patriarch; but essentially it was a fertility symbol based on a rebus, with the meaning, "May your great (or illustrious) descendant have many descendants of his own."

An equally clever but very different toggle (No. 121), shows a crouching monkey mother giving birth to a baby monkey, while another young one stands before her in a worshipful attitude, and a slightly older one clambers up her back. The maker of this toggle, who must have been a man of exceeding skill and ingenuity as well as having an excellent imagination, cleverly constructed it so that the mother monkey's eyes, arranged on movable pegs, can be made to swivel around in realistic fashion, by pulling on a small string that passes in one ear and out the other—like a symbol of gossip. The head of the baby monkey, which is emerging in the act of birth, has also been constructed on a movable peg so that it can turn completely around without slipping out. Though simply carved, the whole group is very realistic, and since it came from

Szechuan, it is possible that the maker had seen actual monkeys on Mount Omei to provide the inspiration.

The horse is shown alone, without the monkey, often richly caparisoned, with bridle, saddlecloth, and saddle, but usually only in the richer substances, such as bronze or jade. This is probably because, in general, only the wealthy could afford horses, or hope to keep one. There were many auspicious phrases involving horses, some of which could account for their use as toggles, but the most likely reason for a horse toggle would be as a birth symbol from the zodiac group.

The twelve animals of the zodiac were: the rat, ox (or cow), tiger, hare (or rabbit), dragon, serpent, horse, sheep, monkey, cock, dog, and pig. As previously mentioned, they were Time symbols, presiding over the twelve double hours of the day, the twelve months of the year, and the years in the sixty-year cycle. In the latter case, each was repeated five times during the period of sixty years, each time being prefixed by the sign of one of the Five Elements (wood, fire, earth, metal, water). People reckoned their birth years by these animals, rather than by reign-dates. The birth animal was important in the construction of horoscopes, to determine one's fortune, and they were particularly significant when one contemplated marriage. For it was forbidden to marry anyone who had a birth animal that might be antagonistic to one's own, as that would inevitably lead to violent discord.[13] We have seen most of these animals used as toggle subjects—except for the rabbit and the rooster. (The former was considered obscene, and the latter was impractical because of the sharp edges of its serrated comb, pointed tail plumes, and sharp-toed feet.)

A good example of this zodiacal usage is found in the pig toggles; although the boar, which was usually represented, was just as likely to be used as a symbol of vigorous procreative powers or masculine vitality. Among the objects reused as toggles, we also find small pigs of opaque glass or jade recovered from tombs. These were usually sleeveweights in origin, once worn by court ladies to hold down their excessively long sleeves on windy days. In this case, their use probably was due partly to convenience in finding them ready-made, though doubtless the symbolic connotations of porcine fertility played their part.

While Chinese toggles could be—and often were—made in the form of a sheep in order to represent a man's birth animal, the three examples in this collection all happen to be of Mongol origin. The first and most distinctive seems to have been a pawn from a fine Mongol chess set, as it has traces of white pigment on its body and of red on the thick base,[14] which was somewhat crudely pierced on the bottom to make a hole for the cord when it was reutilized for a toggle. This one and the second, obviously originally made for a toggle, both represent fat-tailed rams. The fat-tailed sheep were symbols of wealth and security among the Mongol herdsmen, as they can survive in seasons of famine and drought or through bad winters by drawing on the fat that is stored in their grotesquely large tails, when ordinary sheep would perish; while the ram of the species is always aggressively masculine, and is therefore an obvious symbol of procreation. In the case of the ewe with the lamb, on the third toggle (No. 169), we have once again a parent-and-child symbol to denote fertility of the herds, which meant increased wealth, and was therefore also a symbol of riches.

The dog figured quite frequently on toggles, either as a birth-year animal or as a symbol of protection, but the kind that the toggle-makers most favored and enjoyed depicting was a breed for which Old Peking was famous, the lion-dog (shih-tzŭ kou). There was a humorous as well as lovable quality about these little mops of taffy-colored silken hair which appealed to the hearts of the Chinese and aroused their sentiments, so that they never treated them unkindly as they did most dogs.

These lion-dogs, like the ornamental goldfish, were the product of countless generations of careful breeding; and like the goldfish they were also living symbols, because they were specially bred to resemble the semi-mythical Buddhist lion, as the Chinese imagined him, and were thought to share some of that mystic creature's formidable powers.[15]

Few Chinese ever had an opportunity to see a real lion. "Tribute lions" were sent at irregular intervals from Persia as gifts to the Son of Heaven, ever since a Parthian prince began the custom back in the Han Dynasty, during the first century A.D.; but the emperors kept these prized possessions in their private parks or palace zoos, and only the most highly privileged courtiers ever got to see them. However, the lion was an important symbol in Buddhism, and in the Manichaean religion that came to China a few centuries later, so artists had to depict them.[16] For lack of a living model, the Chinese artists gradually evolved a conventionalized monster which had little basis in reality, but was certainly a symbol of formidable power.

The Buddhist lion, as the Chinese evolved him, was a huge blue animal, with powerful jaws, a curly mane which extended the whole length of his back, and a huge bushy tail that had curls like the mane.[17] Traditionally, they were usually displayed in pairs—as gate guards, throne guardians, etc.—one being considered male and the other female, although both had the same powerful build and heavy mane. Originally, the distinction between them was indicated by giving the male lion an open mouth, as though roaring, while the she-one discreetly kept her mouth shut. Later the male lion was depicted with a ball, said to contain his life essence, while the female guarded a cub, and that is the convention that was carried over onto the toggles. One toggle in this collection (No. 129) shows a lion with both ball and cub, perhaps a joking reference to a hermaphrodite. Other conventions for the Buddhist lions, shown on some of the toggles, were: a massive collar or harness supporting one or more huge, round bells, and also flames sprouting from the shoulders and flanks to indicate the supernatural qualities of this mythical creature.

The even more mythical dragon, a composite of several other animals, could not appear in full detail in the folk arts or on the toggles as long as China was an empire, or as long as the imperial power had effective control to enforce its laws (until about 1910). Before that, it was strictly forbidden for anyone below the highest officials to wear the traditional dragon: either the sacred and imperial five-clawed *lung* or the semisacred four-clawed *mang*.[18] Even the Mongols and Tibetans were subject to these laws. But after the fall of the Ch'ing Dynasty in 1911, coin toggles with imperial dragons on them could be used freely.

Meanwhile, if people wanted to use dragons—and they often did, because they were not only birth-year symbols but also sacred beasts endowed with special spiritual powers—they might do so if they altered the dragon so that it would be neither a *lung* nor a *mang*. They could do this by leaving off any claws, and showing only a single horn, or by showing another lesser form of dragon, such as the *ch'ih*, described below.

Aside from the coin toggles with the *lung* dragon and the coin amulet with a pair of clawless dragons, mentioned in Chapter 7, the Bieber Collection has only one other example of the traditional Chinese dragon. Displayed on a spreader toggle, this has its feet discreetly hidden among clouds, so it could also pass as a clawless one.

Another very old toggle in this collection (No. 135) displays two of the *ch'ih* dragons.[19] Catlike, scaleless creatures with forked tails, the *ch'ih* are usually described as "immature dragons," though some are evidently old enough to have cubs of their own. A mother *ch'ih* with a young one made a frequent motif on belt buckles and other ornaments, and that is the combination shown here. The pair are depicted standing on three stalks of sacred fungus and an artemisia leaf. Since both these plants were used in Chinese medicine—the first for healing, and the second for prolonging life—the animals themselves must obviously have had an appropriate symbolic meaning to account for this association. Long ago their name made a pun on another word, meaning "cure" (now pronounced *chih*, without the aspirate),[20] so at that time a big and little *ch'ih* could have formed a rebus meaning "great and small cures." This is the most likely reason for their presence with the curative plants. The toggle itself is very old, and its style is quite antique, so it seems likely that it was made centuries ago when such a pun would still have been possible.

Not only mythical reptiles but actual ones appeared on the toggles, notably frogs and toads. Unattractive as these may seem to us Occidentals, they were revered by the Chinese since ancient times. They were always considered as highly mysterious creatures, because of their strange life cycle, and their ability to live happily in two elements as amphibians. But they were a special source of wonder, because in spite of the lack of obvious generative organs they were extremely prolific. It was probably their powers of fertility that made them such popular folk symbols.

In this category we also find a mythical element in the "money toad" (*ch'ien ch'an*). A grotesque three-legged monster, it was considered as an animated purse of inexhaustible coins, and hence was very popular as a symbol of wealth. Often he is shown on the toggles with a cord strung with cash coins hanging from his mouth, as a token of his legendary powers as a dispenser of wealth. He is often represented as the companion of a youthful immortal named Liu Hai (or Liu Han), who will be described in Chapter 12.

Bats in the Occident are generally considered almost as repulsive as frogs and toads, and are usually associated with eerie spirits, ghosts, and witches; but in China, by contrast, they were extremely popular as lucky symbols. Although the Old Chinese wrote the word "bat" in such a way as to show that they classed them with reptiles and insects (writing it with the insect element), the other half of the character, which gave it its pronounciation, rhymed with the word for happiness,[21] so the bats were much used as pun symbols. In addition to examples already mentioned in connection with other symbols, a favorite motif showed a small bat resting on a cash coin. As these coins had a small, square central hole, called an "eye" (the way we speak of the eye of a needle), they were popularly called "eye coins," *yen ch'ien*;[22] therefore the whole motif was described as *fu tsai yen ch'ien* ("bat on eye coin"), which makes a pun on "Happiness lies before the eyes." (Illustrated on No. 111.)

In studying examples of the Chinese folk arts, whether in carvings or in embroideries, it is often difficult to distinguish between bats and butterflies, as the latter are sometimes rendered with broad heads and without antennae, in some of the cruder representations. The Bieber Collection has one unmistakable butterfly (No. 157), as well as the mushroom toggle in butterfly form described in the last chapter. The Chinese generally call the butterfly *hu tieh*, and the second character of this name makes a pun on "seventy years of age," so it is used as a symbol of longevity, conveying the wish that one might live that long. In some parts of South and Central China, the first character is also pronounced like the word for happiness (*fu*), so the butterfly is used like the bat as a symbol of happiness; but it carries as well the additional idea of a long life in which to enjoy it more fully. Probably this similarity of meanings is one reason for the confusion of the representations of these two creatures.

Another insect associated with longevity was the cicada; but that was used as a symbol for different reasons. Here, it was not the name, but the nature and habits of the original insect that made it symbolically significant. More than three thousand years ago, in China's first historical dynasty, the Shang, observant men apparently noted its peculiar life cycle, and were impressed by it. The cicada begins its existence as an ugly whitish grub (our farmers call them "cutworms"), which lives from seven to thirteen years underground, eventually tunneling back to the surface, where it becomes a long-legged insect. Then this insect form climbs a tree, splits its skin, and leaving behind a fragile shell, it emerges as a free-flying creature that soars away into the empyrean.

It would be difficult to conceive a more graphic example of transformation in Nature as a prefiguring of man's hoped-for transfiguration after death.[23] As such, the men of Shang cast symbolic figures of the cicada on the ritual bronzes which they created as offerings to the dead, and later Chinese placed its image, carved in jade or marble on the tongues of corpses as a passport to immortality.

The Chinese peasants of recent times who found and reused as toggles the ancient stone cicadas like No. 45, or those who carved new ones like No. 159 or the rhinoceros horn one previously mentioned, might not have been able to put these ancient sentiments into words; but they still sensed the meaning, and felt convinced that the cicada toggle amulets could insure them longevity, if not actual immortality, in the world beyond the grave.

11

INANIMATE OBJECTS:
THE REPLICA TOGGLES

Not only the world of Nature but also inanimate things provided subjects for the toggle-makers. Although we tend to consider it a trait more characteristic of the people of Japan, the Chinese have also long displayed as strong fondness for miniature copies of customary things. This is fully expressed in the replica toggles of Old China, which imitated on a tiny scale many familiar objects of daily life, or the tools and utensils of various occupations. It must not be assumed, though, that these often-whimsical models of things were mere toys. In the first place, they always had to be objects well fitted by their size and shape for the primary purpose of serving as functional counterweights.

At a casual glance, it might seem that most of these replica toggles were made only for amusement, or to serve as emblems of their wearers' professions or personal interests. This may be true of some of them; but, on closer inspection, many of the most matter-of-fact-looking ones turn out to have symbolic meanings as well. The deep symbol-minded strain in Chinese life, which we have noticed as a thread running all the way through the toggle tradition, was too strong not to exert its influence here, also. For example, the little saddles (an) of brass or copper (t'ung) which fall into the replica class, made a pun on t'ung an, "peace together," an appropriate marriage wish that made them charms for marital harmony; and similar instances turn up again and again. In short, it would seem that, in addition to providing humor, or a key to the wearer's chief interest, most if not all the small models could probably once have been interpreted as auspicious symbols.

Among the most obvious symbols by association were the copies of the heavy stone weights called t'o-tzŭ, which were used for securing the ropes when erecting tents or temporary pavilions, or for tying up horses.[1] (See No. 183 for an example.) The prototype was a rectangular block of stone, usually tapered at the sides, with a slot cut through it near the top to make a handle to which a rope could be tied. As the function of the original weight was to provide security and stability, this idea carried over into the miniature models used for counterweights, so that these toggles gave a symbolic assurance that they would not fail in their task.

The same general idea of symbolic security was expressed in the models of padlocks. Some of these had much the same shape as the stone weights just mentioned, with a similar crossbar above a slot at their top, but they were generally somewhat thinner, and often highly ornamented on the sides. The peasants had wooden locks for toggles as symbols of security, but the nobles and courtiers in Peking frequently had fine ones of jade, often inscribed on the sides with large characters forming auspicious phrases. Some of the more elaborate padlock toggles were symmetrically lobed at sides and base (as in No. 185), recalling the "baby locks" commonly worn by young children to "secure them to life" and prevent their being seized by evil spirits who might try to drag them off to a premature death.[2] But the toggle locks were much heavier than the "baby locks," which were generally made of light German silver, beaten out in patterns that were very decorative as well as being magically effective according to Old Chinese beliefs.

The same idea of symbolically holding or securing was doubtless intended in the miniature copy of a stone belt buckle in this collection (No. 197). Made of onyx, this has the shape of an oldtime scholar's belt fastening, with a button on the base to slide into a buttonhole on one end of the silk cloth belt, and a hook in the form of a dragon's head, at the narrow end, to slip through a ring at the other end of the belt. In this case, the button is not sufficiently undercut to hold a belt, although it amply serves to secure a cord looped around it. This makes it clear that the object in question was originally made as a replica of a buckle to serve as a toggle, and was not merely a noble child's belt buckle reused for one.

Perhaps the small iron stirrups fell into the same category of securing symbols, since Chinese stirrups were very heavy and were intended to provide greater security for a horseback rider. But there may be another element under consideration here. These obvious equestrian symbols may have been horsemen's charms for protection against falling from the saddle, since many of the toggle-wearers, especially the Mongols and Manchus, were professional horsemen.

Sometimes the miniatures were quite functional, as in the case of the very small flint-and-steel sets such as No. 194, which were made to serve as toggles but still could be used for kindling fires. Since fire was considered most effective in exorcism, fire-making things were held to be especially effective for keeping evil spirits at bay. Sometimes these strike-a-light sets bore other symbols as well, as in the cases where a metal stud engraved with a *shou* character was used to decorate the cover of the flint-pouch, to provide auspicious wishes for longevity.

Also capable of use was the miniature calculator or abacus (No. 204). This was made exactly like the original device, with tiny beads for counters that could be slipped up and down the vertical rods with a sharp fingernail, to make quick calculations.[3] In any case, this would have been a natural symbol for a merchant or businessman in Old China, not only serving as a mark of his profession, but also tending to bring him, by sympathetic magic, skill and ability at reckoning up his accounts.

Less practical, though still functional to a lesser extent, is a miniature Mongol or Manchu knife-and-chopstick set (No. 199). Perhaps it was originally used to support a full-sized one, as an example of ironic folk humor. The tiny knife is still large enough for small cutting work or light engraving, and the chopsticks could be useful as small pegs for securing things, even though they could never be used effectively to pick up food; while the skewer could still be used as a toothpick or nail cleaner.

Another functional miniature is the beautifully made model of a nested food box (No. 208), a tiny copy of the kind the Chinese formerly took on picnics to carry their lunch. This is a fairly obvious symbol of jolly feasting, and good times in general; but, in addition, its three small compartments can be utilized in a practical way, for carrying small pills or other little items, like those of a Japanese *inrō*, which it distantly resembles.

The small silver mirror in the Bieber Collection (No. 182) was another replica intended for use as a toggle. It is not particularly effective as a looking glass—though it may once have been—because the reflecting surface, small to begin with, is now scratched and scored; but it could still fulfill another important function ascribed to Chinese mirrors, namely to act as an exorciser, to ward off or absorb any lurking spirit of evil (*kuei*), and to keep the wearer free from harm. The presence of the Yin-Yang symbol on the boss at the reverse side indicates that the maker deliberately conceived it as a miniature copy of a magic cosmic mirror capable of acting in this way. Also, the addition of the four-character message, saying *fu ju Tung Hai*, "as happy as the Eastern Sea," indicates a belief in a more positive power to bring happiness through wealth and long life, since the Eastern Sea was a legendary source of wealth and the site of the Isles of the Immortals, whose inhabitants enjoyed long life without end.

Miniature drums make up a very familiar category of replica toggles. They are usually carved of wood. The carvers often hollowed them out by working through slits in the sides, between the horizontal bars which were later to become side slats linking the drumheads at each end. In accomplishing this they usually deliberately left a small piece of the core which they carefully rounded to make a free-rolling ball. The reason for this seems to have been an example of folk logic. Since a drum was primarily associated with noise-making, these drums had to be able to produce a sound, and that was provided by the ball rattling around inside, every time the miniature drum was picked up or shaken.

Since early times the sound of a drum has been associated with thunder and rain-making in China and in the neighboring countries to the north and south. Other writers have described the shaman drums of Siberia, and ancient Chinese-style bronze drums are still used for this purpose by the aboriginal tribes of South China, Burma, and Siam. In all these cultures, drums have also been extensively used for chasing off demons. For example, they pound drums noisily at the time of solar eclipses, to make "the evil monster" disgorge the sun, which they imagine he is trying to swallow. By their fancied ability to drive off evil, drums were considered as bringers of good fortune, and hence they were included among the luck-bringing symbols in the folk tradition.

This is by no means the only association to account for the popularity of drum toggles, however. Drums have traditionally played an important part in Chinese warfare and military parades for at least two thousand years. One dramatic instance of the Chinese use of martial music was in 36 B.C., when a small Chinese army made a surprise attack on the King of the Huns in Western Turkestan, advancing with beating drums to frighten the Hunnish garrison into believing that the assault was on a much larger scale.[4] (Incidentally, that was probably the only time that

Chinese troops ever fought against Roman soldiers, as the Hunnish King had hired some Roman guards.[5]) Thus the drum would have been popular as a symbol for the military-minded. But, in the popular mind, one of the chief associations was probably with the idea of holiday-making at festival times, when drummers led the joyful processions, and announced the performances of acrobats, traveling theatrical troupes, or dancing bears.

Any of these connotations might have come into mind on seeing a miniature drum, but the principal reason for using these little drums as toggles seems to have been still another idea. Nearly all the toggle drums are eight-sided, and the Chinese had a small eight-sided drum which they called the "drum of Great Peace" (*T'ai-p'ing ku*);[6] thus the small replicas were probably symbolic of a peaceful and harmonious life. This concept is even emphasized on one little drum toggle in the Bieber Collection (No. 163), on which the characters for *T'ai* and *P'ing* have been carved in relief on the drumheads at each end.

Another very extensive group among the replica toggles is composed of tiny models of shoes, very often in pairs. They are generally carved in minute detail from fine woods. Some of the carved shoes we have seen from China have been so small and so light that they could scarcely have served as toggles, and must have been worn as amulets in other ways. However, all those in the Bieber Collection were definitely functioning toggles.

Psychologists tell us that there is a highly developed form of fetishism based upon shoes—especially women's shoes—and many writers have pointed out the sexual connotations in the bound feet of Chinese women. However, it is not necessary to plunge into the turgid depths of Freud and Krafft-Ebing to explain the use of miniature shoes for toggles. These very clearly belong to the class of rebus symbols, acting as such in two separate ways, depending on regional differences in pronunciation.

In North China, especially around Peking, the word for shoe is pronounced *hsieh*,[7] but there is another word, pronounced in the same way, which means "to agree," "to be in accord," "to harmonize together."[8] Therefore, taking advantage of this pun combination, a pair of shoes can connote a married couple together in harmony.[9] In fact, a typical auspicious wish on behalf of a married couple is *t'ung hsieh tao lao*, "walk together to old age." This idea is sometimes still more openly expressed by a small bronze shoe (*t'ung hsieh*, in Chinese). In fact, with this thought in mind, small bronze shoes, somewhat larger than the miniature toggle ones, were sometimes given as wedding presents, to serve as little containers on table or desk.

Another entire series of pun meanings is afforded by an alternative pronunciation of the same word for shoe, more common in Central and South China, but also known in the North. This is *hai-tzŭ*, or, for a small one, *hsiao hai-tzŭ*, which makes a direct pun on the words for child (or children), which are pronounced the same, though written slightly differently. This second pun possibility has given rise to a number of clever variations, which have been exploited to the utmost by Chinese folk artists, including the toggle carvers.

Its simplest expression is merely a single small shoe or a pair of shoes, to represent the child—or children—desired. (A Chinese word can be either singular or plural, depending on how it is used, without changing its form.) Often the shoe toggle will be inscribed with a *shou* character in relief, representing embroidered decoration on an original cloth or leather one, to extend the pun description and make it say *hsiao hai-tzŭ yu shou*, "May your child(ren) have a long life."

Quite a group of shoe toggles, as well as the little shoe amulets previously referred to, consist of a tiny shoe contained within a larger one, for example, a woman's shoe inside a man's. This can be explained in Chinese as *hsiao hai-tzŭ yu hsiao hai-tzŭ*, literally "Little shoe has little shoe," used as a pun for the wish "May your child(ren) have children," expressing a hope for continuing the family line. This was a profoundly important hope in Old China, where the natural desire for posterity was reinforced by the belief that one needed sons to carry on the ancestral worship, without which the family would die out in the most literal sense.

The smaller shoes, inserted in the large ones or represented alone, were the tiny woman's shoes for the bound "lily feet" that were fashionable in China from the tenth century to the twentieth, in spite of the excruciating torture to the wearers during that thousand years. This type of shoe was described as *lien hai-tzŭ*, literally "lily shoe," but these words in turn made a pun on "successive children," thus increasing still more the idea of prospective fertility. This thought is elaborately expressed in one of the toggles in the Bieber Collection (No. 179), which shows a linked pair of large man's shoes, in one of which is a tiny woman's shoe (*lien hai-tzŭ*) while the other contains a small crab. The Chinese word for crab, *ta chia*,[10] makes a pun on the phrase for "a large family." Altogether then, this toggle represents the pun sentence, *hai-tzŭ yu lien hai-tzŭ, hai yu ta chia*, meaning "May your children have a succession of children, and also have an influential family." This would certainly be an appropriate sentiment for a toggle intended for a wedding present, as many of them were.

Although the last-mentioned arrangement might seem to be an ultimate example of the elaboration of rebus symbols, another toggle in this collection (No. 181) does it one better. This consists of a pair of man's shoes, hollowed out, with a plug in each that is carved in the form of a seated monkey (*hou*); but when each monkey is removed, behind it, carved on the back of the same piece of wood, is a woman's lily shoe. This entire presentation would be described in Chinese as *hsiao hai-tzŭ yu hou, hou hai yu lien hai-tzŭ* (shoes have monkeys; monkeys further have lotus shoes), which provides a series of puns that can be read, "May your children have descendants, who in turn will have successive children." As if this were not enough, each toe of the two man's shoes is carved into the shape of a *ju-i* and is ornamented with an incised circular *shou* character (*yüan shou*), while a conventionalized lotus flower (*lien*) is lightly incised upon the side of each shoe; so by considering these new elements and disregarding the contents of the shoes, we get a whole new pun sequence conveying the wish, "May your children continue to enjoy a full long life, as much as they desire." This ornate rebus figure, with many meanings, is a pun symbol to end all pun symbols, and it would be difficult to find a more intricate one.

A last major category of replica toggles is provided by the flat straw baskets, or winnowing fans, of the type utilized by Chinese peasants for all manner of activities. One of the principal uses was for a dustpan, together with a straw brush, for cleaning floors and doorways. Often the toggles show the basket with a cat or a small lion-dog curled up inside it. This winnowing fan has a number of symbolic interpretations, as any real folk symbol should have. In the first place, the act of winnowing sorts out the good (grain) from the bad (chaff), in the course of which the basket or fan is the chief agent, and hence a force for the good. Secondly, the fan used as a dust basket, together with the broom, is an obvious symbol of sweeping out evil, or, by extension, of exorcism. In fact, the basket and broom are well-known features in Chinese and Japanese rites of exorcism against evil spirits.[11] Then the cat, which is often shown in it, as enemy of rats and mice extends the idea of warding off evil;[12] while the lion-dog as a symbolic—and actual—protector of the home, also carries the idea of providing security against evil. This is therefore an appropriate symbol for a farmer or householder.

An especially interesting old toggle in the Bieber Collection depicts a ewe and a lamb reclining together in a winnowing basket (No. 169). This theme is very simply carved in camphorwood. A very large hole for the cord was originally drilled between the ewe and the lamb, big enough for the passage of a rawhide thong. This, together with the pastoral subject so congenial to a herding people, suggests a Mongol origin. Later, a small hole was bored through the back of the basket, so the toggle might be worn with a smaller cord, in the Chinese or Manchu fashion. Very probably the later owner thought of the animals as a dog with a pup; although close observation reveals that the young one's foreleg is curled under him in sheep fashion, and that the pair are clearly not dogs, but flop-eared sheep with natural, undocked tails, of a kind very commonly found in Mongolia, where Chinese camphorwood was used for incense or for image-making in the Lama monasteries.

The other kind of basket with an arched handle—a type more familiar outside China—also appears as a subject for the replica toggles; but in this case it is not so much the basket itself as what it contains that provides the significant meaning. In the baskets are displayed peaches, or one or more fish. Obviously, these meant the same as peaches alone, or a fish without the basket: that is, longevity and fertility or abundance. However, the basket made an effective decorative background, provided unity for the composition, and even more importantly, its handle provided a convenient and effective loop fastening for the cord.

On other objects as well, it is often the decoration or filling that provides the chief significance. For example, the Bieber Collection has a clever miniature replica of a scholar's arm rest, carved from fine-grained wood to simulate an original made from a section of bamboo. Conceivably, the subject may have been chosen by a writer, professional scribe, or an artist, as a symbol of his occupation, but the real symbolic significance is provided by the decoration carved on it, a blossoming plum tree, as a symbol of youth and rejuvenation. (See No. 205.)

A handsome ivory toggle in the shape of a well-filled cloth purse (ho-pao), which might once have served to secure such a purse to a man's belt, was an obvious symbol of riches. But another symbolic dimension was added to this one (No. 196) by carving upon it a simulated button or stud with a circular *shou* character, to symbolize a long life during which the wearer would have leisure to enjoy his wealth. Still another obvious wealth symbol was provided by a hollow cube or cuboctahedron of light brass, cleverly worked to resemble a mass of coins (No. 203). But the Chinese usually showed more subtlety when expressing their desire for riches.

Before the institution of banking, wealthy Chinese often invested their surplus capital in antique bronzes or jades, so these, too, became signs of wealth. This collection has a small copy in peachwood of an ancient jade sword fitting, of a type much prized by scholar-antiquarians and other connoisseurs in Old China. The original object was so devised as to fit into the side of the sword sheath, to provide a slot for the strap by which it could be hung from the belt.[13] The maker of this toggle slightly misunderstood the form and purpose of the original, but he did succeed in his intent to represent a valued antique as a wealth symbol, and he carved it in an auspicious wood that would be lucky in its own right.

In contrast to entrenched wealth which permitted the ownership of antiques, was the sudden windfall that came through a lucky toss in gambling. A symbol of this was very popular for toggles, especially among the Mongols. This was a sheep's ankle bone (*astragalus*), so commonly used in dice games among the peoples of the nothern borders of China and the steppe dwellers beyond the frontier.[14] The actual bone could be drilled to form a primitive natural toggle, but we often find replicas in other substances: wood, bronze, or even glass (as in No. 200). These need not all have been gamblers' symbols, but their principal association was clearly the gain to be acquired through a trick of fortune.

The subtlest of all the wealth symbols, in this collection at least, is No. 201. It is a simple lathe-turned replica of a diabolo, a dumbbell-shaped top that by deft manipulation could be kept spinning on a string between two sticks. This looks like a simple symbol of joy, to recall the pleasure of a popular leisure pastime, but again we have to do with a pun. The colloquial Chinese name for this kind of top was *mên hu-lu*, a pun on a phrase meaning "money box,"[15] expressing a wish for riches.

One could proceed in this way indefinitely, taking up item by item in the replica category to show the multiple significance in fairly ordinary objects, with reasonably definite assurance that the thing being copied would not have been chosen as a subject for a toggle unless it did have auspicious connotations. Generally the meaning is fairly obvious, as in the case of the brass saddles, or the slightly more subtle one of a miniature straw hat (like No. 192), which had a double interpretation. Since a hat protects one from sun, rain, and wind, the latter was a symbol of protection in general; but because its name *li* is a pun on the word for "strong," it was also a pun symbol, invoking physical strength and stamina for a farmer or coolie who wore it.

Only rarely is the investigator somewhat baffled, but even in these cases, further searching would doubtless reveal an inner association based on pun meanings, obvious to both the maker and the wearer (if they were different persons). The possibilities of pun combinations in Chinese are almost endless, and as yet they have not been investigated at all fully. Most of them are expressions of a limited number of subjects, indicating a constant or recurrent preoccupation with a few essential themes: health and longevity, riches and wealth, marital happiness, mutual devotion, fertility (for crops and herds, as well as for people), and peace with security. These have been the essential human longings of men and women everywhere, regardless of nationality, from the beginnings of civilization: but few people have shown the imagination and ingenuity in expressing them that were found among the folk artists in Old China.

12

MEN AND GODS

THE OLD CHINESE PHILOSOPHERS never considered man as the lord of Creation, master of Nature by his own ingenuity. Although they regarded him as somewhat higher than the other animals, he was still definitely subordinate to the forces of Nature, which enjoyed powers to which he could never aspire. This view was well expressed in the Sung landscape paintings, inspired by Taoist teachings, in which one or two tiny men stand dwarfed by the lofty mountains above them and the down-rushing streams below, almost lost in the immensity of the natural world around them. Since he was not overburdened with human conceit and self-complacency, the average man in Old China could regard himself and his fellow men with a sense of humor, even though his own lot might be a very hard one.

This attitude must often have been present in the toggle-makers. Take No. 216, for example. Its carver has depicted an elderly peasant with bald head and scraggly beard, naked to the waist, with the tops of his trousers rolled down over his belt, holding his grinning, naked grandchild in his lap. Such a sight used to be a familiar one of a summer's evening in the China that is now gone, and the theme of the continuity of generations was certainly very ancient and all-pervading in Old Chinese thought and tradition, as we have seen. But a second glance reveals another note. This pair were carved in the same attitude as the familiar monkey-with-young toggles. Although the monkeys themselves were often depicted in such a way as to give a satirical commentary on human actions, this toggle, by contrast, appears to be a playful parody on the ancient monkey theme. As such, this toggle could provoke humor as well as arousing sympathy or nostalgia for the proud and loving grandparent, while at the same time it served its intended purpose of symbolizing the continuity of generations, and thus acted as a fertility charm.

Even when a toggle such as No. 217 depicts a distinguished elder or dignitary seated on a cushion inscribed with a *shou* character, doubtless alluding to a rise in rank accompanied by long life in which to enjoy its prestige, the face has an air of comic gravity that was probably quite intentional. The toggle-makers seem to have taken a special delight in subtly ridiculing excessive dignity. Here we have a graphic expression of a universal attitude of peasants toward their self-styled "superiors."

A very common toggle subject, especially on flat sections of old ivory, is the figure of an ancient scholar with a long beard, reclining against a rock. The old man is always depicted as being so relaxed and so contented that one automatically forgets one's own problems on seeing him. Here, the main purpose was probably to suggest that by contemplation and meditation one could find the road to immortality; for this was essentially a longevity symbol. As a side thought, it is amusing to contrast the relaxed attitude of the contemplative Chinese, as depicted here, with the rigid poses assumed by the meditating yogis of India. It gives an interesting commentary on the two very different Asian cultures.

Women are rarely depicted on the toggles, except in one small group of "doctors' toggles." These represent a nude woman, usually lying on a giant leaf, and were apparently intended to imitate the little ivory figures formerly carried by old-style Chinese doctors to help them in diagnosing female illnesses. By the old custom, when a male doctor called on a woman patient she remained hidden behind the curtains of her bed; without attempting to look at her, he would then offer her one of these figures, and she would indicate on it with the tip of a fingernail, or a mark with a writing brush, the location of her ailment. After determining this, the doctor would then proceed to take her pulse and calculate from it the precise nature of the illness, for which he would then prescribe the appropriate medicine. In this way, the patient could retain her modesty throughout the examination.

The original medical figures measured up to eight or ten inches in length, but the toggle replicas were much smaller, usually less than three inches long, far too small to be of any use in actual diagnosis. Then, too, they were generally made of jade, which further indicates that they were only replicas and not intended for actual use, since the greasy surface of jade will not take Chinese ink effectively.

The female figure was always represented as nude, except for the feet, which were covered. (This latter detail was required because the bound, lily feet were so repulsively distorted that they were never exposed to view at any time.) The woman usually holds a fan, as a sick woman with a fever would be expected to do, and she is usually shown lying on a huge banana leaf,[1] since the banana plant was also considered as providing relief to the feverish, as its fruit actually does. Because of this anti-febrile motif, such a toggle might have served as a charm against fever and illness, although the subject was doubtless considered primarily as an erotic one, to act as an aphrodisiac. Then again, such a toggle might have been worn by a country doctor, as an easily recognized sign of his profession. On occasion, a single individual might have worn such a toggle for all three of these reasons together.

The only direct representation of this theme in the Bieber Collection is a jade toggle in which the convex underside of the leaf was apparently worn outward, so that the female figure was visible only when it was turned over. Thus it would appear innocuous enough until its owner flipped it around to show the reverse to amuse his friends. Here the erotic intention seems obvious. Although erotic subjects were frequently represented in other phases of Chinese art, they seem to have been very rare on the toggles, in marked contrast to the Japanese netsuke or the fairly numerous pornographic Chinese snuff bottles. Perhaps this was because the toggle was a rather public object, worn openly at the belt, while a snuff bottle was far more personal, generally kept in a cloth purse or tucked inside the outer flap of the upper robe, to be extracted only when the owner wanted to help himself to snuff.

Another toggle in this collection, No. 219, in wood, provides a playful parody of the medical figure motif, by showing a woman very fully clothed lying on a banana leaf in the same way, with a fan in her hand. Although the main purpose for this choice of subject was doubtless either frankly humorous, or erotic—as an allusion to the usual nude variety—and hence conducive to arousing passion, the symbolic leaf could also have made this in the Chinese view a charm against sickness.

Children, although greatly desired and much appreciated in Old China, were also fair game for comedy. Accordingly, they were usually represented on the toggles as jolly, plump, romping infants, with bulging tummies and broad grins on their fat faces. Since boy babies were so highly regarded as potential continuers of the family line (girls married out of the family, so their descendants did not count), the children on the toggles are often portrayed wearing only an embroidered bib that covers the stomach but stops in time to reveal beyond question that they are indeed little boys. Sometimes the toggle carver would even emphasize that they were potent little fellows, well equipped to carry on the line, for these child toggles were essentially charms for potency and fertility, to help their wearers to beget children. As such, they were particularly appropriate as wedding presents, and it seems likely that many of the child toggles were originally made for that purpose.

Often, the fertility theme was further emphasized by the addition of a lotus, in the form of a flower held in the child's hand, displayed in the background, or as an embroidered ornament on his bib, because this made a pun on *lien tzŭ*, "successive sons," thus increasing the idea of fertility. (See No. 24.) Still another way of expressing continuity was achieved by arranging two child figures, connected, with the head of one at the other's feet, and the hole for the cord between them, in such a way that there seemed to be four instead of two; and then, when the toggle was spun around the cord passing through it, it gave the impression of an endless succession, of "sons without end" (*lien tzŭ wu liang*). The Bieber Collection has a fine example carved in jet (No. 212), while the Buffalo Museum of Science has one cast from bronze. In the latter, the material itself contributes an additional thought, since *t'ung*, meaning bronze, is equivalent to *t'ung*, "together," expressing the wish that the wearer might have many children living at the same time, rather than in successive generations.

Lastly, a whole series of the child toggles portray a stout, round infant, often holding a box, as a pun on the word for harmony (*ho*), as in No. 214 of this collection. This motif is described in Chinese as *i t'uan ho ch'i*, literally interpreted as "a bundle of harmony and friendship," making it a symbol of peace and friendliness between individuals and a charm capable of inducing that happy state.

The toggles that represent gods or immortals illustrate the fact that the Chinese had a special attitude toward their divinities, quite different from those held in the West. They believed that almost any individual would be capable of achieving immortality by special practices—such as a diet of sacred fungus or other magic herbs, or following occult rites, or by spiritual meditation—and that the immortals, and even some of the gods, were once living men or women who had discovered the Way, or Tao, and followed it. Therefore, they tended to imagine their gods and immortals merely as highly superior mortals of ancient times, and usually represented them as dignified human beings, generally of advanced age, clad in obsolete styles of clothing. However, the folk artists often tended to emphasize the human element in the divine, sometimes with considerable humor. It would seem as though they wished to stress the fact that, although the figures they depicted had attained divinity or immortality, they still retained some characteristics of mankind, including human foibles and weaknesses. Viewed in this way the gods did not appear so frighteningly superior, and the average man could find it possible to believe that the attainment of their exalted state would not be altogether impossible for him.

Most prominent among the folk divinities were four very popular worthies whose figures recur constantly among the toggles. In each case, their origins go far back in time, and none of them can be said to belong exclusively to any given cult, although they all apparently originated in Taoist teachings.

The first of these was Shou Hsing, literally the "Star of Longevity," god of long life. Although he was only one of a popular triad of star gods, all of which often appeared on the coin amulets sometimes used as toggles, he was the only one of the three to appear alone on the figure toggles. Shou Hsing as a star god was considered to be the presiding genius of the southern constellation known as Nan Tou.[2] He was sometimes identified with P'êng Tsu, the "Taoist Methusaleh," who was said to have lived on this earth for more than a thousand years.[3] Shou Hsing was perhaps the most frequently represented of the lesser deities from the extensive Chinese pantheon, and he was certainly the most popular one.

Shou Hsing was always represented as a bearded old man of vast age. Characteristically he is shown hatless, or wearing merely a small scarf or cap atop an abnormally high cranium. His greatly enlarged brain was supposed to indicate the vast wisdom that had accrued through his abnormally long life. He often holds a peach of immortality in his right hand, while the left one grips a tall staff with a gourd tied to the top of it. In larger carvings, and rarely in more elaborate toggles, he may be accompanied by a deer or a crane, as a further symbol of his longevity, each of these being considered a long-lived creature in its own right. Or else Shou Hsing may have as his attendant a young boy who is the symbol of Youth—or youth renewed through his magic powers. Such a toggle subject would be especially popular for an old man desirous of many more years of life, and it might have been made for a grandfather as a birthday present.

Sometimes, the toggles show a rather similar-looking figure, but with a normally shaped head, usually covered by an archaic cap, who bears a branch laden with peaches. This represents Tung-Fang So, a Taoist scholar of the third century B.C., who is believed to have attained immortality.[4] As an immortal himself and as a carrier of the peaches of immortality he has long been a popular symbol of eternal longevity regardless of his Taoist affiliations.

The third most popular toggle divinity is Liu Hai.[5] He is shown as a youthful figure standing or sitting on a three-legged toad, holding the end of a long cord on which are strung a number of "cash" coins, the other end of the cord being held in the animal's jaws. Modern Western writers attempt to account for this singular combination by explaining that this boyish god of luck once caught and tamed the "evil monster" by using the cord strung with coins as bait. However, this animal itself was a traditional giver of wealth, and often held the coin string when Liu Hai was not present, so it seems far more likely that Liu Hai is actually drawing the string of coins out of its mouth, and that the story is only a rationalization, made up after the original legend was forgotten. In any case, the group as a whole was considered as a symbol of wealth, which in turn was wealth-producing, a charm with which to obtain prosperity. As such, it would be a most appropriate subject for merchant or trader, although the desire for wealth was by no means confined to any one group.

One more figure belonged in the same general category with Liu Hai as a popular luck-bringer. This was Li T'ieh-kuai, "Li of the Iron Crutch."[6] Although he was originally one of the group of the Eight Taoist Immortals, whose symbols or attributes we have already considered, he was singled out as a lucky god in his own right, even by people who did not consider themselves Taoist. (Chinese religions were by no means as exclusive as the Occidental faiths, and popular divinities were traded back and forth quite freely, especially on the folk level.)

According to legend, he was originally a handsome young prince who cultivated magical arts through meditation and austerities. Eventually, he acquired so much occult power that he was able to make his spirit leave his body in order to venture out on long journeys. When doing this, he usually had an attendant keep guard over his empty frame, but one day when his soul was off on a trip, the attendant was careless and wandered away, so the prince's body was found and appropriated by the soul of a dying beggar. Thus, on his return, Li's soul had no choice but to take the beggar's body as its permanent habitation, even though it was still capable of performing superhuman feats and had achieved immortality.

He is traditionally represented as a lame beggar in rags, with the tightly curled hair and the royal fillet that Chinese iconography usually assigned to foreign dignitaries from Central Asia. His characteristic emblems are the gourd and the crutch, previously mentioned: a pilgrim's gourd bottle and a short T-shaped crutch. In this form he is the patron of chemists and druggists, who often used his gourd for the sign to mark their medicine shops.

Li of the Iron Crutch was often treated very humorously on the toggles. Doubtless it was partly because, according to the legend, he was the victim of his own cleverness, and hence an object of derision, partly because he was traditionally a foreigner (foreigners were always a butt for laughter), and partly because he was a sufficiently popular figure to be exempt from reverence.

For example, one toggle in the Bieber Collection (No. 224) shows him with the twisted grimace of a drunkard after having quaffed from his pilgrim's gourd, as though it had contained powerful spirits instead of the medicine of immortality. The very levity with which he is treated here would make it seem that he was not considered very seriously as a divinity; yet the Old Chinese confidently believed he could prolong one's life, like the other immortals, who, having gained eternal life themselves, could impart their secrets to others, to help them to do the same. Therefore, regardless of the degree of humor shown in them, the toggles representing him still belonged in the category of wonder-working charms.

As Shou Hsing and Liu Hai were also strictly popular divinities and not directly associated with any special religious cults, they, too, could be depicted semihumorously, without provoking any wrath in high places; and they frequently are shown, on the toggles and elsewhere, wearing sly grins that would have seemed out of place on a revered divinity. However, the Chinese toggle-makers never treated them with the broad humor amounting to ridicule that one finds in their figures of Li T'ieh-kuai, or in some of the netsuke renderings of Shou Hsing's Japanese counterpart, Fukurokuju.

The more powerful spiritual protectors such as the Buddhas and bodhisattvas, even the popular Kuan Yin, "Goddess of Mercy," were avoided as subjects for the toggles, though their images were frequently worn for protection in the form of amulets. It would probably have been considered very disrespectful to portray them on these casual objects of utility.

The ultimate use of human figures on the toggles is found in the extremely detailed storytelling toggles. Individual examples of these often depict whole episodes from folklore and legend or from popular plays, rendered either on flat plaques or medallions or in groups in the round. As elsewhere in Chinese art, the chief figures often hold objects or attributes especially associated with them, or else they were portrayed in distinctive surroundings, which would help to identify them. A scene that could not be immediately recognized was considered a failure in communication. These traditions also led to a certain conventionality in representing familiar scenes, regardless of the medium used. Thus, we were able to identify the subject of No. 37 as the homecoming climax from a famous play, *San-niang chiao tzŭ*,[7] after seeing the same three persons depicted in almost identical fashion and in a similar setting on North China embroidery patterns.[8]

Sometimes the presentation is so detailed that it almost tells its own tale, even though the specific narrative or story cycle is unknown. One toggle of this type is No. 229, which shows an old Taoist monk in conventional attire, sitting under a tree before a shrine, beating a wooden-fish drum as he prays for the woman who is standing before him. In a wisp of vapor emerging from his head—apparently representing his prayer or a vision—a child appears, holding a peach of immortality and a magic fly whisk. Clearly this represents a Taoist tale in which there figured a prayer for fertility, while a circular *shou* character inscribed on the underside of the base adds the element of longevity, making the whole a charm for long life and fertility. In fact, that was the real purpose of these storytelling toggles; the story was always a tale of gaining wealth, begetting children, or earning official rank, or acquiring great age or immortality—the perennial preoccupations of Chinese ambition—to serve as a magic means for obtaining these very things. In spite of their far greater elaboration, these were essentially no different from any of the simpler toggles in their basic aims.

In addition to Taoist stories, we also find Buddhist folk tales depicted on the toggles. The Bieber Collection has one (No. 228) on which two wonder-working Buddhist monks are shown in the act of creating clouds upon which float temples and shrines. The scene is very graphically presented, even though we do not know the full story. Incidentally, the toggles of this group are the only ones that could strictly be called "Buddhist," for the Buddhist symbols which occasionally appear on other toggles have usually lost all their specifically Buddhistic character, and have merely become popular luck symbols without retaining any real religious connotations.

A supreme example of storytelling is presented on a relatively small toggle in the Bieber Collection (No. 230), which, in spite of its diminutive size, shows in individual scenes several episodes from the well-known Legend of the White Snake Lady (*Pai Shê Chuan*), more popularly known in the Old Chinese theater as "The White Snake Pagoda."[9] These are all carved on the sides and base of a wedge-shaped sliver of boxwood, only two inches long, that has been fashioned into a bar toggle.

On the base, a man accompanied by a coolie who carries his baggage is returning home, bearing a white snake he has rescued on his journey. As a sequel to this scene (but not shown), after his return home, the snake changed into a beautiful woman, whom he married. However, when he later discovered that his wife actually was a snake spirit, he fled and took refuge in a Buddhist monastery called Chin Shan Ssǔ, on the West Lake, near Hangchow.

Next, the prominent scene at the bottom of the flat rear side shows the dramatic "Meeting at the Broken Bridge," which forms the subject of a special play, *Tuan Ch'iao.* The White Snake Lady was on her way back from the monastery where she had made an unsuccessful attempt to find her husband and, when thwarted, had caused a catastrophic flood in revenge. Then, suddenly, she met her runaway husband on this bridge. Her attendant, the Blue Snake, knocked him down and tried to kill him, as is so graphically shown here. However, the White Snake Lady was so glad to see him that a temporary reconciliation followed, and she returned with him to his sister's house to have their child.

After a son was born, the still-frightened husband hurled at her the "spirit-capturing alms bowl" that a monk from the monastery had given him, and changed her back into a snake. He then carried her back to the monk of the flood-ridden monastery, who imprisoned her in the "Thunder Peak Pagoda" (Lei Fêng T'a) at Chin Shan Ssǔ, on the edge of the lake. This series of episodes is minutely portrayed in three panels on the narrow side of the wedge. The bottom panel shows the wise monk handing the magic bowl to the husband; the middle one, immediately above, shows him carrying his wife, already half a snake, back to the monastery; while the top panel depicts the monk laying bricks, as he builds the pagoda around the White Snake to restrain her from further mischief.

The action once again shifts to the flat side of the toggle. At the top, the now-grown son is portrayed at his home-coming, after having returned in triumph from the capital, where he had taken first place in the Triennial Imperial Examinations, earning the title of Chuang-yüan. His new status is indicated by his special hat and by the presence of the horse, the Chuang-yüan's traditional steed, from which he has just dismounted.[10] The scene goes on to show his aunt telling him the story of his parentage, as she had promised him she would do if he won the coveted title.

In the final episode, "The Offering at the Pagoda" (*Chi T'a*), the young man went to the Emperor and obtained from him a special decree ordering the local officials to prepare a sacrifice to the White Snake Lady at the pagoda, to soothe her soul. The carrying out of this decree is illustrated on the third side of the wedge, with the pagoda itself occupying the prominent ridge between the second and third flat sides. To the right of it, under a tree, stands the offering table, set out with candles and an urn of incense sticks. Before this, the son kneels in prayer, as other dignitaries look on, while the White Snake Lady writhes out of an upper window of the pagoda to converse with her son. The son was unable to release her, because she still had the power to work evil, and she also had to suffer further punishment to atone for the damage she had caused by the flood; but by his sacrifice her son calmed her spirit and brought her a measure of peace, thus creating a happy ending.

Although the decoration on this toggle is unusually complex, the maker's choice of just these specific scenes, from this particular story, clearly indicates that he intended them to be symbolic. Indeed the meanings are quite obvious. As we analyze them, we shall see that this is, in fact, an epitome of Chinese toggles, summing up in itself everything that we have been trying to say about the nature of Chinese toggles and their symbolism.

In the first place, the tale of the White Snake Pagoda is primarily a story of exorcism, of the exposure and neutralizing of potentially malevolent spirits, the snake-women. We have seen that the Chinese, especially the humbler folk who wore the wooden toggles, were very much concerned with the fear of evil spirits—many of which, incidentally, were thought to be half-animal, as the White Snake was—and the desire to drive them away was a prominent motive in their use of charms and amulets. The fact that this toggle-amulet was made from an auspicious, evil-averting, long-life wood (box), suggests to us that the idea of a long life uninterrupted by evil influences must have been present in the mind of its maker, who doubtless intended it to be an exorcising charm in itself. The first meaning of this storytelling toggle apparently was: "May harmful spirits of evil be exposed and kept away."

Secondly, "The White Snake Pagoda" was a success story, telling how the White Snake's son became a Chuang-yüan, and ultimately a distinguished official. Hope for success was always a dominant theme in Chinese symbolism (as we have seen in discussing the meaning of the *shêng* jewels and the *ju-i*), and the highest form of success was to have one's son obtain official rank, thus raising the status of the whole family. In short, the second message on the toggle was a hope for success, with the special additional thought: "Anyone's son can become the highest scholar in the land, even a snake spirit's, so there is hope for mine."

Thirdly, "The White Snake Pagoda" is a tale of wrongs righted, with the good rewarded and the wicked justly punished, a restoration of order and harmony in the universe, a reassertion of the *Tao*. Therefore, on this little toggle we see stated once more the basic theme that constantly recurs in the decoration on the toggles; it is even expressed on the most abstract ones which simply have two different kinds of carving on the opposite sides to indicate the balanced contrast of the Yin and Yang. That is, the deep conviction that there is a basic harmony regulating all things spiritual and material, uniting all in the Tao, the Way of the Immortals, the Universal Way.

It might seem strange to find so clear an expression of the core philosophy of Taoism conveyed in scenes from a Buddhist tale, that was originally intended to display the magic powers of a certain Buddhist monk. However, from the Neo-Confucian philosophy of the scholar-gentry down to the folk beliefs of the humblest peasants, Chinese thought was characteristically given to synthesis. A person could take from any religion or philosophy those elements which seemed most appropriate to the immediate case, freely borrowing ideas and symbols from one to express the beliefs of another, even if this meant mixing things that would seem basically incompatible, as has been done here. We have noticed this tendency repeatedly, throughout this study, but seldom was it carried out as clearly as it was in this example.

With all its significant meanings, this little carving was at the same time a highly efficient bar toggle, with a gap for the cord ingeniously contrived between the elements of the pattern. Also, in spite of its richness of decoration, the details have been kept flat and smooth enough to be pleasant to the touch, with no sharp edges to chafe or tear the wearer's clothing.

In short, this was an almost perfect combination of a functional toggle and an auspicious amulet, made from a medicinally potent substance, yet still infused with the power to divert and amuse the viewer. Altogether, it possesses the well-roundedness and faithfulness to purpose that we have found to be a principal characteristic of Chinese peasant art, and of these toggles as a primary expression of that art, revealing once again the deep sense of practicality which balanced the rich imagination in the creative minds of the Old Chinese people.

NOTES

CHAPTER 1

1. The Manchu belts with side fittings are illustrated in the Official Regulations of the Ch'ing Dynasty, *Ta Ch'ing Hui-tien-t'u*, Peking, 1899, Chs. 57-75. A similar style of belt from Tibet is illustrated in W. W. Rockhill, "Notes on the Ethnology of Tibet," *Report of the U.S. National Museum for 1893*, Washington, 1895, Plate 10.

2. See Rockhill, *ibid.*

3. The extensive literature on Japanese netsuke includes: Albert Brockhaus, *Netsuke*, Leipzig, 1905; F. M. Jonas, *Netsuke*, London, 1928; R. Ueda, *Shumi no Netsuke*, Osaka, 1934; Y. Okada, *Netsuke: a Miniature Art of Japan*, Tokyo, 1953; M. R. Tollner, *Netsuke*, San Francisco, 1954; and F. Meinertzhagen, *The Art of the Netsuke Carver*, London, 1956.

4. See Hazel H. Gorham, "Netsuke, their Origin and Development," *Cultural Nippon*, VI, No. 3, November, 1938, p. 86.

5. Korea in the 1590's was still a dependency of Ming China, and the Koreans also used belt toggles, having probably received the idea from China, during the Yüan or Ming dynasties. On the other hand, Japanese visitors to China or Chinese traders in Japan could have brought them to Japan directly. The exact means of introduction seems never to have been noted.

6. Brockhaus illustrated some carvings purporting to be *tōbori*, in his *Netsuke*, pp. 93-98, figs. 103-134, having taken them from Inaba Michitatsu's *Sōken Kishō*, Kyoto, 1781, vii, pp. 15-17b. Actually, these represent a strange mixture of small carvings from many

lands, including a few truly Chinese human figures (figs. 108, 111, 121, 131, and 132), an Indonesian *kris* handle (fig. 104), and a "knight" from a Siamese chess set (fig. 109). These can give some idea of the diverse influences that must have combined to influence the early Japanese netsuke carvers; but still more it shows the confusion regarding foreign things in the mind of an eighteenth-century connoisseur in self-isolated Japan.

7. Cf. No. 135 in the Bieber Collection, which appears to be a Ming example.

8. Illustrated in the *Ku-kung chou-k'an*, No. 269, Aug. 5, 1933, p. 2.

9. *Ibid.*, No. 334, March 21, 1934, p. 4.

10. For a brief discussion of the Manchu formal belts, see S. Cammann, "Chinese Mandarin Squares," *The University Museum Bulletin*, XVII, No. 3, Philadelphia, June, 1953, pp. 40-41, 43, and the reference in note 1, above.

11. Some particularly exasperating Ch'ing paintings from the mid-eighteenth century, also in the Palace Museum Collection, show Chinese farmers wearing pouches or purses hanging by cords that must have been attached to toggles, because of their location; but again the outer jackets prevent seeing the actual mode of attachment. See *Ku-kung chou-k'an*, Nos. 252, 256, 257, 265, all 1933.

12. For an example, see Laurence Binyon, *Painting in the Far East*, London, 1908, Plate 12.

13. While many refinements of the *inrō* boxes were due to later development in Japan, again their origin was apparently in Old China. The Chicago Museum of Natural History has, in its Jade Hall, a small Sung Dynasty box in the form and shape of the much later *inrō*, but with only a single compartment, and it was also intended to hang from the girdle (No. 183488). Furthermore, the Tibetan collection in the same museum has a number of small wooden boxes, made on the same principle, from Eastern Tibet. When a similar culture trait appears in both Japan and Tibet, experience tells that it can almost always be traced to a Chinese origin, even though it may have died out in China without leaving any traces there.

14. The only marks on Chinese toggles are the signs of the silversmiths on some of the metal caps or other fittings, or on the all-metal

toggles; but these are usually only commercial trademarks, not actual names.

15. For the changing fashions in Chinese symbols, see S. Cammann, "Types of Symbols in Chinese Art," in *Studies in Chinese Thought* (American Anthropological Association Memoir, No. 75), Chicago, 1953, pp. 195-231.

16. See Nos. 124 and 135 in the Bieber Collection.

17. See Paul Pelliot, "Sceaux-amulettes de bronze avec croix et colombes, provenant de la boucle du Fleuve Jaune," *Revue des Arts Asiatiques*, VII, No. 1, 1931, pp. 1-3, and plates.

18. For examples of Old Asian bird symbolism with both single- and double-headed eagles, see S. Cammann, "Ancient Symbols in Modern Afghanistan," *Ars Orientalis*, II, 1957, pp. 5-34.

19. Illustrated in W. Bogoras, *The Chukchee* (Memoirs of the American Museum of Natural History, II, Part 1), Leiden, 1904, p. 259, figs. e and f.

20. *Ibid.*, p. 224, fig. 155.

21. See E. W. Nelson, "The Eskimo about Bering Strait," *U.S. Bureau of American Ethnology: 18th Annual Report*, Part 1 (1896-97), Plate 27, and pp. 61-62.

22. See the comment on these by Arthur Diósy, in *Transactions and Proceedings of the Japan Society, London*, 1894-95, III, Part 4, 1897, p. 19.

23. See Malanyay Dezsö, A *Magyar Nép Müvészete*, Budapest, 1911, Vol. III, figs. 316-317 (facing p. 244); and M. Bing, "The Crafts of the Puszta Herdsmen," *Ciba Review*, No. 45, March, 1945, p. 1642, and picture on top of p. 1644.

24. University Museum No. AF 43-21.

25. For further information on this substance, see S. Cammann, "The Story of Hornbill Ivory," *The University Museum Bulletin*, XV, No. 4, Philadelphia, December, 1950, pp. 19-47.

26. University Museum No. P 1258.

27. For a hornbill ivory one, see Cammann, "Story of Hornbill Ivory," fig. 13, center.

28. See references in note 3, above.

29. The date of the introduction of toggles to China and the exact amount of time required for their development in China are

still unknown. We pass the questions on to others, in the hope that someone may find some more definite literary or pictorial evidence to supplement the scanty material presented here.

CHAPTER 2

1. Ueda's *Dai ji-ten*, a Sino-Japanese dictionary, under No. 1851, p. 477, lists the Chinese characters for *chui-tzŭ* and defines the term as meaning *netsuke*. H. A. Giles, *Chinese-English Dictionary*, 1912 edition, under 2818, p. 352, defines the term as "small eardrops," but the other meanings listed under this word *chui* clearly show how it came to be used to refer to toggles as counter-weights.

Another Chinese term *hsüan-ch'ui* was sometimes used by Japanese writers (who pronounced it *kensui*), and in Ueda's *Dai ji-ten*, under No. 3586, p. 894, this also is defined as meaning *netsuke*. (Inaba uses this term in *Sōken Kishō*, Ch. 7.)

Although we know that the expression *chui-tzŭ* was, until recently, actively used in North China (usually in the form *chui-'rh*), we have not heard *hsüan-ch'ui* used there, and it may have been a purely literary expression.

2. See Giles, Dictionary, No. 8832, p. 1081.

3. *Ibid.*

4. Giles, No. 10,183, p. 1262, and 13,129, p. 1627.

5. Among the cubo-octahedron toggles as well as the Chinese bolt-heads, one finds a considerable variety of shapes, ranging from a simple cube with flattened corners (technically, a cube truncated by an octahedron) to the pure cubo-octahedron. For convenience, we shall use the term cuboctahedron to cover all.

6. It does not matter very much what particular system of classification is adopted by an individual student or collector, although some kind of system is clearly needed to reduce this rather vast subject to any sort of order. The main point is to avoid too long a listing. The one outlined here, worked out by the writer in the process of cataloguing the Bieber Collection, has proved both practical and convenient in studying other collections also, and is recommended for general use.

CHAPTER 3

1. Old Chinese philosophy and folklore held that trees, shrubs, and plants possessed souls or spirits, just as did men or animals. See J. J. M. de Groot, *The Religious System of China*, IV, pp. 272-273, 290, 294 ff., and V, p. 652; also I, p. 300.

2. See G. A. Stuart, M.D., *Chinese Materia Medica: Vegetable Kingdom*, Shanghai, 1911, p. 250. He calls it *Lycium chinense*.

3. de Groot, IV, p. 320. For the mandrake root itself, see *ibid.*, pp. 314-317.

4. *Ibid.*, p. 320.

5. See C. A. S. Williams, *Outlines of Chinese Symbolism*, Peiping, 1931, p. 181.

6. Frequently in jade carvings the characters for *ta chi* were inscribed directly on the gourd, and it is possible that this usage may also be found among the toggles.

7. The full Chinese term was *k'o-t'êng-tzŭ* See Li Shih-chên, *Pên-ts'ao kang-mu* (first published in 1591), Ch. 18, p. 19*b*. Hereafter, this basic source will be abbreviated as *PTKM*.

8. Also described as *Pursaetha scandens, Lens phaseloides, Entada phaseloides*, etc. We are grateful to George Kalmbacher, taxonomist at the Brooklyn Botanical Garden, for first identifying for us the giant bean from a specimen in the Chinese collections of the Brooklyn Museum.

9. The *Kuang-chou chi*, quoted by Li Shih-chên in *PTKM*, ch. 18, p. 19*b*.

10. *Cf.* George Watt, *Dictionary of the Economic Products of India*, III, London and Calcutta, 1890, p. 246.

11. *PTKM*, ch. 18, p. 19*b*. In this passage Li uses the expression "medicine gourd" to signify "container."

12. See H. B. Guppy, *Plants, Seeds and Currents in the West Indies and Azores*, London, 1917, pp. 22-24, etc.

13. *Ibid.*, and Nathaniel Colgan, "On the Occurrence of Tropical Drift Seeds on the Irish Atlantic Coasts," *Proceedings of the Royal Irish Academy*, XXXV, Section B, No. 3, September, 1919, pp. 29-37.

14. Colgan, *ibid.*, p. 35.

15. Meinertzhagen, *Art of the Netsuke Carver*, Plate XX, No. 29.

16. The West China Union University Museum in Chengtu, Szechuan, also had some examples of conch shell toggles in its extensive Tibetan ethnological collections.
17. See B. E. Read, *Chinese Materia Medica: Turtle and Shellfish Drugs*, Peiping, 1937, p. 70.

CHAPTER 4

1. For Chinese woods in general, see Norman Shaw, *Chinese Forest Trees and Timber Supply*, London and Leipzig, 1914; and Hang-fan Chow, *The Familiar Trees of Hopei* (Peking Natural History Bulletin Handbook No. 4), Peiping, 1934.
2. Dr. B. Francis Kukachka, Acting Chief of the Division of Timber Growth and Utilization Relations, in the U.S. Department of Agriculture's Forest Service, Forest Products Laboratory, Madison, Wisconsin, very kindly undertook the task of analyzing the woods in these toggles. As they are very small and might easily be damaged, he did not immediately use the customary method of removing small pieces from each one for microscopic analysis, but first segregated them into a number of separate groups based on combinations of features visible with the hand lens. (These included such things as texture [pore diameter classes], tyloses, ray width, ray height, included phloem, etc.) Then two or three toggles were selected from each group, and radial and tangential sections were taken from them for microscopic study. At the same time any toggle that deviated from the group was also checked microscopically. Hand lens examination permitted exact identification only in the case of *Osmanthus* and *Aquillaria*, because of their unique structure; for precise determination of all the other genera, microscopic examination was required. While this method determined the genus, it was usually impossible to identify the species, except when other information was available.
3. Shaw, *op. cit.*, p. 212, and Stuart, *Chinese Materia Medica*, pp. 76-77.
4. T. F. Carter, *The Invention of Printing in China and Its Spread Westward*, New York, 1925, p. 26, says that pearwood was generally used for printing blocks, and the revised edition by L. C.

Goodrich (New York, 1955), p. 34, says that pear or jujube wood was used. Pearwood was indeed commonly used, but boxwood was considered better.

5. Stuart, *Materia Medica*, p. 77.

6. Also known as *Betula japonica*, var. *mandschurica* Winkl. See Chow, *Familiar Trees of Hopei*, p. 96.

7. Stuart, *Materia Medica*, p. 68.

8. Chow, *Familiar Trees*, p. 98.

9. The first reports from the Forest Products Laboratory simply listed one group of plain wood toggles as *Prunus* and another group of allied burl toggles as *Rosaceae*; however, after further checking, Dr. Kukachka wrote that he now believed that it would be reasonably safe and quite logical to say that all the *Prunus* material as well as those burls first simply indicated as *Rosaceae* were actually of peachwood (*P. persica*).

10. For a discussion of *hsien* trees in general, see de Groot, *Religious System*, IV, p. 303.

11. For beliefs regarding the peach tree and its wood, see *ibid.*, pp. 303-362, and VI, pp. 956-962.

12. Stuart, *Materia Medica*, pp. 356-358.

13. *Ibid.*, pp. 355-356, and Chow, *Familiar Trees*, pp. 218-220.

14. The persimmon is a member of the ebony family, and although its dark heartwood is rather narrow, it would have provided enough for a toggle. For its medical uses, see Stuart, pp. 152-153.

15. *Ibid.*, pp. 164-165.

16. *Ibid.*, pp. 466-467.

17. See note 9.

18. de Groot, VI, p. 290.

19. *Ibid.*, VI, p. 1080.

20. Shaw, *Chinese Forest Trees*, pp. 214-219.

21. de Groot, I, p. 301.

22. Stuart, *Materia Medica*, pp. 87-88.

23. No. 37.374.113.

24. Also called gharu wood, kalambak, calambac, etc.; its properties and the extensive international trade in it are described in S. Wells Williams, *Chinese Commercial Guide*, 5th ed., Hongkong, 1863, p. 105; George Watt, *Dictionary of the Economic Products of India*, pp. 278-281; and F. Hirth and W. W. Rockhill, *Chao Ju-*

kua: His Work on the Chinese and Arab Trade in the Twelfth and Thirteenth Centuries, St. Petersburg, 1911, pp. 204-208.

25. Stuart, *Materia Medica*, pp. 44-45.

26. For a discussion of rosewood in China, and especially the long-standing controversy regarding *tzŭ t'an*, whether it was from a kind of *Dalbergia* or from *Pterocarpus santalinus*, see Gustav Ecke, *Chinese Domestic Furniture*, Peking, 1944, p. 22, and E. H. Schafer, "Dragon's Blood and Lac," *Journal of the American Oriental Society*, LXXVII, 1957, p. 129.

27. The *chin-ssŭ tzŭ-t'an* is described and discussed in George N. Kates, *Chinese Household Furniture*, New York and London, 1948, p. 21.

28. See Stuart, *Materia Medica*, p. 360. Although he discusses *tzŭ-t'an* under the scientific name of *Pterocarpus santalinus*, the reader should bear in mind that the Chinese use the term *tzŭ-t'an* very loosely to cover several kinds of wood that are definitely *Dalbergia*, and it is not yet certain how much of the *Pterocarpus santalinus* was actually used in China under the name of *tzŭ-t'an*.

29. See E. Bretschneider, *Botanicon Sinicum*, II, Shanghai, 1892, p. 387, and also his *History of European Botanical Discoveries in China*, London, 1898, pp. 511-512.

30. For some of the uses of this palm in China, see *The Chinese Repository*, III, No. 6, October, 1834, pp. 267-270.

31. See Stuart, *Materia Medica*, p. 102. He describes this under the name of *Chamaerops excelsa*, which is an alternative name for *Camaerops fortunei*.

32. See Kates, *op. cit.*, p. 21.

33. de Groot, IV, p. 290.

34. Apart from brief remarks by Kates and Ecke in their works cited, there is only Arthur Stanley, "Chinese Wood Carving," *Journal of the North China Branch of the Royal Asiatic Society*, XLV, 1914, pp. 76-84.

35. For the woodworker's drills, see Rudolf P. Hommel, *China at Work*, New York, 1937, pp. 247-249.

36. For the woodworker's lathes and turning methods, see *ibid.*, pp. 252-254.

37. This is also known as the Dutch rush. The Chinese call it *mu tsei*, literally "wood robber," probably because of its effectiveness in

grinding down wood. See *ibid.*, p. 253; Stuart, *Materia Medica*, p. 163; and Giles, Dictionary, No. 11,701.

CHAPTER 5

1. See Bernard E. Read, *Chinese Materia Medica: Animal Drugs*, Peiping, 1931, No. 354, *ya.*
2. See the illustration of a Shang dynasty carved ivory mask in the Musée Guimet, Paris, accompanying the writer's articles on Ivory Carving in *Encyclopaedia Britannica*, 1958 edition, Vol. XII, "Ivory Carving," Plate VIII, fig. 1 (following p. 838).
3. Peking radio reported two herds of wild elephants in southern Yünnan in the year 1957, according to *The Philadelphia Inquirer*, Sunday, March 3, 1957.
4. See B. Laufer, *Ivory in China* (Field Museum of Natural History, Anthropological Leaflet 21), Chicago, 1925, pp. 17-18.
5. *Ibid.*, pp. 27-30.
6. See B. Laufer, "Arabic and Chinese Trade in Walrus and Narwhal Ivory," *T'oung Pao*, Series 2, XIV, 1913, pp. 315-364.
7. See T. K. Penniman, *Pictures of Ivory and Other Animal Teeth* (Pitt Rivers Museum, Oxford, Occasional Papers on Technology, 5), Oxford, 1952, Plates I-III.
8. See *ibid.*, Plates VIII and IX.
9. For walrus ivory carving in general, see S. Cammann, "Carvings in Walrus Ivory," *Bulletin of the University Museum*, XVIII, No. 3, December, 1954, pp. 3-31. Some of the illustrations clearly show the use of the core.
10. See Penniman, *Pictures*, Plate X.
11. Penniman, *ibid.*, p. 29, gives the impression that narwhal ivory was very commonly used for the Japanese netsuke. Although the Japanese occasionally used it, there is no evidence that they used it very commonly. A typical cross section is shown in *ibid.*, Plate XI.
12. In the collection of Rev. Stephen D. Pyle, in Oakland, California.
13. See Penniman, *Pictures*, Plates VI and VII for cross sections of hippopotamus teeth. For a typical Cantonese carving, preserving

the distinctive shape of the canine, see *Encyclopaedia Britannica*, 1958 ed., Vol. XII, "Ivory Carving," Plate VIII, fig. 6.

14. See S. Cammann, "The Story of Hornbill Ivory," fig. 13, center.
15. See *ibid.*, pp. 19-47, for a full discussion of the use of hornbill ivory in China and elsewhere.
16. See B. E. Read, *Animal Drugs*, No. 327, under *ku, t'ou ku* for horse bones, and No. 326, *ku* for cow bones. *Ibid.*, No. 328, also lists donkey bones as a medical substance.
17. Penniman, *Pictures*, Plate XV, shows a somewhat exaggerated example from a whale's jawbone.
18. See *ibid.*, Plates XVI-XIX.
19. For more specific abilities ascribed to deer's antlers, see Read, *Animal Drugs*, No. 364, under *jung* and *chüeh*.
20. See Williams, *Outlines of Chinese Symbolism*, p. 98.
21. See Read, *Animal Drugs*, No. 365.
22. No. 37.371.127; this is 2¼ inches in diameter.
23. Read, *Animal Drugs*, No. 326.
24. *Ibid.*, No. 355, under *hsi chüeh*.
25. See Soame Jenyns, "The Chinese Rhinoceros and Chinese Carvings in Rhinoceros Horn," *Transactions of the Oriental Ceramics Society*, 1954-55, London, 1957, pp. 31-59, especially Plates 20-26, illustrating the cups.
26. No. 37.137.110.
27. For the symbolism of the cicada, see Chapter 10.
28. See note 24, above, for reference.

CHAPTER 6

1. For example, *shui yü*, literally: "water jade," is used for quartz crystal; and *huang yü*, "yellow jade" is one Chinese term for topaz.
2. See *PTKM*, Ch. 8, pp. 44-46.
3. The Europeans seem to have taken over the medical ideas of the Mayas along with the stone; see J. Alden Mason, "Native American Jades," *The Museum Journal*, XVIII, No. 1, Philadelphia, March, 1927, p. 50.
4. Pao P'u-Tzŭ, quoted by B. E. Read and C. Pak, *A Compendium of Minerals and Stones used in Chinese Medicine*, 2d ed., Peiping, 1936, p. 18, top.

5. More specifically, nephrite belongs to the amphibole group, and is a silicate of calcium and magnesium, with a little iron, etc.; while jadeite, one of the pyroxenes, is essentially a silicate of aluminum and sodium, with small quantities of iron, calcium, and magnesium. Jadeite is a little harder, with a slightly higher specific gravity. The distinction between these two kinds of "jade" was not known even in Europe until 1868. The contrast is strikingly presented in two photomicrographs of thin sections of the respective types of "jade" in S. Howard Hansford, *Chinese Jade Carving*, London, 1950, Plate I.

6. See Hansford, *ibid.*, pp. 78-79, and Plate IV*b*, or H. P. Whitlock, "Modern Methods of Carving Jade," *Natural History*, XXXI, No. 5, September, 1931, p. 513, top.

7. See Hansford, Plates V*a* and VI*a*, and Whitlock, p. 13, bottom.

8. The lathe drill is illustrated in Hansford, Plate IX; the bow drill in *ibid.*, Plate X, or Whitlock, p. 512, bottom; and the wire saw in Hansford, Plate X*b*.

9. The abrasives used in Peking in 1939 are described in Hansford, pp. 67-71.

10. *PTKM*, Ch. 8, pp. 52*b*-53.

11. *Ibid.*, Ch. 10, pp. 16-17*b*.

12. See B. Laufer, *Notes on Turquois in the East* (Field Museum of Natural History, Anthropological Series, XIII, No. 1), Chicago, 1913, pp. 5-20.

13. *Ibid.*, p. 61, text and note 1.

14. *Ibid.*, pp. 65 and 20.

15. See reference in Chapter 1, note 2.

16. *PTKM*, Ch. 8, pp. 50-51, coral; Ch. 37, pp. 7*b*-10, amber.

17. For an account of coral in Asia, see B. Laufer, *Sino-Iranica* (Field Museum of Natural History, Anthropological Series, XV, No. 3), Chicago, 1919, pp. 523-525.

18. See B. Laufer, *Historical Jottings on Amber in Asia* (American Anthropological Society Memoirs, I), Lancaster, Pa., 1907, pp. 233-243.

19. See *PTKM*, Ch. 37, 7*b* ff. Some of this material is quoted in translation by Laufer, in *Amber*, pp. 217-222.

20. Laufer, *ibid.*, pp. 243-244.

21. References in note 19, above.

22. *PTKM*, Ch. 37, pp. 10-10*b*, and Laufer, *Amber*, pp. 222-225.

23. *Ibid.*
24. For remarks on Chinese glass, see W. B. Honey, "Chinese Glass," *Transactions of the Oriental Ceramic Society 1939-40*, London, 1940, pp. 35-47; and C. G. Seligman and H. C. Beck, "Far Eastern Glass," *Bulletin of the Museum of Far Eastern Antiquities*, Stockholm, X, 1938, pp. 1-64.
25. *PTKM*, Ch. 8, pp. 52*b*-54.
26. *Ibid.*, Ch. 8, pp. 53-53*b*.
27. *Ibid.*, Ch. 9, pp. 38*b*-42*b*, soapstone; 38-38*b*, calcite.
28. Most of the references to "jewels" in Japanese folklore and literature refer to the ancient *magatama*, comma-shaped pendants characteristic of the ancient Korean culture, and apparently brought from Korea; or else they refer to pearls: either Buddhist symbolic pearls or actual ones from the sea.

CHAPTER 7

1. For a general discussion of metals in China, see S. Couling, *Encyclopaedia Sinica*, Shanghai, 1917, pp. 373-374.
2. For metals in Chinese medicine, see *PTKM*, Ch. 8, pp. 1-4, gold; pp. 4-6*b*, silver; pp. 8*b*-9*b*, copper, bronze, and brass; pp. 13-16*b*, lead; pp. 26-27, tin; pp. 32-34, iron. Read and Pak, *Compendium of Minerals and Stones used in Chinese Medicine*, 2d ed., Peiping, 1936, pp. 2-14, also discusses these.
3. See B. Gyllensvärd, *T'ang Gold and Silver*, Stockholm, 1957, pp. 33-35.
4. The Gotō family were famous for stippled backgrounds in this technique, called *nanako* in Japanese.
5. This is apparently the only illustration of this fable in Far Eastern art.
6. Nos. 37.371.135-1 and -2.
7. Nos. RXII-18*d* and B-2863.
8. The "cloud collar motif" is discussed and explained in Chapter 8.
9. Many types of coin amulets are illustrated in the *Hsi Ch'ing kuchien, ch'ien-lu*, Chs. 14-16.
10. Several are illustrated in *ibid.*, Ch. 16, p. 5*b* ff.
11. *Ibid.*, Ch. 15, pp. 6*b* and 8.

12. See S. Cammann, *The Land of the Camel*, New York, 1951, p. 68. For Tibetan examples, see Rockhill, *Ethnology of Tibet*, Plate 20, Nos. 4, 5, 6.
13. No. 37.371.181.
14. For some of the beliefs regarding old Chinese mirrors and their significance in Chinese culture, see S. Cammann, "Chinese Mirrors and Chinese Civilization," *Archaeology*, II, 1957, pp. 5-42.
15. See *PTKM*, Ch. 8, pp. 27-99.
16. No. 37.371.143a.
17. For similar Tibetan seals, see Rockhill, *op. cit.*, Plates 11 and 29.

CHAPTER 8

1. For a general survey of Chinese symbols and their historical development, see S. Cammann, "Types of Symbols in Chinese Art," in *Studies in Chinese Thought* (American Anthropological Association Memoir, No. 75) Chicago, 1953, pp. 195-231.
2. This basic philosophy is also found in other civilizations, as well as in modern Western psychological writings. See for example Erich Fromm, *The Art of Loving*, New York, 1956, pp. 33-37.
3. For a concise presentation of the trigrams, see Williams, *Outlines of Chinese Symbolism*, pp. 121-123, especially the diagram on p. 123.
4. For the commentary on the *I Ching* which discusses the trigrams, see James Legge, *The Sacred Books of China: Part II, The Yi King*, Oxford, 1882, Appendix V, pp. 422-432. For further comments, see de Groot, *Religious System of China*, III, pp. 960-967.
5. For a combination of the Yin-Yang symbol and the eight-petaled flower on a toggle (not recognized as such), see H. F. Whitlock, "Jade," *Natural History*, XXXII, No. 5, September, 1932, final illustration, p. 507. Note also the variations on the *Shou* symbol, shown on p. 498.
6. See S. Cammann, "The Symbolism of the Cloud Collar Motif," *The Art Bulletin*, XXXIII, No. 1, March, 1951, pp. 1-9.
7. For two different sets of "The Hundred Shou Characters," see Nozaki Seikin, *Kisshō zuan kaidai*, Tientsin, 1928, No. 46, pp. 170-171.

8. Two examples of the *fu* character in jade are illustrated in Whit-lock, "Jade," p. 506, top.

9. For the Eight Immortals and their attributes, see Williams, *Outlines*, pp. 125-128.

10. In South China, the highly conventionalized palm leaves are some-times misunderstood as banana leaves, and represented as such.

11. See S. Cammann, "A Rare T'ang Mirror," *The Art Quarterly*, IX, No. 2, Spring, 1946, p. 106.

12. See de Groot, *Religious System*, IV, pp. 306-312, for a discussion of the sacred fungus. He frequently miscalls it a "mushroom" in his writings.

CHAPTER 9

1. For a comprehensive discussion of Chinese gardens and their philo-sophical background see Osvald Sirén, *Gardens of China*, New York, 1949.

2. Especially, to illustrate the auspicious phrase *chin yü mang t'ang.*

3. Very useful for examples of stylized flowers are books on the Chinese paper cutouts or embroidery patterns, such as Alfred Koehn's *Embroidered Wishes*, Peking, 1943, or his *Window Flowers*, Peking, 1948, or the *Man-shi zuan seika daijō*, compiled by Ibara Shizuka, Tokyo, 1936. See also Nozaki's *Kisshō zuan kaidai*, Tientsin, 1928.

4. The convention of showing an auspicious flower on an inappropriate vine is particularly common on porcelains, where a single vine may even be shown sprouting several different kinds of flowers.

5. In some cases the seeds seem to have been carved *in situ*; in other cases the top of the seed pod seems to have been removed, the seeds inserted, and the top replaced; still others may have been produced by making the seeds separately, and then thoroughly drying both seeds and pod to shrink them, so that the seeds could be inserted, then when restored to a normal, moister temperature, both swelled sufficiently so that the seeds could not fall out.

6. One of the more extreme interpretations identifies Hsi Wang Mu with the Greek goddess Hera, on the grounds that Hsi-wang is an attempt to reproduce the name of Siwah in North Africa where

Zeus Ammon and Hera were worshiped. (See Giles, *Chinese-English Dictionary*, under No. 8067.) This seems very far-fetched. However, it is still possible that the Mother Queen of the West (the literal translation of Hsi Wang Mu) with her garden of magic fruits might have preserved a dim memory of Hera's garden as described by Bactrian Greek traders.

7. See Stuart, *Chinese Materia Medica*, p. 114.

8. Laufer, *Sino-Iranica*, pp. 276-287.

9. See Mathews' *Chinese-English Dictionary*, Shanghai, 1931, No. 6607. Giles, Dictionary (No. 10,558) gives an alternative meaning for *tai*.

10. See John Ramsbottom, *Poisonous Fungi* (King Penguin), New York, 1945, p. 21, and *ibid.*, *Mushrooms and Toadstools*, London, 1954, pp. 45-46; and Borgoras, *The Chukchee*, pp. 205-207.

11. See the *P'ei-wên yün-fu*, Commercial Press edition, Shanghai, 1937, III, p. 1811, under *hsiao chün*; see also V. P. and R. G. Wasson, *Mushrooms, Russia and History*, New York, 1957, II, pp. 320-321.

12. De Groot speaks of the mushroom as inheriting the auspicious qualities of the sacred fungus, in *Religious System*, IV, p. 312, but the reader will observe that he is actually talking about another kind of fungus which the Chinese call *mu-êrh*, one of the *Auriculariae*, and not a true mushroom of the types we are discussing.

13. C. A. S. Williams, *A Manual of Chinese Metaphor*, Shanghai, 1920, p. 148.

14. One is in Mrs. Gleysteen's collection, the other is in the Brooklyn Museum (No. 37.371.115).

CHAPTER 10

1. For Chinese goldfish breeding, see A. C. Moule, "A Version of the Book of Vermilion Fish," *T'oung Pao*, XXXIX, 1950, pp. 1-87.

2. Giles, Dictionary, No. 13,615.

3. For other, more complex examples of catfish rebuses, see S. Cammann, *China's Dragon Robes*, New York, 1952, pp. 106-107.

4. See W. F. Mayers, *Chinese Reader's Manual*, Shanghai and London, 1924, p. 321, No. 49.

5. See Carl Schuster, "A Perennial Puzzle: The Motive of Three Fish

with a Common Head," *Art and Thought* (Coomaraswamy Memorial Volume), London, 1947, pp. 116-125.

6. For an early example of the paired magpie motif, see S. Cammann, "Significant Patterns on Chinese Bronze Mirrors," *Archives of the Chinese Art Society*, IX, 1955, p. 52 and fig. 11.

7. From the *Shou shên chi* by Kün Pao, quoted by de Groot, *Religious System*, II, pp. 470-472.

8. See Henri Doré, *Recherches sur les Superstitions en Chine*, II, No. 4, Shanghai, 1912, figs. 197, 198, following p. 382, for two eagle charms.

9. See S. Cammann, "Temples in the Clouds," *Travel*, LXXXVIII, No. 5, March, 1942, p. 8, for a description of the monkeys on Mt. Omei.

10. The legendary tale of this monkey rogue is amusingly told in a sixteenth-century novel, the *Hsi-yü chi*, beautifully translated by Arthur Waley in *Monkey*, New York, 1943. The theft of the peaches is described in Chapter V. The legend of Sun hou-tzŭ is also retold, more briefly, in E. T. C. Werner, *Myths and Legends of China*, London, 1922, Chapter XIV.

11. For a discussion of the Chuang-yüan motif and its probable origin in Classical triumph scenes from the West, see Carl Schuster, "A Comparative Study of Motives in Western Chinese Folk Embroideries," *Monumenta Serica*, II, Peiping, 1936, pp. 40-76.

12. Our reconstruction of the Chinese phrase may not be exact in this second rebus; but the meaning given here seems to have been the intended one. Although we have been unable to find any literary reference to it, it was apparently a fairly common theme, as we have seen it reproduced elsewhere. Miss Bieber has another small Chinese wood carving (not a toggle), which also shows a monkey crouching beneath a horse on the off side.

13. For fortune-telling with the zodiac animals, see Doré, *Recherches*, II, No. 3, pp. 221-222, and fig. 154.

14. For details on Mongol chessmen, See S. Cammann, "Chess with Mongolian Lamas," *Natural History*, LV, No. 9, November, 1946, pp. 407-411.

15. For more about lion dogs, see A. C. Dixie, *The Lion Dog of Peking*, New York, n.d.; and V. W. F. Collier, *Dogs of China and Japan in Nature and Art*, London, 1921.

16. See S. Cammann, "The Lion and Grape Patterns on Chinese Bronze Mirrors," *Artibus Asiae*, XVI, 1953, pp. 284-291.
17. For a late lion, see S. Cammann, "Development of the Mandarin Square," fig. 8*a*.
18. For more about these, and other dragons, see S. Cammann, *China's Dragon Robes*, pp. 77-81, and "Some Strange Ming Beasts," *Oriental Art*, New Series, II, No. 3, Autumn, 1956, pp. 94-102.
19. See Giles, Dictionary, No. 1973, and "Some Strange Ming Beasts," pp. 100-101 and fig. 6.
20. Giles, Dictionary, Nos. 1957 and 1845.
21. *Ibid.*, No. 3709.
22. *Ibid.*, under No. 13,129.
23. The only natural symbol at all comparable to this is the snake, as described earlier in this chapter, which also figured with the cicada on China's most ancient bronzes.

CHAPTER 11

1. Giles, Dictionary, No. 11,351.
2. See Mrs. M. L. C. Bogan, *Manchu Customs and Superstitions*, Tientsin and Peking, 1928, p. 104; and Doré, *Recherches*, I, p. 13 and fig. 10.
3. For details on the Chinese abacus and methods of reckoning with it, see D. H. Leavens, "The Chinese Suan P'an," *The American Mathematical Monthly*, XXVII, April, 1920, pp. 180-184, and other sources cited by him. The Japanese also had abacus toggles, known as *soroban netsuke* (see Okada, *Netsuke*, p. 50), but the Japanese abacus has only one bead in the upper section of each column, while the Chinese type has two, so one type of toggle could not be mistaken for the other.
4. See W. M. McGovern, *The Early Empires of Central Asia*, Chapel Hill, 1931, p. 192.
5. See Homer H. Dubs, "A Military Contact between Chinese and Romans in 36 B.C.," *T'oung Pao*, Series 2, XXXVI, 1942, pp. 64-76.
6. Giles, Dictionary, under No. 10,573, refers to it as a "tambourine," but he uses this word in other cases to refer to a small drum, rather

than a tambourine in the usual sense of that term, and he is probably doing so here.

7. *Ibid.*, No. 4377.

8. *Ibid.*, No. 1438, lists this under *chieh*; but Mathews' *Chinese-English Dictionary*, revised American edition, Cambridge, Mass., 1943, n. 621, explains that this is also read *hsieh*,[2] like the word for shoe.

9. For a specific use of this rebus combination, elsewhere, see Nozaki Seikin, *Kisshō zuan kaidai*, No. 95, pp. 331-332.

10. Literally, "great pincers," see under Giles, No. 4427.

11. See de Groot, *Religious System*, VI, p. 972; and John Hersey, "Red Pepper Village," *Life*, Aug. 26, 1946, p. 95, describing a modern use of the winnowing basket for a form of divination.

12. See Doré, *Recherches*, II, No. 4, pp. 472-473.

13. For this particular sword-fitting, see R. P. Hommel, "Notes on Chinese Sword Furniture," *The China Journal*, VIII, No. 1, January, 1928, pp. 3-6. (This was reprinted in *Hobbies*, VIII, No. 5, July, 1951, pp. 144-45, 149.)

14. For a discussion of some Mongol games with "sheep's knuckles," see Steffan Skallsjo, "Hsia," *Ethnos*, 1952, pp. 15-23.

15. Literally, it means a "money gourd," for the Chinese sometimes used gourds as we would use a "piggy bank." See Giles, Dictionary, under No. 4937.

CHAPTER 12

1. The leaf was not always present, either in the original doctor's figures or the toggles imitating them. See, for example, the Chinese medical figure included among the "tōbori netsuke" in the *Sōken kishō* (7.16), reproduced in Brockhaus, *Netsuke*, p. 95, fig. 111.

2. For Shou Hsing and his fellow star gods, see Doré, *Recherches*, Part II, vol. 11, Shanghai, 1916, pp. 966-970.

3. For P'êng Tsu, see de Groot, *Religious System*, IV, p. 303; VI, p. 1032.

4. For Tung Fang-so, see Doré, *Recherches*, Part II, vol. 11, pp. 1006-1012.

5. See *ibid.*, Part II, vol. 9, pp. 521-524, and H. A. Giles, *Chinese*

Biographical Dictionary, London and Shanghai, 1898, No. 1305 (p. 505).

6. See Doré, *op. cit.*, pp. 514-515.

7. For a synopsis of this famous tale, see Cecilia S. L. Zung (Ch'êng Hsien-ling), *Secrets of the Chinese Drama*, Shanghai, 1937, pp. 175-176.

8. For a typical example on a Chinese embroidery pattern, see the *Man-shi zu-an*, 18, No. 25.

9. For the full story with its various episodes, each of which was made the subject of individual plays, see Zung, *Secrets*, pp. 213-217.

10. Regarding the Chuang-yüan, see reference in Chapter 10, note 11.

Catalogue of Chinese Belt
Toggles in the Bieber Collection

CATALOGUE OF CHINESE BELT*
TOGGLES IN THE BIEBER COLLECTION

I. SIMPLER TOGGLES

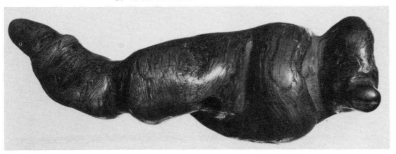

1

A. NATURAL OBJECTS

1. LONG, TWISTED NATURAL ROOT, pierced through center to make bar toggle. Length: 3⅞".

2. NATURAL GLOBULAR CLUSTER OF *Aquillaria* ROOT. Pierced for cord. Height and diameter: approx. 2".

2

3. NATURAL ROOT IN THE SHAPE OF A DOG, only slightly assisted by whittling. Hole pierced down through center of body for cord. Length: 2¾"; max. breadth: 1"; max. height: 1¼".

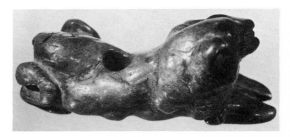

3

* Unless otherwise specified, these toggles were acquired in Peking, mostly in the Jade Market, during the late 1920's and early 1930's.

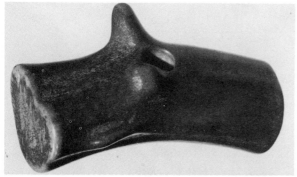

4. SECTION OF DEER ANTLER, intended to resemble a log of wood. Pierced through center to make bar toggle. Dark from age and handling. Length: 2½″.

4

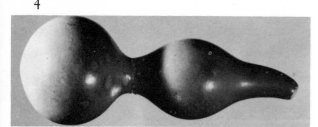

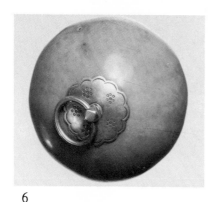

5. SMALL DOUBLE BOTTLE GOURD, with cord knotted around slender waist. Length: 3″.

5

6. LITTLE ROUND GOURD, full of rattling seeds, pierced by a slender ringbolt, with silver guard-plates at each end. Height: 1½″; diameter: 1¾″.

6

7. ARTIFICIALLY SHAPED GOURD, tied by wires during growth to form six rounded lobes. Transfixed by slender pin of white bone, carved at the top to represent a hand clutching the cord, which passes through it. Ornamental washers at top and bottom. One like a *hai-t'ang* flower. Length: 1¾″, including hand; gourd diameter: 1⅝″.

7

8. SMALL COWRIE SHELL. Ivory color mottled with blue-gray and light brown, darker brown spots. Hole pierced through narrower end. Length: 1⅞"; max. width: 1⅛".

9. SMALL GILLA BEAN (*Entada* family), mounted as bun-pendant toggle. Pierced lengthwise by slender silver bolt with cuboctahedral head holding ring for cord. Double washers of silver at top and bottom, shaped to represent *hai-t'ang* flowers (top pair twice as long as bottom pair). Dark brown surface apparently finished in clear transparent lacquer, through which dark natural veining is slightly visible. Length: 1½"; breadth: 1¼"; thickness: ½". (Acquired in America.)

8

9

B. Natural Substances, Simply Carved or Shaped

10. LARGE GILLA BEAN, made into bun-shaped toggle, transfixed through center by small iron pin with cuboctahedral head holding ring. Small iron washers (once gilded), in form of six-petaled flowers at top and bottom. Top surface lightly engraved with river scene, showing sampan with boatman and two passengers; bottom surface inscribed with long poem in minute Chinese characters, dated "Ming Dynasty, reign of Yung Lo" (date of poem, not necessarily date of inscription, though possibly so). Diameter: 1¾"; thickness: ⅝".

10a

10b

11. BUTTON TOGGLE OF PEACH BURL. Hand-shaped (not lathe-turned) to suggest mushroom head. Hole for cord tunneled under circular projection on base. Diameter: 1¼″; thickness: ⅝″.

12. LARGE, SLIGHTLY CONVEX BUTTON TOGGLE of peachwood. Hand-shaped, smoothed, and polished to show fine burl figure. Small projection at back undercut for cord. Diameter: 2¾″; thickness: approx. ⅛″. (Acquired in America.)

13. VERY LARGE, SLIGHTLY CONVEX BUTTON TOGGLE of peachwood, like the preceding, except for much larger size and prominent projecting lug at back, pierced for cord. Traces of reddish stain. Diameter: 5″; thickness: approx. ¼″.

14. SLIGHTLY FLATTENED, CIRCULAR BUTTON TOGGLE of light brown antler. Hand-shaped, with flat circular projection at back undercut for cord hole. Diameter: 1½″; thickness: ½″. (Acquired in America, attached to Mongolian flint-and-steel set, as originally used together in Asia.)

15. ROUNDED, CIRCULAR BUTTON TOGGLE of light creamy antler. Apparently lathe turned and hand finished. Resembles a mushroom head with a short stem at back; latter has been drilled for cord. Diameter: 1¾″; thickness: ½″.

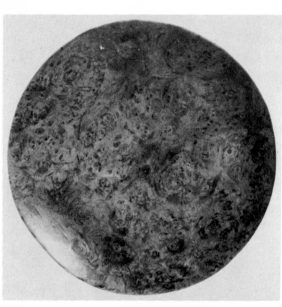

12

14

16. ROUNDED, CIRCULAR BUTTON TOGGLE of antler, dyed deep green with a verdigris solution and highly polished. Apparently lathe turned. Flat circular projection at rear tunneled for cord hole. Diameter: 1⅝"; thickness: ⅜".

17. FLATTER, CIRCULAR BUTTON TOGGLE of green-dyed antler, lighter than the preceding. Lathe turned. Cord eye pierced through circular projection at back. Diameter: 1 ⅝"; thickness: ⅜".

18. ROUNDED IVORY DISC from section of mammoth tusk with yellow rind around outside edge, inscribed with four cursive Chinese characters. Secured by a silver-plated copper button with a metal loop on the underside to a rawhide thong passing through hole in center, attached to Mongol knife set. Diameter: 1½"; thickness: ¼". (Acquired in America.)

18

19. BUN TOGGLE MADE OF A FLATTENED DISC of old ivory with rounded edges, mounted between two decorated silver plates. Upper plate has five *hai-t'ang* flowers in high relief against a punched background; lower plate incised with a stylized *shou* character in concentric bands of ornamentation. The whole is pierced by a silver pin with a cuboctahedral head holding a silver ring. Diameter: 1⅜"; thickness: ⅝".

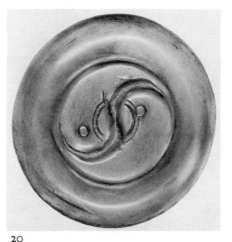

20

20. BUTTON TOGGLE made of a slightly convex circular disc of light cow's horn with *Yin-Yang* motif in low relief at center. The "eyes" in the two comma-shaped elements of the latter are formed by the heads of copper rivets, which secure to the back a ring of dark rosewood and a central button of white horn with a flat circular projection at the center undercut for the cord. Diameter: 2¼″; thickness: ½″.

21

21. DISC TOGGLE of dark polished *Dalbergia* wood (*chin ssŭ t'an mu*) with inlay of thin metal wire, representing an ancient ritual jade ring (*pi*), wrapped in a silken scarf, with the ends of the scarf tied at the center to form a bar for attaching the cord. Some of the wire inlay has dropped out, leaving part of the pattern simply indicated by incised lines. Both in style and appearance this seems very old. Diameter: 2¼″; thickness: ⅜″.

22. SLIGHTLY CONVEX BUTTON TOGGLE of *Prunus* wood with the background cut away to leave a pattern in low relief, consisting of a large plant or tree with prominent leaves, among the branches of which are four highly stylized animals and a happiness bat. Small lug at back, undercut to make cord hole, almost worn through from long use. An old, folk toggle. Diameter: 2⅛″; thickness: ¼″.

23. VERY OLD BUN TOGGLE of boxwood burl with relief carving on both sides. Outer face carved to represent four large fish circling around a disc surmounted by another disc labeled "moon" in Chinese. The underside has two entwined snakes in high relief, the body of one being undercut for the cord where it crosses the center of the disc. Diameter: 2⅜"; thickness: ¾".

23a

24. LARGE FLAT BUTTON TOGGLE of birchwood, carved in low relief to show an infant boy in a bib, holding a peach, with a vase of auspicious flowers on each side of him. The border contains a continuous rinceau band of lotus flowers, the lotus itself being a symbol of continuity. Round, projecting lug on underside pierced for cord. Diameter: 3⅜"; thickness: ⅜".

23b

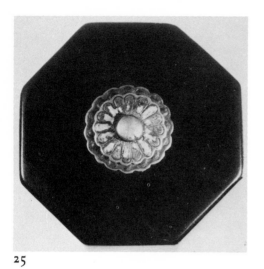

25

C. SIMPLE STONE TOGGLES

25. SLIGHTLY CONVEX FLAT OCTAGON OF JET, mounted as a bun toggle, pierced through the center by a metal bolt with cuboctahedral head holding a ring. Two washers on the face and one at the rear in the form of sixteen-petaled flowers, with traces of turquoise blue and pale green enamel on the engraved petals. Greatest diameter: 2⅜"; thickness: ½".

26

26. DISC TOGGLE formed of a perforated disc (*pi* form) of mottled gray jade, secured by a silver pin with cuboctahedral head holding a ring, passing through large silver guard-plates. Three-layered silver plate on face is worked to represent a multipetaled chrysanthemum, with each petal outlined in relief. Rear plate in the shape of a flower with six bilobed petals, each lightly engraved at the tip. Diameter: 1½"; thickness of the jade: ³⁄₁₆".

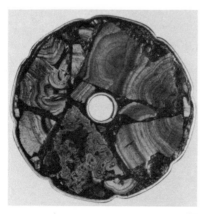

27

27. FLAT DISC formed of irregular chips of malachite set in a dark cement, with sleeve core around central perforation, and six-lobed flat rim around outside, both of gilt bronze. Originally a rawhide cord was passed through the central hole and knotted. Diameter: 2"; thickness: ⅜". (Purchased by S. C. in Zagulao, on the Sino-Tibetan border of West China.)

28. SIMILAR DISC set with malachite fragments, but enclosed by a circular rim of gilt bronze with rounded edges. Secured by a heavy silver bolt with cuboctahedral head holding a ring; outer end of bolt flattened into a smaller circular disc, worked to represent the Yin-Yang symbol surrounded by the Eight Trigrams (*pa kua*). Small flat washer under head of bolt, at rear, shaped to resemble a six-petaled flower with light engraving on petals. The head of the bolt itself is inscribed with three Chinese characters, Li Jun Hsiang, probably the name of the silversmith or the owner. This appears to have been a Tibetan toggle of the previous type, altered to Chinese taste by the addition of the silver fastening. Diameter: 1⅞″; thickness: ⅜″.

29. DISC TOGGLE formed of a flat ring of white nephrite jade, with two silver plates covering the central aperture on each side. The front plate, ornamented in high relief, has the figure of a Chinese lion playing with silk scarfs and an embroidered ball, against a lightly punched background enclosed by ornamental borders; the rear plate is undecorated, but has at its center a triple loop of wire securing a ring for the cord. Total diameter: 2½″; diameter of silver button: 1¼″; jade: approx. ⅛″ thick.

30. BUN PENDANT of amethyst fashioned into a seven-lobed form to resemble a pumpkin or squash. Center pierced by a pin with a cuboctahedral head holding a ring for the cord. At the lower end, a three-tiered metal flower in the shape of a multipetaled chrysanthemum; below head of bolt, at top, a simpler seven-petaled flower with light engraving on its petals. Total length: 1⅜″; diameter: 1½″.

31. BALL TOGGLE consisting of a sphere of pink agate, slightly flattened at top and bottom. Pierced by a metal pin with a cuboctahedral head holding a ring. At lower end, a double washer represents a multipetaled chrysanthemum; at top, a plain silver cap with an illegible silversmith's mark. Total length: 1½″; ball: ⅞″ high, 1¼″ thick.

32. AUSPICIOUS GOURD, formed by two carnelian beads on a silver pin, which also secures plain silver caps with scalloped edges: two at the base, two on each side of the slender neck around which the cord is knotted; and a longer silver cap at the top represents the stem. Total length: 2¼″; diameter of largest bead: ¾″.

32

II. MORE ELABORATE TOGGLES

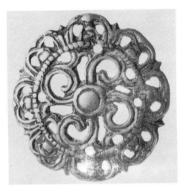

33

35

36

A. METAL BUTTON AND DISC TOGGLES

33. SLIGHTLY CONVEX OPENWORK TIBETAN TOGGLE of gilt bronze, representing a highly conventionalized swastika superimposed on the Buddhist eight-petaled lotus. Loop for cord soldered on reverse. Diameter: 1¾"; thickness: 1⁄16". (Purchased by S. C. in the Sino-Tibetan border country, 1937.)

34. HEAVY SILVER BUTTON TOGGLE, with Chinese lion in high relief against a stippled background, enclosed in a double rim. Silver loop soldered to base. Silversmith's mark (Tsu Wên) repeated three times on lower edge of rim. Diameter: 1"; rim: ¼" thick.

35. OLD MONGOLIAN DISC TOGGLE representing a fox under a grapevine within an ornamental border, done in high relief with openwork in copper, on brass. At back, a much worn cuboctahedral bolthead holds an iron ring. Diameter: 1½"; thickness: ⅛". (Acquired by S. C. in Inner Mongolia, 1945.)

36. THIN REPOUSSÉ SILVER BUTTON showing a crane in high relief, holding in its mouth the sacred fungus (ling chih), enclosed in a stylized rope frame with an outer border of star-shaped punch marks, making a flower petal effect. Silver loop at back holds silver ring. Diameter: 2"; thickness: 1⁄32".

37. THIN CONVEX REPOUSSÉ SILVER BUTTON TOGGLE showing a scene from the popular story and play, *San Niang Chiao Tzŭ*. A seated matron (the San Niang, or third concubine) and a kneeling youth in an official cap (her foster son), greet a bearded old man with a staff (the boy's father). These, with other details, are all presented in relief against a punched background. A thin rope border encloses the scene, with an outer border of lightly stamped figures making a continuous Greek fret. At back, a silver loop holds a ring. Diameter: just under 2"; thickness: ⅟₃₂".

37

38. THIN CONVEX REPOUSSÉ SILVER BUTTON showing water animals in high relief. At center a fantail goldfish, surrounded by a crab, a clam, a crayfish, a snail, a small minnow (silver darter?), a water spider, a hermit crab in a periwinkle shell, and a frog. The background consists of tiny circular punch marks, which is again used to set off the toothed border. A double loop of thin silver wire at the back holds a silver wire ring. Diameter: just over 2"; thickness: ⅟₃₂".

38

B. DOUBLE-UTILITY TOGGLES: SEALS, ETC.

39. SMALL ANTIQUE JADE SEAL representing a little bear, standing with bandy legs on a square base with upper edges beveled. Of brown-stained "Han" jade with its original gray color partly visible on the base. Two characters in old seal script (Chung Hsin) are deeply incised on the bottom. Gap for cord between bear's legs. Over-all height: 1"; base: 1" square.

39

40

40. SMALL   SINO-TIBETAN   SEAL-TOGGLE.
Tibetan Buddhist lion in gilt bronze,
seated on a flat square base of iron
inscribed with two elongated characters in Tibetan seal script, enclosed
in a typical Tibetan T-fret border.
Over-all height: 1¼"; seal: ⅞"
square. (Acquired by Bailey Vander-
hoef from a Tibetan yak driver from
Lhasa, near Shigatse, Tibet, in July,
1938.)

41

41. TYPICAL TIBETAN SEAL, with lump of
"sealing wax," mounted on a rawhide thong to serve as a counterweight
for a knife set. Ch'ing dynasty copper
cash coins lend additional weight and
help to protect against wear. Upper
part of seal of gilt bronze with typical
foliate design in openwork; circular
iron base inscribed with the Tibetan
syllable *tsa*, probably an initial of the
original owner. Seal: 1⅝" high; diameter: ⅝". (Purchased by S. C. from
a Tibetan pilgrim near Zagulao, in
the Tibetan border country, in January, 1938.)

For other forms of double-utility
toggles, see Nos. 73, 74, 194 and
199.

C. OTHER OBJECTS REUSED AS TOGGLES

42a

42. TWO SILVER COINS REUSED AS TOGGLES.
a. A Yünnan provincial dollar,
reign of Kuang-hsü (1875-1908);
obverse, imperial Manchu dragon
coiled around a flaming pearl, surrounded by plain circular border;

inscription all on back, where a soldered wire loop holds a silver ring for the cord. Diameter: 1½"; thickness: nearly ⅛".

b. British trade dollar of 1901 reused as toggle. Face (originally the reverse) shows a "cloud collar" motif surrounding a highly stylized *shou* character with a T-fret meander in the outer border. The Chinese characters for "one dollar" (*i yüan*) and the equivalent in Malayan (Arabic) script are shown in the lappets of the cloud collar. The reverse side, which shows the figure of Britannia as Queen of the Seas, has a wire ring soldered to it, holding another ring for the cord. Diameter: 1⁹⁄₁₆"; thickness: nearly ⅛".

42b

43. PLAIN BRICK TOGGLE of mammoth ivory. Undecorated flat rectangle pierced by two holes, probably originally made to serve as a "spreader" for a large bag or quiver suspended on two stout cords. Length: 1¾"; breadth: 1⅛"; thickness: ⁵⁄₁₆".

44. BRICK TOGGLE of carved cinnabar lacquer, dark brown from age, with Ming-style dragon in low relief set off by openwork on convex upper portion, with plain, slightly concave base. Length: 1⁹⁄₁₆"; breadth: 1⅛"; thickness: ½".

44

45

45. ANTIQUE CICADA IN DISCOLORED JADE, from old Chinese tomb, with holes bored through head end to receive cord for toggle or pendant. Simple carving, but rather naturalistic. Overall length: 2¼″; max. breadth: 1 3/16″; thickness: 5/16″. (Acquired by S. C. in West China, 1945.)

46. TWO BRONZE LUCKY PIECES, described in Chinese as coins (*ch'ien*), though not used for actual currency, and differing from coins in having open-work designs and a round hole in the center, instead of a square one. Through the center hole a thong was passed and knotted to make each into a toggle.

46a

a. A pattern of three fish, swimming around in the same direction. Diameter: 1¾″.

46b

b. Two dragons, one ascending, one descending. Diameter: 1⅞″.

For other examples of reused objects, see Nos. 107, 109, 124.

III. BOTANICAL TOGGLES

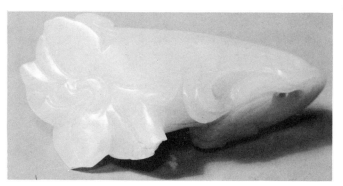

47

A. FLOWERS, PLANTS, AND TREES, IN GENERAL

47. DATURA FLOWER AND BUD with two stylized leaves, in pale green nephrite jade. Lower part of the small bud arches outward to form loop for cord. Length: 2⅞"; breadth: 1¾"; thickness: ¾".

48. MORNING GLORY (*Convolvulus*) flower, with a small leaf on either side of the curling stem. In camphor jade, pale gray-green with minute white speckles. Loop of vine makes cord attachment. A groove cut around the outer convex edge of the flower may have had some practical purpose. Length: 2¼"; max. width: 1½"; thickness: ⅜".

49. MAGNOLIA BLOSSOM with three leaves and a short length of stem, simply carved from mammoth tusk rind. Hole under arching stem for cord. Length: 1½"; max. breadth: 1"; thickness: ⅞".

48

50

50. SECTION OF CHRYSANTHEMUM FLOWER with two characteristic buds and three leaves, carved on the convex surface of a section of mammoth ivory rind. Openwork holes on either side of stem provided a means for attaching the cord. (Originally rectangular, one corner with a bud has broken off.) Length: 2⅛″; width: 1¼″; thickness: ¼″.

51

51. SECTION OF PINE TREE, part of trunk with branch, carved in low relief on the flat inner surface of a segment of elephant tusk; convex outer surface roughened, apparently in an attempt to represent a rock which, like the pine tree, was a symbol of longevity. Hole at one side, between branch and trunk, for passing the cord. Length: 1⅝″; width: ¼″; max. thickness: ⅜″.

52

52. SECTION OF PLUM TREE, trunk with flowering branch (two blossoms and two buds), carved in low relief on rounded inner surface of a segment of old elephant tusk. As in the preceding example, a branch is curved to leave a hole for the cord at one side. Length 1⅝″; width: 1⅜″; max. thickness, ¾″.

53. SECTION OF BAMBOO PLANT, with two stalks, simulated in boxwood, carved in very naturalistic fashion. Cord looped around one of the stalks. Max. length: 4⅜″; max. width: 1⅛″; max. thickness: ¾″.

For other pine tree motifs, see Nos. 223 and 224; for other plum trees, see Nos. 152 and 205.

53

B. Lotus Motifs

54. EXTREMELY SIMPLE CARVING of a lotus seed pod on a short stem, in birchwood, with seven movable seeds. The pod proper seems to have been turned on a lathe. Three tiny holes at end of stem, indicate natural ducts in original stalk. Hole for cord drilled through base of stem where it joins pod. Length with stem: 1⅝″; diameter of pod: 1⅛″.

55. LOTUS SEED POD with seven movable seeds on one stalk, with lotus leaf on adjoining stalk; the two stalks are looped to hold the cord. Carved in boxwood burl. Length: 1⅝″; max. diameter of pod: 1¼″.

55

56

56. LOTUS POD with seven movable seeds on one stem, with highly conventionalized leaf on adjoining stem, both stems arching outward to form a bar around which the cord can be looped. In finely figured boxwood burl. The back is flattened and smoothed, but uncarved. Length: 3¼″; max. width: 1¾″; max. thickness: 1⅛″.

57

57. VERY NATURALISTIC LOTUS POD with seven movable seeds on one short stem, with a closed bud on another stem, in boxwood. Sensitive rendering of top of pod and fine dotting on stems to indicate plant hairs, show the carver's keen observation. The joined stems form a loop for attaching cord. Length: 1½″; breadth, with bud: 1½″; max. diameter of pod: 1⅛″.

58. LARGE LOTUS POD with seven very large movable seeds on a short stem, with two miniature stems each bearing a very small conventionalized lotus flower on each side of the pod; done in birchwood, very dark from age and

long handling. Base of shorter stem pierced for cord hole. Height: 1¼″; max. diameter of pod: 1¾″.

59

59. SMALL LOTUS POD with six movable seeds on a long stem, that is entwined with the equally long stem of a large lotus leaf in which is enwrapped a small fish; like the seeds, the latter is movable, but not removable. The whole is carved in lightly figured maple burl. Length: 2″; max. width: 1½″; max. thickness: 1⅜″.

60

60. LOTUS SEED POD in elephant ivory, with seven movable seeds, and attached to it four remaining petals of the original flower, while another stem holds a miniature leaf. The arching stems leave two holes for the cord. Length: 2″; width: 1⅜″; height: 1¼″.

61. LUMP OF AGATE carved to represent a whitish lotus seed pod with seven seeds (barely indicated by lightly incised circles), and on an adjoining stem a bud on which is perched a small red butterfly. A darker red portion has been carved to represent a water chestnut and a water caltrop pod. The bud stem is cut free to form a loop. Length: 2″; height: ⅞″; breadth: 1⅜″.

62a

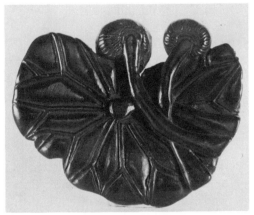

62b

62. FLAT, RATHER NATURALISTIC LOTUS LEAF with upturned edges on a short stem, with two small pods on separate stems, one of them being undercut so the cord can be looped around it. The whole is represented as floating upon the surface of a pond, with a tiny crab and a small water beetle riding on opposite sides of the leaf. Carved from boxwood burl, with considerable realism shown in the rendering of the veins in the leaf and hairs on the stems. Length 2½″; width: 2⅛″; thickness: ¼″.

63. RATHER PRIMITIVE CARVING in aloes wood of a lotus leaf and two conventionalized lotus flowers, one on a stalk with another kind of leaf, and a butterfly in one corner. Two of the stems are undercut to provide gaps for the cord. Length: 2¼″; width: 1¾″; thickness: ½″.

63

64. SECTION OF DARK BROWN *Prunus* BURL carved into a button toggle representing a large lotus leaf with two conventionalized lotus flowers and a seed pod on its surface, in low relief, and the complete figure of a small frog riding along on the leaf. The underside, which is tunneled at the center to make a hole for the cord, has been only partly smoothed, to leave the intricate burl figure projecting slightly in a way that suggests swirling waters. Diameter: 1⅞"; max. height, with frog: 1".

65. LARGE LOTUS LEAF or lily pad, with small frog sitting on it, done in birchwood. A short section of the stem at the center underneath is arched and undercut for attaching the cord. Diameter: 2½"; height, with frog: ½".

66. VERY LARGE, ROUGHLY CONVENTIONALIZED LOTUS LEAF, partially folded to contain a fish, with a small frog clambering up the outside. Leaf stalk cut free at one side to form loop for cord. Carved from boxwood burl, with bottom left rough to show the original surface with warty protuberances. Natural mat finish, without any polish. Length: 3⅜"; width 2⅛"; height: 1½".

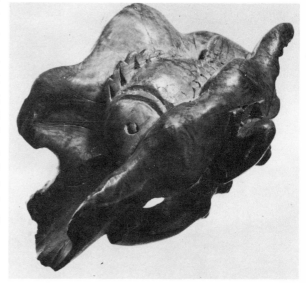

66

67. SECTION OF LOTUS RHIZOME with miniature lotus flower and leaf, carved from light brown gypsum. Seven perforations in rhizome to represent natural ducts, with additional hole for cord between flower and leaf. Someone has scratched on the outer rim the character for "lotus root" (*ou*). Max. width: 1⅜"; thickness: ¼".

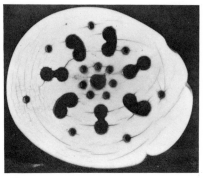

68

68. CROSS SECTION OF ELEPHANT TUSK worked to represent a slice of lotus rhizome by drilling holes to represent the root passages. Cord was passed through the central hole and knotted. A very common type in Old China. Length: 2″; width: 1⅝″; thickness: ⅜″.

For other lotus toggles see Nos. 147 and 181.

C. THE AUSPICIOUS PEACH

69. LARGE FLAT TOGGLE representing a peach on a branch with four leaves and a small bud, made of dark purple rosewood (*Dalbergia*), rounded on the face and flat at the rear. Holes between fruit and branch offer several possible places for the cord. Length: 2¼″; width: 1¾″; thickness: ⅜″.

70

70. LARGE PEACH ON STEM with two leaves, made of boxwood burl. Outer side concave, smooth, and highly polished to display handsome burl figure; underside retains original surface with warty protuberances (like No. 66). Hole for cord between stem and fruit. Length: 2½″; width: 1½″; thickness: 1″.

71. TWO PEACHES ON A BRANCH with four leaves, in boxwood. Finely balanced composition. Open space at center, between branch and two stems, for attaching the cord. Length: 2¼"; breadth: 1¼"; thickness: ⅞".

71

72. BOX TOGGLE in the shape of a stylized peach, carved from a single piece of peachwood burl. Outer part forms a sheath for inner drawer, hinged by a brass pin behind stem at upper center (actual base of the fruit); hole under stem, attached to inner section, provides loop for cord. Over-all length: 2"; width: 1⅞"; height: 1⅜".

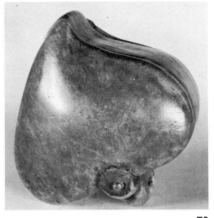

For other toggles that contain peaches, see Nos. 114-119 and 189.

72

D. GOURDS AND MELONS

73. HEAVY BRASS PESTLE in the form of a bottle gourd (*Lagenaria vulgaris*) to make a double-utility toggle. The large gourd grows from one strand of a pair of vines. A branch of the same vine, bearing four small bottle gourds and a number of leaves, loops around the upper portion of the large gourd; while the other vine, which encircles its lower half, is a grapevine, on which two squirrels are playing. The entire surface of the main gourd is beautifully chased with patterns of flowers, leaves, and vines, except for a circular patch at the base that has been left plain for use as the striking part of the pestle. The latter bears scars of much pounding, perhaps in powdering medicine. Length: 2". Max. width: ⅞".

73

74

75

76

74. SMALL SILVER BOTTLE in the shape of a bottle gourd, with screw-on top, serving as a double-utility toggle. Both the upper and lower sections have patterns of auspicious symbols standing out in high relief against a punch-stippled background, leaving a plain area at the narrow neck between them for looping the cord. The pattern on the upper section depicts in miniature seven jewels (symbols of wealth), while the lower section has seven of the Eight Symbols of the Taoist Immortals (the eighth, the gourd of Li T'ieh-kuai, is already present in the form of the whole toggle). Length: 2″ including stem; max. diameter: ¾″.

75. CLUSTER OF SEVEN BOTTLE GOURDS on a vine with five leaves and numerous tendrils, artistically carved in fragrant aloes wood (*Aquillaria*). Length: 2½″; width: 1¾″; thickness: ¾″.

76. TWO LARGE GOURDS on a vine with two large leaves and tendrils, beautifully rendered in palmwood. Undercut stem at top provides place for the cord. Height: 2⅜″; max. breadth: 1¾″.

77. LARGE PUMPKIN WITH EIGHT LOBES, fashioned from a lump of light green and brown turquoise. Pierced vertically through the center for a knotted cord. The calyx is indicated by simple carving around the aperture at the base. Max. diameter: 1⅞"; thickness: ⅞".

77

78. PUMPKIN WITH ELEVEN LOBES on a stalk with one large leaf, carved from ivory, with a hole in one side from which appears the head of a movable (but not removable) worm, arranged like the seeds of the lotus pods (Nos. 54-60). There is a similar hole in the other side, but if that too had a worm, it has fallen out. The small worm has eyes made from tiny iron nailheads and a carved slit mouth. The arching stem provides a place for attaching the cord. Height: 1½"; max. diameter: 1⅜".

For other gourd toggles, see Nos. 5, 6, 7, and 32.

78

E. Mushrooms and Fungus

79. IRREGULAR CLUMP OF TEN MUSHROOMS carved in boxwood burl. Horizontal perforation between stems near base for passing cord. Length: 1½"; breadth: 1¾"; thickness: ¾".

79

80

81

80. CLUSTER OF THIRTEEN LONG-STEMMED MUSHROOMS carved in *Prunus* burl, represented in an erect clump. The undersides of the caps, facing forward, are beautifully rendered in fine line carving. On the rear side, the stem of the largest mushroom arches outward, away from the rest, to make a loop for the cord. Length: 2″; breadth: 1⅝″; thickness: 1″.

81. ERECT CLUSTER OF TEN MUSHROOMS carved in *Prunus* burl; five on each side, with the undersides facing out. Hole for cord pierced through shank, between the stems. Length: 2⅝″; breadth: 1⅝″; thickness: ¾″.

82. TWO CLUSTERS OF FIVE MUSHROOMS EACH, carved in boxwood, with undersides facing out; the two sets of stems are separated to leave room for cord. Height: 2½″; breadth: 1⅛″; thickness: ¼″.

83. GROUP OF TEN MUSHROOMS, carved in boxwood, arranged in a semicircular grouping in the shape of an old Chinese purse (*ho-pao*), five on each side: four clearly visible, with undersides out, and a fifth shown vertically, with only its stem and the top of its cap visible behind the rest. The center is hollowed laterally, making a passage for the cord between the two sets of stems. Breadth: 2″; height: 1¼″; max. thickness: ½″.

84. GROUP OF TEN MUSHROOMS, in box-wood, composed in much the same way as the preceding, but arranged slightly differently, with four on one side, three on the other, and the last three along the top. Cord eye pierced transversely between the two sets of stems. Breadth: 2″; height: 1¼″; thickness: ¼″.

84

85. BUTTERFLY MADE UP OF EIGHT MUSH-ROOMS with undersides up, arranged on either side of the insect body. Re-verse plain, except for simple indica-tion of the body in low relief; other-wise merely smoothed and polished to show the fine burl figure, with a hole drilled through the body for passing the cord. Height: 2″; breadth: 2½″; thickness: ⅜″.

85

86. CLUSTER OF EIGHT MUSHROOMS carved in fine *Prunus* burl, cleverly composed to form a button toggle. A bar for fastening the cord is provided by one of the large stems crossing the central aperture at the rear. Highly polished. Diameter: 2¼″; max. thickness: ½″.

87. TRIANGULAR GROUP OF MUSHROOMS carved in boxwood, making a button toggle. One very large round-topped mushroom in center, with eleven smaller ones arranged around it, underside up, producing the effect of an eight-petaled flower with three projecting leaves. Loop for cord pro-vided by arching stem of largest mush-room on reverse. Max. diameter: 1¾″; thickness: ¾″.

86

87

88. FLAT CLUSTER OF THIRTEEN MUSHROOMS carved in *Prunus* burl for button toggle. One very large round-topped one in center, with twelve much smaller ones arranged irregularly around it, to give an effect like the sun among clouds. Cord loop formed by arching stem of the large central one. Diameter: 2¼″; thickness: ⅞″.

89. LARGE CLUSTER OF MUSHROOMS carved from *Prunus* wood to form a bun toggle, with the center hollowed out for lightness. The outer side has eight mushrooms arranged radially around a central one to provide a most symmetrical grouping; while the reverse has eleven mushrooms arranged in a bisymmetrical but far more casual-looking composition. A silver cotter pin passing through the center holds a ring for the cord. Ornamental washers on each side are decorated, with a highly conventionalized *shou* character, incised, and a double-tiered flower with petals in relief, respectively. Diameter: 2¼″; height: 1¼″.

89

90. VERTICAL CLUMP OF MUSHROOMS, apparently intended to represent *Caprinus micaceus*, very naturalistically carved from a yellowed piece of antler. Vertical perforation for cord passed down through center of the cluster. Height: 1¾″; max. thickness: 1″.

91. HIGHLY CONVENTIONALIZED SACRED FUNGUS (*ling chih*), symbol of longevity, simply carved in a section of ivory tusk. Convex, outer side very

90

plain and highly polished; inside well carved, with deep engraving, but much worn from use. Holes pierced on either side of the main stem at the center offer passage for cord. Length: 1⅞"; breadth: 1¼"; max. thickness: ⅝".

91

For other sacred fungus toggles, see Nos. 100, 117, 135, 149, and 150.

F. FRUITS AND VEGETABLES, ETC.

92. OVAL LUMP OF GRAY AND WHITE QUARTZ mounted to resemble the fruit of an eggplant by the addition of a stem and a five-petaled calyx in iron. Base of stem pierced with small hole for cord. Length: 2¼"; max. diameter: 1¼".

93. CLUSTER OF GRAPES in dark "root amber" with a broad leaf behind it. The leaf has been left severely plain, to show to best advantage a section with golden streaking, and also to afford a space to enjoy the characteristic feel of amber. Length: 2¼"; width: 1⅜"; thickness: ¾".

93

94. UNKNOWN FRUIT WITH FOUR LOBES and circular *hilum*, on a short stem with one thin narrow leaf (both arched to form a loop for the cord), made from a beautifully figured fruitwood burl. Length: 1¾"; max. diameter: 1⅛".

94

95

95. "BUDDHA'S HAND" CITRON, with stem and small leaves, in a handsomely figured maple burl. Arching stems provide cord attachment. Length: 2″; diameter: ⅞″.

96a

96b

96. VERY NATURALISTIC BOXWOOD CARVING of two pea pods on a stem with two broad leaves (one, half broken off). The artist's close observation is indicated by a cleverly rendered small spider hiding under broken leaf, and seven tiny perforations in the end of the stem to indicate canals. Vine with leaf stems arched outward to form cord loop. Length: 2″; breadth: 1¼″; height: ⅝″.

97. SLIGHTLY CURVED, FLAT BAR TOGGLE of nephrite jade, representing a section of beanstalk with three bean pods and several leaves. The inner (concave) side is very realistically rendered in high relief, while the outer (convex) side is more conventionalized, and treated in flat relief with

line engraving. The original cord hole was drilled under the prominent leaf at the center of the concave side; later, a new hole was pierced at one end for a smaller cord, probably for alteration into a pendant. Max. length: 3″; max. breadth: ⅞″; thickness: ⅜″. (Purchased in New York City.)

98. GREEN PEPPER WITH CALYX, represented in green-dyed bone, with iron pin inserted to represent stem. Fashioned into a bar or spike toggle by inserting through middle a small brass cotter pin holding a ring for the cord. Length: 3⅝″; max. diameter: ½″.

99. HEAP OF NUTS AND FRUIT: a chestnut, two peanuts, and a couple of Chinese dates (jujubes), very realistically carved from red and brown agate (sard). Two gaps for passing the cord deliberately left between the nuts by the carver. Length: 1⅞″; width: 1⅜″; thickness: ½″.

99

IV. THE ANIMAL KINGDOM

A. ANIMALS IN GENERAL

100. RECLINING STAG in "mutton fat jade" (white nephrite), carrying in its mouth the sacred fungus. Outer side of body convex and rather plain; inner, concave side intricately carved with undercutting. Dappled hide of *sika* deer simply indicated by lightly incised stars. Main stalk of fungus cut free to provide a place for attaching cord on inner side. Length: 1½″; height: 1″; thickness: 1⅝″. (Acquired by S. C. in Sian, West China, 1945.)

100

101. RECUMBENT WATER BUFFALO in black soapstone (steatite). Vertical hole through body for passing cord. Length: 2″; breadth: 1″; height: ¾″.

101

102

102. RECLINING BUFFALO, with small boy climbing up on his back, resting on a giant leaf; handsomely carved in light boxwood. Leaf stem arching up to meet head of buffalo provides loop for cord. Leaf deeply ridged to indicate coarse veining, in contrast to smoothness of the figures upon it. Height: 1″; length: 1⅝″; max. width: 1¼″.

103

103. SMALL BRASS HORSE very simply cast, with smooth finish except for mane. Vertical cord hole through body at withers. Height: 1¼″; length: 1¾″; max. width: ⅜″.

104

104. TWIN CATS in mutton fat jade (white nephrite). Left leg of each cat arched outward to form a loop, providing two possible cord attachments. Max. length: 1¾″; width: 1½″; height: ⅝″. (Purchased in Changsha by S. C., in 1936.)

105. TWIN CATS reclining on a giant leaf, carved in old, brownish jade. Arching leaf stem makes loop for cord. Length: 2⅛″; width: 1″; height: ½″.

106. RECUMBENT BOAR PIG, in gray and orange jade. Simply carved, but showing the drooping ears, long wrinkled nose, high sharp back, and straight tail of typical Chinese pigs. Two holes bored through back behind ears, meeting inside body, for cord. Length: 1¾″; height: ⅞″; width: ¾″.

106

107. SMALL RECLINING PIG in opaque white glass. Even more simple than the preceding one, and less characteristic of modern Chinese pigs, as it has small ears and curly tail. Type of object used by Han and T'ang court ladies for sleeve weights; probably originally one of these, adapted for a toggle by drilling a small hole transversely through the mouth. Length: 1⅝″; width: ½″; height: ⅝″.

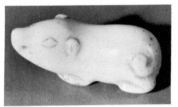

107

108. RECUMBENT RAM of Asiatic fat-tailed sheep, carved in *Prunus* wood. Though carving is simple and much worn, realism is shown in neck folds, characteristic broad tail, and the pose of scratching neck with hind foot. Hind legs undercut to form loops for inserting rawhide cord. Length: 1⅞″; width: 1″; height: ⅞″. (Acquired by barter from a Mongol lama at Lo-pei Chao lamasery in the Ordos Desert, by S. C., in 1945.)

108

109

110

111

109. MONGOLIAN RAM standing on a rectangular base, in boxwood. Traces of white paint on animal and bright red on base indicate that this was originally a pawn from a Mongol chess set. Two holes crudely drilled on underside of base for inserting cord when it was altered for a toggle. Almost total erosion of paint, and a high patina from much handling, attest to long use as a toggle. Height: 1¼″; length: 1¼″; width at base: ¾″.

110. HIGHLY SIMPLIFIED TURTLE, of birch, with movable feet and tail. Body partially lathe turned. Projecting lug left at bottom, pierced for passage of cord. Length: 1½″; breadth: 1″; height: ⅝″.

111. CONVENTIONALIZED HAPPINESS BAT resting on a pair of Ch'ing dynasty cash coins, with Manchu script visible on one of them. Simply carved in peachwood burl; bottom left smooth to permit tactile enjoyment. Length: 2⅛″; breadth: 1¾″; thickness: ⅜″.

B. MONKEY TOGGLES

112. SMALL SEATED MONKEY in brass, holding a peach between his hands. Simply but amusingly done. Worn loop at center of back once held ring for cord. Height: 1¼″; breadth: ⅝″; thickness: ⅝″.

113. SEATED MONKEY with hands on knees. Simple folk carving in box-

wood. Hole drilled through rear of body under shoulder blades. Height: 1⅞"; breadth: 1"; thickness: 1".

114. SEATED MONKEY, the folk-hero Sun Hou-tzŭ, wearing a hat and holding a peach. Carved in birch, with tiny chips of coral for eyes; neck arranged so head can nod or turn completely around. Hole for cord through center of body at abdomen, but right arm is also curved so that it could serve as a loop for alternative attachment. Height: 2⅞"; width: 1"; thickness: 1".

115. MONKEY STEALING A PEACH in orchard. Skilfully carved in birch, with openwork carving and hollow center. Many possible places for looping cord around branches, but specific hole for this in base. Height: 2⅛"; width: 1⅜"; thickness: 1".

116. SEATED MONKEY embracing two peaches: one in hands and one between legs, done in outer piece of ivory tusk with coarse rind. Although much worn, it still shows the face with its wrinkles and a frame of soft hair, very realistically rendered. Traces of red dye. Hole for cord between arms and body, at center of toggle. Height: 1¾"; breadth: 1¼"; thickness: ⅝".

117. SEATED MONKEY holding a giant peach and a *ju-i* scepter shaped like a fungus of immortality; in clear quartz crystal. Arm undercut for cord attachment. Height: 1¾"; breadth: 1⅞"; thickness: ¾".

114

116

117

118. SEATED MONKEY holding a baby monkey and a peach branch with fruit, in light boxwood. Though much worn, it shows traces of careful rendering of spine, body fur, etc. Right arm bowed outward for cord. Height: 2″; breadth: 1″; thickness: ¾″.

119. LARGE MONKEY embracing a giant peach with baby monkey playing below. Carved in brown-stained nephrite jade, with the parent monkey predominantly in brown, the peach green and light brown, the child in white. Very naturalistic work, with light line engraving on each side of spine to suggest fur. Large monkey's right arm, raised to scratch back of neck, forms a loop for attaching cord. Height: 2¼″; max. width: 1¼″; max. thickness: 1″. (Purchased by S. C. in Kunming, Yünnan, winter 1945.)

119

120. SEATED MONKEY embracing young, carved from an outer piece of old mammoth ivory with rind, in general style of No. 116. Very old and much worn, but has traces of line engraving to represent fur. Hole for cord passes under chin and behind left elbow. Height: 1½″; breadth: 1″; thickness: ⅝″.

121. SEATED MONKEY MOTHER with young, in boxwood. A baby stands upright before her with hands in an attitude of prayer, while an older one climbs on her back, and a new one is in process of being born below; apparently intended to suggest the idea of successive generations of

121

descendants, as a fertility charm. The parent's goggle eyes are skilfully arranged on movable pegs, so that by pulling a small string that passes in one ear and out the other, they can be made to swivel around in amusingly realistic fashion. The head of the baby being born is also represented by a movable peg, so that it can turn completely around without slipping out of the parent's body. The parent monkey's arms are both cut free, so that either can serve as a cord loop. Height: 1⅝"; breadth: 1¼"; thickness: ⅝". (Purchased in West China by Carl Schuster.)

122. A MONKEY FAMILY showing eighteen small monkeys crowded around an elderly patriarch monkey seated in a formal armchair, which is upheld by some of the younger ones, apparently as a parody on a human family, as well as a symbol of fertile descendants. Carved in birchwood with detail and openwork. Cord perforation through back of toggle between side legs of patriarch's chair. Height: 2¼"; width: 1"; thickness: 1¼".

122

123. VERY LARGE TOGGLE in cypress wood showing one monkey leaping up to mount a horse, standing with its front hoofs on a mounting block, while another monkey is crouching to help prop up the horse on the off side. On bottom of base is carved in low relief a top view of the traditional three-legged toad. The wood is worn and shiny from long handling. Height: 2¾"; breadth: 1¾"; max. thickness: 1¾".

123

C. Buddhist Lions and Other Mythical Beasts

124

124. MYTHICAL BUDDHIST LION with flames rising from shoulders, and collar strap with bell. Ming dynasty carving in old ivory. Muzzle, bell, and flowing tail in browner rind of tusk. Very small rectangular base in proportion to animal, looks as though it had been intended for mounting in a larger base of another material. Probably this figure was originally made for another purpose, and re-used as a toggle. Height: 2″; length: 1⅞″; thickness: 1″. (Purchased by S. C. at the Tibetan Fair in Tali, Yünnan, Spring, 1938.)

125

125. MYTHICAL LION carved in convex segment of old ivory. Cord hole pierced through center of base, emerging at top between head, body, and tail. Rather simply carved, but monumental in general effect. Length: 1¼″; breadth: 1⅜″; height: ⅞″.

126. MYTHICAL SPOTTED LION in a triangular segment of old ivory, with rind at bottom. Face and head rather detailed, spots on body rendered by nucleated circles. Hole through chest emerging at base, for cord. Length: 1⅜″; height: ¾″; width: 1″.

127. MYTHICAL LION, male, holding an openwork ball under left paw. Exceedingly well carved, in birch, with movable eyes and a rolling ball for his tongue. Eyes, broad collar, strap over head, and prominent raised curls on back, dotted with tiny metal nailheads. Gap between body and right paw for attaching cord. Length: 1⅝″; height: 1¼″; breadth: ⅞″.

128. VERY PREGNANT FEMALE LION in birchwood, with small cub between her forepaws, wearing a collar with three bells. Body pierced vertically from middle of back to stomach, for passing cord. Length: 1⅞"; height: 1½"; breadth: ⅞".

128

129. MYTHICAL LION standing on open-work ball and holding a cub. Beautifully carved in birch with fine detail, rolling ball for tongue. Height: 2⅛"; breadth: 1⅛"; thickness: ⅞".

129

130. MOTHER LION WITH CUB, standing on empty willow basket. Originally carved from birchwood, with great detail, but now much worn and polished from use. Hind legs cut free to leave gaps for cord. Height: 1½"; length: 1⅜"; width: ⅞".

130

131. MYTHICAL MALE LION with ball and scarf. Cast in white brass with silver cuboctahedral bolthead holding ring, affixed to top of head. Height (without bolt): 1⅛"; length: 1¼"; width: ¾".

131

132. MYTHICAL LION'S HEAD, handsomely worked in polished jet. Mouth hollowed, with rolling ball for tongue. Cord hole drilled through curls at back of head, emerging at base. Height: ⅞"; length: 1⅛"; width: 1".

134

133. MYTHICAL LION or lion dog in glossy, creamy white marble (calcite), forelegs and other details badly eroded. Cord hole between projecting left hind leg and body. Length: 1½"; height: ⅞"; width: 1". (Purchased by C. F. Bieber from the Manchu wearer, Summer Palace, Peking, 1937.)

134. MYTHICAL HORNED DRAGON-LION, carved in segment of ancient mammoth ivory. Reddish-brown surface color and dark yellow core. May be Ming, or older. Hole between head, body, and legs for passing cord. Length: 1⅝"; height: ⅝"; width: 1⁵⁄₁₆".

135

135. TWO *ch'ih* DRAGONS, mother and child, standing on three branches of sacred fungus and an artemisia leaf. Extremely well carved in time-darkened boxwood, this toggle seems very old; the style suggests Ming workmanship. Cord holes at center, between legs of the animals. (More recently, a small hole has been drilled at one end to make this into a pendant.) Length: 1⅞"; breadth: 1⅜"; height: ⅝".

For another mythical lion, see No. 29; for lion-dogs, see Nos. 166 and 170.

D. FROGS AND MYTHICAL TOADS

136. FROG IN CLEAR RED AMBER with slight mottling of opaque yellow. Simply carved, with few details, to leave broad, smooth expanses for tactile

appreciation. Two holes bored in stomach, meeting within, for passing cord. Length: 1½″; breadth: 1⅛″; height: ¾″.

137. FROG CARVED IN GRAY AND YELLOW PEBBLE OF CHALCEDONY. Top, flat with surface discolorations in light brown. Little detail, broad spaces left for feeling texture of stone. Hole for cord drilled in chest behind joined forelegs. Length: 1⅝″; height: ¾″; max. width: 1¼″.

138. LARGE FROG ON LILY PAD, carved in fine *Prunus* burl. Well polished to show figure in wood; also worn from use. Hole pierced through center of lily pad at base, emerging under frog's body, for tying knotted cord. Length: 1¾″; breadth: 1¼″; height: 1¼″.

139. REALISTIC FROG on a highly conventionalized lily pad with upcurled edges, carved in mottled gray nephrite. Very humorous expression on frog's face. Right leg looped outward for tying cord. Length: 1½″; breadth: 1⅝″; height: ⅞″.

For other frogs, see Nos. 64 and 66.

139

140 WARTY TOAD carrying a pomegranate branch with leaves and two fruits, worked in particolored onyx, ranging from pinkish gray to dark brown, with impurities utilized to represent the sepals on the fruits. Undercut left leg offers gap for passing cord. Length: 1¾″; width: 1¼″; height: ⅞″.

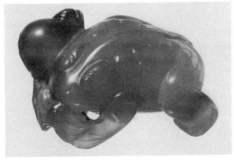

140

141

141. MYTHICAL THREE-LEGGED TOAD, simply shaped from a yellow and white pebble of nephrite with numerous flaws. Protruding eyes, small ears, and simple indications of legs, rest left plain for tactile appreciation. Head drilled transversely behind mouth for passage of cord. Length: 2¾"; max. breadth: 1¾"; height: 1½".

142. THREE-LEGGED TOAD in elephant ivory, apparently from half of the tip of a tusk. Head rather elaborately done, rest of body very simple. Hole through chest, emerging at bottom, for cord. Length: 1¾"; max. breadth: 1⅛"; height: ⅞".

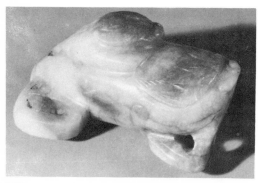

143

143. THREE-LEGGED TOAD with young one on back, and in its mouth a double string attached to a circular *shêng* jewel (instead of the usual coin), worked in gray and red jadeite. A hole between body and string, leaves a place for the cord. Length: 2¼"; breadth: 1¼"; height: 1".

144

144. VERY SMALL THREE-LEGGED TOAD in boxwood· burl, with natural, rough warty surface on top, and smooth, polished surface below. Hole for cord through chest. Although very small, it still has length enough to secure an object in the belt, perhaps for a child. Over-all length: 1¾"; breadth: ⅞"; height: ¾".

For other three-legged toads, see Nos. 123 and 225.

E. Fish Toggles

145. FISH FOLDED IN LEAF, carved in a thin chip of boxwood. Reverse unworked. Style suggests that this was carved by the maker of No. 152. Two holes on either side of leaf stem between leaf and branch offer a place for tying cord. Length: 2⅞″; breadth: 1⅞″; height: ½″.

145

146. FANTAIL GOLDFISH bearing a plant with long narrow leaves and small berries (*Nandina?*), in calcined white jade with many small cracks and fissures. Very fine workmanship. Hole under fish's gills on right side, passing under leaf, makes space for cord. Length: 1¾″; width: 1″; height: ¾″.

146

147. LARGE FANTAIL GOLDFISH carrying lotus flower, in translucent jadeite, color varying from watery blue-green to yellow. Stalk of the lotus arches out to make a loop for the cord; later two small holes were drilled in the fish's mouth for suspension as a pendant. Length: 2¾″; height: ⅞″; thickness: ½″. (Purchased by S. C. in Kunming. Yünnan, Winter, 1945.)

147

148. CONNECTED TWIN FISH, in fossil mammoth tusk, with outer rind left to form darker upper bodies. Fine details in line engraving. Length: 1¾″; breadth: 1½″; thickness: ½″.

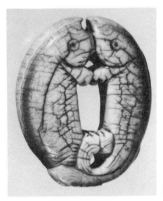

148

149. A MUDFISH (*Parasilurus asotus*), carrying in its mouth a sacred fungus as a symbol of longevity, in white nephrite. Hole for cord between fish's body and stem of fungus. Length: 2⅜″; width: 1⅜″; thickness: ½″.

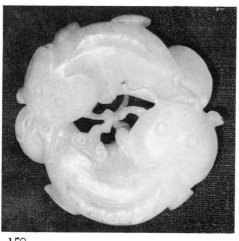

150

150. PAIR OF MUDFISH with *ju-i* fungus and artemisia leaf, in white camphor jade. Very fine detailed carving. Cord can be looped around stems at center. Diameter: 2¼″; thickness: ½″.

For other fish patterns, see Nos. 23, 38, 59, 66.

151

F. BIRD TOGGLES

151. EAGLE PERCHED ON A ROCK, done on a curved section of old ivory. Very primitive carving; worked on upper (convex) side only, back left rough. Four holes to serve as possible cord attachments. Height: ½″; width: 1¾″; thickness: ⁷⁄₁₆″.

152. MAGPIE ON A ROCK with a highly conventionalized flowering plum tree in background. Done in boxwood, with high relief carving on one side only, in the same general style as No. 145, probably by same maker. Cord holes on either side of branch, under bird's beak. Height: 2⅜″; breadth: 1⅜″; thickness: ⅜″.

152

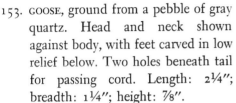

153a

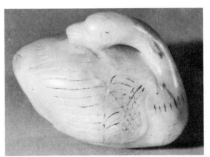

153b

153. GOOSE, ground from a pebble of gray quartz. Head and neck shown against body, with feet carved in low relief below. Two holes beneath tail for passing cord. Length: 2¼″; breadth: 1¼″; height: ⅞″.

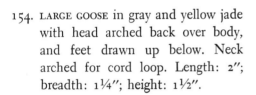

154. LARGE GOOSE in gray and yellow jade with head arched back over body, and feet drawn up below. Neck arched for cord loop. Length: 2″; breadth: 1¼″; height: 1½″.

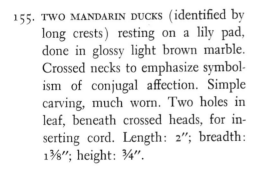

154

155. TWO MANDARIN DUCKS (identified by long crests) resting on a lily pad, done in glossy light brown marble. Crossed necks to emphasize symbolism of conjugal affection. Simple carving, much worn. Two holes in leaf, beneath crossed heads, for inserting cord. Length: 2″; breadth: 1⅜″; height: ¾″.

156. TWO MANDARIN DUCKS with exaggeratedly long crests and necks, in mottled light gray nephrite. Vertical hole for cord passing down between necks. Length: 1½″; width: ⅝″; height: ¾″.

For another bird, see No. 36.

G. INSECT TOGGLES

157. LARGE BUTTERFLY in convex section of old ivory. Patterns on wings indicated by line engraving, with spots formed by nucleated circles; interior plain, but highly polished. Cord holes in carving below abdomen. Length: 1¾″; width: 1⅝″; thickness: ¼″.

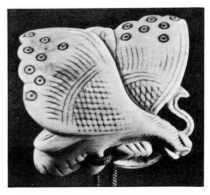

157

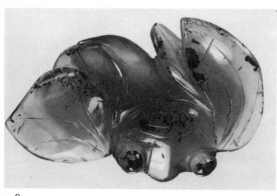

158

159

158. FLYING CICADA (or bat?), done in translucent yellowish onyx with black stains, which have been cleverly used to accent the eyes and to create shading behind the head and along the edges of the wings. Highly polished to enhance the natural luster. Two small holes in creature's thorax for attaching cord. Length: 2¾″; breadth: 1½″; height: ½″.

159. RATHER NATURALISTIC CICADA in box-wood, resting on an artemisia leaf, with a tiny ladybug on underside of leaf. The carving of the cicada's head, jointed legs, and finely segmented abdomen, as well as the veining of the leaf, show careful observation; while the introduction of the ladybug, to contrast the very small with the very large, illustrates an element of folk humor. Two holes on either side of the leaf stem below the cicada's head provide gaps for the cord. Length: 2¼″; breadth: 1″; height: ⅝″.

For other butterflies, see Nos. 63 and 85; another cicada, No. 45.

V. REPLICA TOGGLES (Inanimate Objects Copied in Miniature)

A. DRUM TOGGLES

160. SIMPLE EIGHT-SIDED DRUM in clear blue glass. Small hole through angle between two side panels, at middle, for stringing cord. Length: 1⅛″; diameter: 1″.

161. CRUDE WOODEN DRUM, carved from gold-thread *t'an mu* (a form of *Dalbergia*). Solid, tapered ends connected by eight irregular bars, with a rounded piece left free within to rattle when drum is shaken. Any of the side bars could serve for cord attachment. Length: 2⅜″; diameter: 1⅛″.

161

162. SIMPLE DRUM of the same type as the preceding, but more carefully carved, in birchwood. Six smooth, tapering slats (instead of the usual eight), and suggestions of the nails fastening down the skin drumheads on the original; rolling ball within to provide sound. Cord can be looped around any of the slats. Length: 1½″; diameter: ⅞″.

163. FINELY CARVED DRUM in birchwood, with thirteen slender slats. Elaborate drumheads, each secured by twenty-six nailheads, one end inscribed with the character *T'ai*, the other with the character *P'ing*. Small free-rolling ball within, for sound. Piece of wood left between slats at center of one side, pierced by a metal cotter pin holding ring for cord. Length: 1⅜″; max. diameter: 1¼″.

163

164. LARGE DRUM of polished birchwood. Sides carved to represent eight panels with interlocking *shêng* symbols in openwork. Drumheads each secured by sixteen nails, with a transparent blue glass bead inset at the center of each. Openwork holes in side can be used for looping cord. Length: 2⅛″; max. diameter. 1⅜″.

165

166

165. OCTAGONAL DRUM with eight side panels of green-dyed bone, separated by narrow brass ribs along the angles between them. Drumheads of antique yellow ivory with circular insets of white ivory surrounded by double circles of black horn. White brass bolt holding ring for cord, set off at top and bottom by delicate washers representing sixteen-petaled flowers. Solidly made, with exceedingly fine workmanship. Length: 1⁵⁄₁₆″; max. diameter: ⅞″.

B. WINNOWING FANS OR BASKETS

166. LION-DOG PUPPY reclining in winnowing basket, carved in transparent pale blue glass. Puppy simply carved in low relief, with line engraving on ears and tail; bolder line engraving on bottom to simulate wicker plaiting. Hole drilled through back of basket, emerging at bottom, for passing the cord. Length and breadth: 1⅛″; height: ⅜″.

167. SMALL PIE DOG lying in winnowing basket, carved in boxwood. Dog rather crudely done, much worn. Wicker plaiting indicated by line engraving both inside and out, more finely done on bottom. Hole through back of basket, emerging at bottom, for cord. Length: 1½″; breadth: 1½″; height: ⅝″.

168. WINNOWING BASKET with cat crouching inside it, while a rat or lizard clings to the underside to escape it, done in birchwood. Though much worn so that the details of the ani-

mals are almost obliterated, this shows very careful carving of the wicker work. Body of animal on underside is arched to form loop for cord. Length: 2″; width: 1⅝″; height: ¾″.

169. EWE AND LAMB lying in a winnowing basket, simply carved in camphorwood. Very large hole for cord between ewe and lamb, big enough for rawhide thong, suggest a Mongol origin. Small hole later bored through back of basket to pass smaller cord in Chinese or Manchu fashion. Length: 2″; width: 1¼″; height: ⅜″.

169

170. LION DOG AND PUP sitting in winnowing basket. Very well carved in yellow boxwood, with touches of black paint to indicate pupils of eyes. Wicker plaiting well rendered. Hole for cord through back of basket. Length: 1½″; width: 1⅝″; height: ⅝″.

170

171. TWO SMALL PUPPIES in a winnowing basket, with forepaws resting on a straw sweeping-brush. Done in boxwood, with fine details of fur and wickerwork rendered in line engraving. Handle of brush resting against side of basket offers place for looping cord, much worn from long use. Length: 1⅝″; width: 1⅞″; height: ⅞″.

172

172. WINNOWING BASKET containing a straw brush and a small pile of grain, which is being nibbled by a mouse, while two cats circle around the outside, ready to pounce. Carved in birchwood. Ornate carving on bottom shows the basket resting on a very elaborate jar carved in flat relief, ornamented by a conventionalized lotus flower. Right paw of one cat meets the tail of the other, leaving a slot behind them for passing a narrow strap or cord. Length: 1⅜″; breadth: 1¾″; height: ⅜″.

C. SHOE TOGGLES

173. MAN'S SHOES in mammoth ivory; solid, plain, except for indications of stitching around insole, up the toe, and down the heel, and tiny stitching around the edges of the cloth sole at bottom. Hole drilled through front end of sole for cord, emerging at middle, so whole would have formed a short bar toggle. Length: 1⅞″; width: ¾″; height: ⅞″. (Found in a New York shop.)

174

174. WOMAN'S SOCK AND SHOE in bright lacquer over a composition base made from bark fiber and glue. Shoe predominantly red (the wedding color) with embroidery represented in gold, including a pomegranate for fertility; red sole, gold heel. Sock predominantly black with continuous border pattern in gold, representing embroidery. Center hollow, with hole at base, passing through center of sole, for attaching cord. Length: 1¾″; diameter: 1⅛″.

175. PAIR OF MAN'S SHOES, joined, simply rendered in yellow amber glass, with crossing lines incised on bottom to indicate separation between shoes and between soles and heels. No decoration. Two small holes drilled in top for passing cord. Length: 1⅜"; width: 1"; height: ½".

175

176. SMALL PAIR OF WOMAN'S SHOES for bound feet, in highly polished *Dalbergia* wood. Stitching and embroidery indicated by carving. Small silver pin pierces hole between joined shoes, holding ring for cord. Length: 1½"; width: ⅝"; height: ½". (Acquired in Northeast Harbor, Maine.)

176

177. PAIR OF MAN'S SHOES in hollow country pottery, with whitish glaze and details in black slip (Tz'ŭ Chou style). Black outlines top edges, simple embroidery on outside of toes, and heel tabs. Hole between shoes from top to bottom, for passage of cord or thong. Length: 1⅝"; breadth: 1⅛"; height: ¾".

177

178. PAIR OF MAN'S SHOES beautifully carved in yellowish birchwood. Very thick "platform" soles perfectly smooth and plain in contrast to the highly decorated uppers, on which rich embroidery is indicated by delicate relief work. Hole for cord pierced between them. Length: 1⅜", width: ⅞"; height: ⅞".

178

179. PAIR OF MAN'S SHOES in polished boxwood. Left shoe has tiny woman's
shoe within it; right shoe contains a
small crab. Otherwise, the only decoration is a simple indication of the
stitching around the insole and down
the back. Ingot-shaped lug between
shoes, at base, undercut for cord.
Length: 1½"; width: ¾"; height:
⅝".

180. COMPOUND TOGGLE showing man's
shoe with heavy sole, in polished
birchwood, with tiny woman's shoe
inside. Hole for cord pierces through
sole of large shoe, passes through
small one, and fastens to underside
of small oval lid which closes aperture. Lid inscribed with a conventionalized *shou* character. Low relief carving represents appliqué
decoration on the large shoe and
embroidery on the small one.
Length: 1¾"; width: ⅝"; height:
⅞".

181. PAIR OF MAN'S SHOES in birchwood.
Cord, inserted through a single hole
in the base between them, passes
through a plug in each (both plugs
are carved to represent a seated monkey, with a woman's shoe behind
it), then back through the hole in
the base. The toes of the man's shoes
are each carved in *ju-i* shape and
ornamented with a stylized *shou*
character, while a conventionalized
lotus flower is lightly incised on the
outside of each. Length: 1½";
width: 1"; height, with monkeys:
1⅛".

181a

181b

D. Assorted Miniatures

182. MINIATURE SILVER MIRROR, copying the familiar bronze variety of Old China. Four characters, *fu ju tung hai*, jutting in relief against a stippled (punched) background; raised circle in center worked to resemble twin fish uniting to form a Yin-Yang symbol. In center of this, a bolthead with ring for cord. Obverse polished to serve as reflector. Diameter: 1 3/16″; height: 1/8″.

182

183

183. MINIATURE STONE WEIGHT, rectangular with cylindrical handle on top, simply cut from mottled yellow calcite. Handle offers natural place for looping cord, and shows erosion from this use. Length: 1 1/2″; height: 1″; width: 1/2″.

184. STONE WEIGHT (or Chinese padlock?) simply carved in *Dalbergia* wood. Length: 1 7/8″; height: 1″; width: 5/8″.

185. METAL LOCK imitated in birchwood. Carved to suggest three thicknesses of metal, fastened together by rivets, the heads of which form a border around the panels on each side. Panels decorated with highly stylized emblems of the Eight Immortals outlined in relief. Crossbar at top shows much erosion from the cord, after long wear. Length: 3″; width: 1 7/8″; width: 1/2″.

185

186. MINIATURE COPY OF ROADMAKERS' EARTH-TAMPER, with four vertical bars for four men simultaneously to lift and pound. Simply carved in wood. Height: 2 1/2″; max. width: 5/8″.

186

187

187. MINIATURE MORTAR AND PESTLE, lathe-turned from *Osmanthus* wood, dark and polished from long use. Contrived so that the pestle will not slip out. Two cord holes drilled through one side under the rim. Over-all height: 1¾″; mortar: 1⅜″ high, 1¼″ in diameter; pestle: 1¼″ long.

188

188. WELL-WATER BASKET with stick across mouth for handle, serving also as cord attachment. Wicker surface cleverly simulated. In boxwood. Height: 1¼″; diameter: 1⅛″.

189

189. FLOWER BASKET containing peach blossoms and peaches (one of each on either side), in boxwood. Flowers and fruits in relief and openwork. Basket solid, its handle serves as loop for cord. Height: 1¾″; width: 1⅞″; thickness: ⅞″.

190. TWIN FISH IN BASKET, rather crudely carved in boxwood. Again, the basket handle serves as cord loop. Length: 1½″; height: ⅞″; width: 1⅛″.

191. BUDDHIST HOLLOW FISH DRUM, globular bell shape with the joined heads
of two dragon-fish at the top. Original would have been in wood, but
this is made of old ivory from a
section near the tip of a mammoth
tusk. No attempt was made to hollow
the interior to make it conform with
the original, but the artist has indicated the round openings at each
side, and the slit between them.
Handle of drum provides cord loop.
Height: 1¼"; breadth: 1½"; thickness: 1".

191

192. MINIATURE BROAD-BRIMMED HIGH-
PEAKED HAT, topped by a round
button, in darkened birchwood,
turned on a lathe. Fine concentric
lines produce effect of straw original.
Round projection at bottom undercut for cord hole. The general shape
with this bottom projection makes it
possible to use this toggle as a child's
top, and probably it was so used, on
occasion, to amuse the young. Diameter: 1⅝"; height: ¾".

192

193. FURLED UMBRELLA in brown wood,
fluted to indicate twenty-three ribs,
with ornamental handle, upper cap-
ping, and tip of dark brown horn,
apparently turned on a lathe. Small
hole through top of handle for cord.
Length: 2⅜"; diameter: ⅝".

193

194

194. VERY SMALL FLINT-AND-STEEL SET, capable of actual use. Purse of coarse yak leather for holding flakes of flint, and lint for tinder, and heavy steel shoe at bottom for striking sparks. Plain silver trimmings on front flap. The characters *t'ung hsiang* lightly incised on the surface of the steel at the back. Length: 3⅜″; height (without loop): 1⅝″; thickness: ⅝″.

195

195. FLINT-AND-STEEL SET simulated in two-colored slate. Light brown portion used for the leather pouch above, and a dark gray streak for the steel shoe at bottom. Loop at top for securing cord, as on original. Length: 2¼″; width: 1½″; thickness: ¼″.

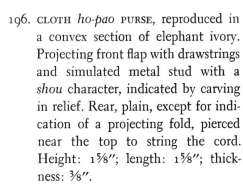

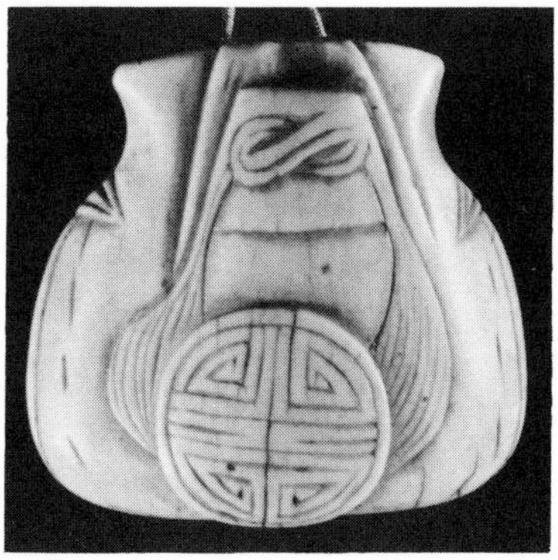

196

196. CLOTH *ho-pao* PURSE, reproduced in a convex section of elephant ivory. Projecting front flap with drawstrings and simulated metal stud with a *shou* character, indicated by carving in relief. Rear, plain, except for indication of a projecting fold, pierced near the top to string the cord. Height: 1⅝″; length: 1⅝″; thickness: ⅜″.

197. MINIATURE BELT-HOOK in translucent gray onyx with tinges of yellow brown. Simple, conventionalized

dragon's head on hook, rest left plain to display natural color and texture. Button at base not sufficiently detached to attach to belt, but prominent enough to permit looping cord for toggle. Length: 2⅛"; breadth: ⅞"; height: ⅞". (Purchased by S. C. in Kunming, Yünnan, Winter, 1945.)

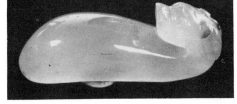

197

198. MINIATURE REPRODUCTION of an antique jade sword fitting, of a type much prized by Chinese scholar-antiquarians, copied in *Prunus* burl. Square hole at back suitable for passing cord or strap, to make a bar toggle. Length: 2"; width: ⅝"; height: 9/16.

198

199. MINIATURE MONGOL OR MANCHU KNIFE-AND-CHOPSTICK SET. Tiny, usable knife, with handle of black horn and white horn on opposite sides, in Mongol-Tibetan style, fastened to tang of blade by copper rivets. Hilt capped by a sliver of white bone to match the white bone chape at the end of the sheath. Pair of tiny chopsticks and skewer in bone. Three-section wooden sheath, bound by five brass straps riveted to vertical brass bar at back; small ring near top holds cord, as on original large knife. Over-all length: 3⅝"; knife: 3" long; sheath: 2¼" long, ½" broad, and 5/16" thick.

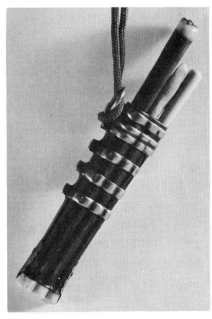

199

200. SHEEP'S ANKLE BONE (astragalus) reproduced in transparent pale blue glass. Small round projection at base pierced for cord. Length: 1½"; width: ¾"; height: ¾".

200

201

202

201. MINIATURE DIABOLO, the popular stick-top, lathe-turned from birch, with one end flattened so it can stand upright. Central bar provides a natural place for looping the cord. Length: 1⅝"; diameter: 1".

202. COMPLETE SET OF THIRTY-TWO CHINESE DOMINOES, represented on a hollow octagonal cylinder of bone by fine dividing lines and small drilled holes marked with dark coloring matter. Diameter at center pierced by an iron cotter pin, the upper end of which makes a loop for the cord, producing a bar toggle. Length: 2⅛"; diameter: ⅞". (Purchased in London.)

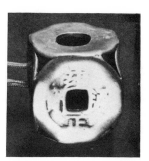

203

203. HOLLOW CUBE (or cuboctahedron) of brass, made to resemble a box formed of cash coins, five of them worked to represent Manchu cash of the Yung-chêng reign (1723-1735) with the four-character inscription, *Yung-chêng t'ung-pao;* lower one left plain. Holes pierced through top and bottom sides for passing a knotted cord or thong. 1" square.

204

204. MINIATURE CHINESE ABACUS (*suan p'an*), with nine double rods carrying two tiers of tiny wooden beads each (two above and five below), enclosed in a simple *Prunus* wood frame. Two tiny wire staples on the top probably once held a larger metal loop handle, but they themselves could still serve as cord attachment. Length: 2"; height: 1⅛"; thickness: ⁵⁄₁₆".

205. MINIATURE SCHOLAR'S ARMREST of boxwood carved to simulate a bamboo original. Convex side has a picture of a blossoming plum tree in low relief on a sunken surface. Small convex lug underneath, pierced for cord. Length: 2″; breadth: 1″; thickness: ⅛″.

205

206. MINIATURE CHINESE OR MONGOLIAN SADDLE, cast in light brass, with center of seat pierced for cord. Length: 1¼″; width: 1″; height at pommel: ¾″.

206

207. MINIATURE CHINESE OR MONGOLIAN IRON STIRRUP, in cast and chiseled iron. At top, finely rendered dragon's heads facing out on either side of slot for stirrup leather, here used for passage of tape or cord. Height: 1⅝″; width: 1⅜″; breadth: 1″.

208. MINIATURE MODEL OF FOOD- OR PICNIC-BOX, in metal. Three covered compartments in white brass trimmed with copper, supported in a brass carrying frame, with a movable loop handle which served for attaching the cord. The individual compartments are secured by a flat metal strip passing through a vertical slot on the lid of the topmost one, and locked on the far side by a tiny metal hasp. Height: 2″; width: 1⅜″; thickness: ⅝″.

For another type of replica, see No. 218.

207

208

VI. HUMAN FIGURES

A. CHILDREN

209. GRINNING BOY IN full jacket and embroidered stomach bib, holding a bowl of treasures, cast in white brass. Lotus flower embroidered on bib indicated by low relief casting. Loop on back for cord. Height: 1⅝"; width: ⅞"; thickness: ⅝".

210. SMALL BOY, fully clothed, reclining on stomach with knees drawn up, resting chin on hands, done in a half tusk of elephant ivory. Gaps for cord within bowed arms. Length: 1½"; breadth: 1⅜" height: ¾".

210

211. SMALL CHILD with two broad hair tufts at sides of head, lying on his stomach on two giant leaves; holding between his hands a cat, on which he pillows his chin. Done in boxwood. Large hole for cord or thong through leaf under his arched body. Length: 2¼"; width: 1³⁄₁₆"; height: ⅞".

211

212. TWO BOYS WEARING STOMACH BIBS, so arranged that when rotated there seem to be four (alternate front and rear views) worked in polished jet. Two holes for cords pierced through the solid rectangle left between the boys at the center. Length: 1½"; width: 1½"; height: ½".

212a

212b

213a   213b

213. CHILD WITH HAIR TUFTS, seated, holding a large basket, carved in box.
Front rather detailed, back very
simply yet effectively rendered. The
handle of the basket projects at one
side to serve as cord loop. Possibly
this represents the immortal Lan
Ts'ai-ho. Height: 1½″; length: 1½″;
thickness: ½″.

214. ROTUND CHILD WITH HAIR TUFTS, carrying a bowl. Worked in the outer
portion of an ivory tusk, with the
heavy yellow-brown rind at back.
Pierced with three holes: two to
indicate crooks of arms; the third, at
center, for passage of knotted cord.
Height: 1¾″; breadth: 1½″; thickness: ⅜″.

214

For another child figure, see No.
24.

B. MEN

215. ELDERLY SCHOLAR OR SAGE reclining
against a rock, stroking his beard,
simply carved in a section of old
ivory, face almost obliterated from
long wear. Hole through center passing under left arm, for cord. Length:
2″; width: 1″; thickness: ⅝″.

215

216a

216b

217a

217b

216. OLD MAN SEATED WITH GRANDCHILD on his lap. In yellow boxwood. Man's arms both cut free, so that either could serve as a cord loop. Height: 2″; breadth: 1½″; thickness: 1″.

217. MAN IN CH'ING DYNASTY (MANCHU) DRESS, squatting on a cushion, with arms clasped in front of chin, elaborately executed in birchwood. Bottom of cushion has decorated design centering on a *shou* character. Small of back cut away behind center of queue to make a gap for the cord. Height: 2½″; max. breadth: 1⅜″; thickness: ⅞″.

C. WOMEN

218. MINIATURE REPLICA IN JADE OF IVORY FIGURE OF A WOMAN, carried by Old Chinese doctor for diagnosing female illnesses. Woman, nude except for foot-coverings on her bound feet, reclines on a giant leaf, holding a leaf fan in one hand. Carved from white nephrite, with traces of brown on the underside of the leaf. Stem of the leaf loops back against leaf to make a loop for attaching a small silver chain. Length: 2¾″; max. breadth: 1″; max. height: ¾″. (Purchased by S. C. in Kunming, Yünnan, Winter, 1945.)

218

219

219. A SMILING WOMAN, very fully clothed, lying on a giant leaf with a fan in her hand, done in handsomely figured *Prunus* burl. Undoubtedly this was intended as a parody on the preceding type. Holes for cord on either side of leaf stem, under the lady's neck. Length: 3⅛″; breadth: 1⅜″; height: ⅞″.

D. DIVINE FIGURES

220. TRIANGULAR FIGURE OF TUNG-FANG SO, carrying a peach branch, in a section of old ivory tusk. Hole for cord pierced through back. Height: 1¾″; max. width: 1½″.

220

221. SHOU LAO, GOD OF LONGEVITY, with very high forehead, carrying a long-life peach. Arched left arm leaves gap for cord. Height: 1½″; width: 1¼″; thickness: ½″.

222. SHOU LAO WEARING A LONG, HOODED CAPE, holding a peach. Simply carved in multicolored jadeite; head and peach blue-green shading down through pale violet to white at feet; brown cloak and hood frame figure. Hole through back of cloak for attaching cord. Height: 2⅛″; breadth: 1⅛″; thickness: ¾″.

222

223. SHOU LAO WALKING WITH A YOUNG DISCIPLE, carved in fragrant aloes wood. Rocks and pine in background. Hole for cord between the two figures. Height: 2¾″; breadth at base: 1⅞″; thickness: ¾″.

224. THE IMMORTAL LI T'IEH-KUAI, leaning on his iron crutch under a pine tree, with a tipsy smile after drinking from his gourd. Arching branch of pine tree at back returns to main trunk, making a loop for the cord. Made of highly polished yellow boxwood. Height: 2½″; max. breadth: 1½″; thickness: ⅞″.

225. THE IMMORTAL LIU HAI, drawing from the three-legged money-toad a string of cash coins, handsomely carved in *Prunus* burl. Originally the cord passed through a hole under his belt behind his back; but after the belt broke away, a new hole was bored through the back of his coat, emerging between his legs. Height: 2⅜″; width: 2″; thickness: ⅞″.

225

VII. SCENIC AND STORYTELLING TOGGLES

226. A TALL, SLENDER MOUNTAIN, SHOU SHAN, the Mount of Longevity, with pine trees and bamboos, carved from fragrant aloes wood. Hole pierced for cord through the upper part of the peak. Length: 3¼"; max. breadth: 1½"; max. thickness: 1".

227. SCENIC TOGGLE, perhaps illustrating a legend, carved on the convex surface of a half-section of a branch of loquat (*Eriobotrya*). A small human figure is shown crossing a bridge below a Buddhist monastery, built on successive levels up a steep hillside, with shrines and pavilions, culminating in a stupa or pagoda at upper left. Reverse, undecorated, has two holes for cord, just above center. Height: 2½"; breadth: 1⅜"; thickness: ½".

226

227

228a

228b

228. TWO MAGIC-WORKING BUDDHIST
MONKS shown creating clouds from
which spring temples and shrines, illustrating a Buddhist legend. Reverse
carved with highly conventionalized
pattern, with central column deeply
undercut for passage of .cord. Done
in *Prunus* burl. Height: 1⅞″;
breadth: 1¾″; thickness: ⅝″.

229

229. SCENIC TOGGLE portraying the story
of an old Taoist monk, seated before
a shrine under a tree, apparently
praying for a woman suppliant who
stands before him. In a wisp of
vapor over his head a child appears,
holding a pack and a magic fly whisk.
Carved in yellow box. A circular *shou*
character is inscribed under the base.
Hole behind trunk of tree at the
back for attaching cord. Length: 2″;
max. diameter: 1⅛″.

230. THE STORY OF THE WHITE SNAKE
PAGODA (*Pai-shê T'a*) represented in
seven scenes on three sides of a
wedge-shaped section of boxwood
and on its base, with a conventionalized leaf across the top. In spite of
the smallness of the scenes (which
are described in detail in Chapter
12), each contains a surprising
amount of detail. Hole for cord
through narrowest part of wedge, between figures. Height: 2"; max.
width: 1⅛"; max. thickness: ⅝".

For other scenic toggles, see Nos.
37 and 115.

230a

230b

230c

GLOSSARY OF ORIENTAL TERMS

CHINESE TOGGLE TERMS

chui-tzŭ 墜子   belt toggle
p'ei-ching 佩經   girdle pendant
p'ei-yü (or *yü-p'ei*) 佩玉   girdle pendant
so-tzŭ yen 索子眼   hole for cord
yang wên 陽文   carving in relief
yin wên 陰文   sunken carving
ho pao 荷包   belt purse

JAPANESE TERMS

netsuke 根付   Japanese toggle
inrō 印籠   small box worn with netsuke
obi 帶   man's belt or girdle
karamono 唐物   Chinese-style early netsuke
tōbori 唐彫   Chinese-style early netsuke
manjū netsuke 饅頭根付   a bun-shaped toggle
kagami-buta 鏡蓋   a metal-faced toggle
soroban netsuke 算盤根付   a miniature abacus toggle
nanako 魚子   stippling on metal things

CHINESE TERMS FOR WOODS

chang mu 樟木   camphor wood
ch'ên hsiang mu 沈香木   eaglewood or Lignaloes

hai t'ang 海棠	crabapple
hsien mu 仙木	"spirit wood"
huang hua-li 黄花梨	light rosewood
huang yang 黄楊	box
p'i-pa 枇杷	loquat
t'an hsiang mu 檀香木	sandalwood
t'an mu, tzŭ t'an 檀木，紫檀	dark rosewood
t'ao mu 桃木	peachwood
tsung 棕	palm
hua mu 花木	burl (from any kind of tree)

ANIMAL SUBSTANCES USED FOR TOGGLES

chüeh 角	horn, or antler
hsi chüeh 犀角	rhinoceros horn
hsiang ya 象牙	ivory (not only elephant's)
ho-ting 鶴頂	"hornbill ivory"
ku-t'ou 骨頭	bone
tzŭ pei 紫貝	purple cowry shell

MINERAL SUBSTANCES IN TOGGLES

yü 玉	jade
Han yü 漢玉	old jade (supposedly Han)
shui ching 水晶	clear quartz, rock crystal
ma nao 瑪瑙	agate, onyx, carnelian, etc.
hu p'o 琥珀	amber
liu-li 琉璃	opaque glass
po-li 玻璃	clear glass

AUSPICIOUS SYMBOLS

yin-yang 陰陽	the cosmic poles
pa kua 八卦	the eight trigrams
shou, ch'ang shou 壽，長壽	long life; long, long life
shuang hsi 囍	the marriage symbol

pa pao 八寶	the eight precious things	
pa chi hsiang 八吉祥	the eight Buddhist symbols	
pa chu 八珠	the eight jewels	
ju-i 如意	the wish-granting scepter	
ju-i chu 如意珠	the wish-granting jewel	
shêng 勝	square or circular jewels	
pao yeh 寶葉	sacred palm leaf	
yen ch'ien 眼錢	coin with hole through center	
yün-chien 雲肩	cloud collar	
t'ai p'ing ku 太平鼓	an eight-sided hand drum	

Auspicious Flowers and Plants

kou-ch'i 枸杞	dog root
hu-lu 葫蘆	bottle gourd
ta chi hu-lu 大吉葫蘆	lucky gourd
k'o-têng-tzŭ 榼藤子	Entada bean
hsiang tou 象豆	Entada bean (popular term)
ho hua, lien hua 荷花，蓮花	lotus flower
ho yeh 荷葉	lotus leaf
lien tzŭ 蓮子	lotus seeds
ling chih 靈芝	sacred fungus
t'ao-hua-êrh 桃花兒	peach flower
p'an t'ao 蟠桃	peach of immortality
fu-shou 佛手	Buddha's hand (citron)
wan shou hua 萬壽花	marigold

Birds, Animals, and Fish

fêng-huang 鳳凰	an auspicious bird; the "phoenix"
hsi ch'iao 喜鵲	magpie
ch'i-chih 鸂鶒	mandarin duck
shih-tzŭ 獅子	lion
shih-tzŭ kou 獅子狗	lion dog
lung 龍	five-clawed imperial dragon

mang 蟒	four-clawed dragon
ch'ih 螭	young, immature dragon
ch'ien ch'an 錢蟾	the three-legged "money toad"
pien fu 蝙蝠	bat
hu-tieh 蝴蝶	butterfly
chin yü 金魚	goldfish
nien 鮎	catfish

Auspicious Phrases

chin yü mang t'ang 金玉滿堂	"a hall filled with gold and jade."
i t'uan ho ch'i 一團和氣	"a bundle of harmony and friendship."
ju t'ung chao chün 如同朝菌	"like mushrooms in the morning."
shou pi Nan Shan 壽比南山	"long-lived as the Southern Mountain."
fu ju Tung Hai 福如東海	"happy as the Eastern Sea."
ta fu ju i 大福如意	"as happy as you wish."
wan shou wu chiang 萬壽無疆	"endless life."

Punning Symbols or Rebuses

chia kuan 茄冠	egglant cap (calyx)
加官	promotion in official rank
chin yü 金魚	goldfish
金餘	gold (wealth) in abundance
ho pao chin yü 荷包金魚	goldfish enwrapped in lotus plant
荷包金餘	an abundance of gold in the purse
hou pei fêng hou 猴背瘋猴	monkey carries (on back) crazy monkey
後輩封侯	may your descendants become marquises
hou tai fêng hou 猴戴瘋猴	monkey carries crazy monkey
後代封侯	may the later generations be marquises
ma shang fêng hou 馬上瘋猴	crazy monkey on horseback
馬上封侯	may you quickly become a marquis
hsiao hai-tzǔ 小鞋子	little shoes
小孩子	small children

lien tzŭ 蓮子	lotus seeds
連子	successive children
ta chia 大鋏	a sea crab (literally: huge pincers)
大家	a man of influence; an important family
t'ung an 銅鞍	brass saddle
同安	peace and harmony, together
shêng 勝	a kind of jewel; success
笙	a form of mouth organ
升	to rise in rank
wan tai 蔓蒂	gourd (or melon) vines and stems
萬代	ten thousand generations

PEOPLE AND GODS

Chang Tao-ling 張道陵	the founder of Taoism
Li T'ieh-kuai 李鐵拐	one of the Eight Immortals
Liu Hai 劉海	child god of wealth
Nan Tou 南斗	southern star god
P'êng Tsu 彭祖	the Taoist Methusaleh
Shou Hsing 壽星	god of longevity
Tung-fang So 東方朔	a Taoist immortal
Chuang-yüan 狀元	a successful scholar
kuei 鬼	an evil spirit, demon

TITLES OF CHINESE PLAYS

San-niang chiao tzŭ 三娘教子
Pai-shê chuan 白蛇傳
Chin-shan ssŭ 金山寺
Tuan ch'iao 斷橋
Chi t'a 祭塔

TITLES OF CHINESE BOOKS

Hsi-ch'ing ku-chien 西清古鑑
Hsi-yu chi 西遊記

I Ching 易經

Kuang-chou chi 廣州記

Ku-kung ch'ou-k'an 故宮週刊

P'ei-wên yün-fu 佩文韻府

Pên-ts'ao kang-mu, by Li Shih-chên. 李時珍，本草綱目

Sou-shên chi, by Kan Pao. 干寶，搜神記

Ta Ch'ing hui-tien t'u 大清會典圖

JAPANESE BOOKS

Man-shi zuan seika daijō, by Ibara Shizuka, 庵原諡，滿支圖案精華大成

Sōken kishō, by Inaba Michitatsu, 稻葉通龍，裝劍奇賞

Kisshō zuan kaidai, by Nozaki Seikin, 野崎誠近，吉祥圖解題

Shumi no netsuke, by Ueda Reikichi, 上田令吉，趣味乃根付

INDEX TO TEXT AND NOTES